THORSTEIN VEBLEN
a reference guide

A
Reference
Guide
to
Literature

Jack Salzman
Editor

THORSTEIN VEBLEN
a reference guide

JERRY L. SIMICH *and* RICK TILMAN

G.K.HALL &CO.

70 LINCOLN STREET, BOSTON, MASS.

Library of Congress Cataloging in Publication Data

Simich, Jerry L.
  Thorstein Veblen : a reference guide.

  (A Reference guide to literature)
  Includes index.
  1. Veblen, Thorstein, 1857-1929—Bibliography.
I. Title. II. Series.
Z8927.53.S55 1985   016.33′0092′4   84-25177
ISBN 0-8161-8358-9

Contents

The Authors

Jerry L. Simich teaches political science at the University of Nevada, Las Vegas. He earned his Ph.D. at the University of California, Santa Barbara, and has contributed articles to the History of Political Economy, the American Journal of Economics and Sociology, and the Journal of Economic Issues.

Rick Tilman is also a member of the political science faculty at the University of Nevada, Las Vegas. He earned his Ph.D. in history at the University of Arizona and did postdoctoral study in government and economics at the University of Texas. He is currently a member of the editorial board of the Journal of Economic Issues and has contributed to that journal, the American Journal of Economics and Sociology, the Western Political Quarterly, the History of Political Economy, Polity, and Dissent. His book, C. Wright Mills: A Native Radical and His American Intellectual Roots, was published by Pennsylvania State University Press in 1984.

Preface

In preparing this guide the authors utilized various indexes and other sources to obtain citations to writings on Veblen. Although the indexes were indispensable for citations, they are by no means exhaustive. We found the following indexes and reference sources to be the most helpful in our search for material on Veblen:

Biography Index
Book Review Digest
Comprehensive Dissertation Index
Current Sociology
Economic Abstracts
Essays and General Literature Index
Historical Abstracts
History of Economic Analysis
Humanities Index
International Bibliography of Economics
International Bibliography of Political Science
International Bibliography of Social Sciences
International Index to Periodicals
Journal of Economic Literature
London Bibliography of the Social Sciences
Readers Guide to Periodical Literature
Selected Bibliography of Modern Economic Theory
Social Sciences Citation Index
Social Sciences Index
Sociological Abstracts
Widener Library Shelflist, Harvard University

We have attempted to annotate any book, chapter or portion of a book, dissertation, article, significant portion of an article, or book review on Veblen that we could obtain. Our aim was to be inclusive, thus in some cases we have abstracted relatively brief treatments of Veblen because we felt them to be important. We have also abstracted reviews of books on Veblen when it was obvious that the reviewer was making an independent judgment on Veblen.

Our searches also turned up information on Veblen in several foreign languages--namely, Italian, French, German, Dutch, Spanish, Japanese, Norwegian, and in one instance, Czech. The guide also contains abstracts of items published in Canada, England, Switzerland, Sweden, and Australia.

While we have attempted to secure any material on Veblen, we have undoubtedly not found all of it--particularly portions of books dealing with him. Occasionally we found citations to a piece on Veblen but were unable to secure it through interlibrary loan. These few titles are listed in the guide and are designated with an asterisk (*).

We found Joseph Dorfman's book, Thorstein Veblen and His America (1934.9; 1966.4) and his lengthy essay, "New Light on Veblen," in his edition of Thorstein Veblen: Essays, Reviews, and Reports (1973.8) to be rich sources for bibliography on Veblen. A significant number of items were also obtained from bibliographies in dissertations, books, and articles. In some instances, systematic searches through library stacks yielded books with enough information on Veblen to warrant abstracting. By searching these sources, we often discovered material on Veblen that could not be located in indexes.

The index to this volume is primarily an author-title index, but it also includes personal names used as subjects. In addition, we have included selected subject categories. The reader is advised that these categories refer to the annotated entry. Books or articles listed in this bibliography might often treat subjects omitted in the index for reasons of space and convenience.

Acknowledgments

The authors wish to thank the following persons for their kind assistance in the preparation of this volume: Pat Hudson for patiently typing and retyping the entire manuscript; Bob Ball, Ida Bowser, Bill Marion, and Lee Wahrer of Interlibrary Loan, Dickinson Library, University of Nevada, Las Vegas, for obtaining material for us from libraries both in the United States and abroad; Julia Angelica and Lori Randall for their efforts in searching, proofing, and indexing; David Cotter, Terry Lamuraglia, Lisa Miller, Jennifer Simich, Paula Whitney, and Julie Wilcox for research assistance; Robert Bigler, Andrea Fontana, Haruhiro Fukui, Scott Locicero, Christian Søe, Herman Van Betten, and Thomas C. Wright for translations of material in foreign languages. We also wish to thank John Diggins, Joseph Dorfman, Vern Mattson, and Andrew Tuttle for encouragement and friendly suggestions.

Introduction

Biographical Note

The critical literature on Thorstein Veblen that began to appear
slightly before the turn of the twentieth century continues unabated
up to the present time. Although critics and commentators disagree
about the significance of his work, interest in Veblen has not dimin-
ished. Born in 1857, Veblen was a true son of the middle border.
Reared in a Scandinavian-Lutheran community in the Midwest, he was
the fourth son of Norwegian immigrant farmers who raised a large
family, most of whom received higher education. Several of the
Veblen children went to Carleton College in Minnesota; there
Thorstein obtained his training in economics and philosophy under the
tutelage of John Bates Clark, who later became a prominent neoclassical economist. After receiving his bachelor's degree at Carleton,
Veblen taught for a year and then enrolled at Johns Hopkins for graduate study. After a short stay he transferred to Yale, where he
obtained his Ph.D. in philosophy and economics in 1884 while studying
under such noted academicians as Noah Porter and William Graham
Sumner. He was then idle for seven years, most of which was spent on
the farms of relatives or in-laws in the Midwest. Veblen's agnosti-
cism made him unemployable in schools with religious affiliations and
he had not yet established a reputation in economics. Finally, in
1890 he obtained a graduate position at Cornell University, where he
once again became a Ph.D. candidate, this time in economics. The
economist A. Laurence Laughlin was impressed by him and in 1892, when
Laughlin moved to the newly founded University of Chicago, took
Veblen with him. Veblen soon became editor of the Journal of Political Economy and began publishing in the field of economics. In 1899
his most famous book, The Theory of the Leisure Class, appeared and
achieved a notoriety all its own. But Veblen's personal idiosyncra-
cies and his failure to properly "advertise" the university offended
the administration at Chicago and he was forced to move. His next
job was at Stanford where, in a few short years, he encountered

similar difficulties that were exacerbated by his "womanizing." He
was compelled to move again, this time to the University of Missouri.
World War I found Veblen briefly in Washington as an employee of the
Food Administration. After the war he served for a short time as one
of the editors of the Dial, a journal of literary and political
opinion, and as a member of the faculty of the recently founded New
School for Social Research in New York City. By then, even though
his reputation as a scholar and publicist was at its peak, his academic career was at an end. Veblen retired and moved to California,
near Stanford, where he lived an isolated existence in an old house
in the hills. He died in August 1929, shortly before the onset of
the depression (1934.9; 1966.4).

Veblen's Orientation

Veblen was critical of classical and neoclassical economics because they were, in his view, pre-Darwinian and unscientific. Under
the influence of Spencer, Sumner, and Darwin he emphasized process
and claimed that economics should become an evolutionary science.
Conventional economics was wrong in refusing to abandon static equilibrium models and psychological hedonism and deficient in its inability to incorporate the critical-genetic method used by Veblen in
his own work. In short, the important social and economic implications of Darwinian evolutionary biology were largely ignored by
mainline economists, to their own and society's detriment.

Veblen's most important analytic tool was his distinction between
business and industrial pursuits or the "ceremonial-technological
dichotomy," as it is now known. This concept was apparent in his
early belief in the liberating impact of machine technology, ultimately eradicating the effects of cultural lag by undermining the
barbarian residues of the past that plagued mankind. The predatory
culture of the capitalist order might give way to a society that
would incorporate the traits Veblen prized, including efficient work
(instinct of workmanship), altruism (the parental bent), and scientific inquiry (idle curiosity). The existing system of waste, exploitation, and predation might wither away as an egalitarian society
based on the brotherhood of man emerged.

Veblen's Audience

Veblen has attracted attention primarily from intellectuals,
those who make a living from the production and dissemination of
abstract ideas. This group includes economists, sociologists, historians, critics, journalists, philosophers, literary figures and
critics, political scientists, psychologists, anthropologists, and,
on occasion, scientists, political leaders, and activists.

A survey of the secondary literature on Veblen reveals several
patterns that warrant mention. It is noteworthy that Veblen is more
often compared with Karl Marx than any other figure owing, no doubt,
to the fact that both thinkers were profound critics of capitalism.
Much of the secondary literature points to Veblen's having been

influenced by Darwinian thought; there are also a significant number
of references to the impact of Immanuel Kant and Herbert Spencer on
Veblen. Not a few commentators have made comparisons between Veblen
and such thinkers as Bernard Mandeville, Jean-Jacques Rousseau,
Sigmund Freud, Max Weber, and John Maynard Keynes. In terms of
Veblen's influence on subsequent thinkers, the names that appear most
frequently include Wesley C. Mitchell, John R. Commons, John Kenneth
Galbraith, and C. Wright Mills. Several authors likewise maintain
that Veblen provided a powerful stimulus to such novelists as Robert
Herrick, Sinclair Lewis, and John Dos Passos (1966.3).

The secondary literature on Veblen demonstrates that he has
enjoyed a very broad appeal indeed. Books, articles, reviews, and
comments have ranged over Veblen's ideas concerning waste and exploitation, emulation and display, war and peace, and evolution and
revolution; his critical and positive contributions to economic theory; and his views on social class, culture lag, and the importance
of the machine process on our thinking. Veblen has been treated as a
great critic of American capitalist culture and also as a profound
visionary on the subject of the relationship between technology and
history.

Veblen has been accused of pessimism while some see in him elements of utopianism. He has been called an elitist by some and a
democrat by others. For many Veblen is a prophet with an ethical
message, while other followers view him simply as an insightful
social scientist. Although Veblen's significance is widely disputed,
the secondary literature dealing with his ideas indicates that he was
an original thinker responsible for introducing and popularizing a
host of important concepts and insights. A partial catalogue would
include the ideas of conspicuous consumption, display, and emulation.
These have been shown by writers to have significance in explaining
not only ruling class hegemony, but also consumer behavior, corporate
behavior, exploitation by the military, school district spending,
recreational activities, sports, and fashion changes. Veblen is also
credited with demonstrating the linkage between conspicuous display
and the oppression of women (1978.6-7).

Sociologists and students of modernization have responded sympa-
thetically to such Veblenian concepts as "the penalty for taking the
lead" in industrialization, the notion of "trained incapacity," and
the idea of "conscious withdrawal of efficiency." Veblen is also
recognized for his major contributions to the theory of latent and
manifest functions so popular in recent sociology. He has been
praised for his ideas regarding social class stratification and the
sociology of knowledge (1949.14). Radical social theorists often
refer to his critique of social institutions and their linkage to
corporate power centers.

Veblen was not an orthodox or mainstream economist and, in traditional economics, is often viewed as a dissident thinker. Nonetheless, his critique of orthodox economics and his efforts to place the
study of economics within an historical and sociological context have
attracted wide attention. Credited with having influenced economists
who stress empirical and statistical approaches to such topics as

business cycles and price fluctuations, he is also cited by Kenneth Arrow, for example, for his contributions to microeconomic theory and other insights that remain amenable to modeling and/or testing (1975.1).

In speaking of the social sciences as a whole, Veblen is seen as having helped in establishing a new paradigm, one based largely upon an evolutionary, anthropological foundation (1978.7). He is likewise held in high regard for his contributions to disciplines outside sociology and economics. Writers have studied his impact on American novelists and he has been treated as a cultural critic on a par with fiction writers. Other scholars have assessed Veblen's prose style and his use of irony and satire. He is believed to have remarkable insights into the nature of linguistics and rhetoric. Even his efforts at journalism and translation have received attention.

Critics and interpreters of Veblen's work may be classified into categories of: (1) liberal, (2) radical, (3) conservative, and (4) cutural-aesthetic. This classification assumes that the perspective of his critics, in the case of the first three categories, clearly reflects either political-ideological propensities or, in the case of the fourth, an interest in the cultural and aesthetic implications of Veblen's work.

The Liberal Critics

Early liberal critics of Veblen, while impressed with some of his insights, believed that his obsession with the morbid aspects of business enterprise blinded him to the wholesome side of it (1905.3). Others suggested that while Veblen was a master at locating traces of teleology in others he nevertheless fell prey to it himself (1916.3). Veblen's attacks on orthodox economics were regarded by many liberal economists as too extreme. A commonly voiced opinion was that Veblen should have improved upon orthodox economics and not called for its abandonment. Other liberals, in assessing Veblen's contribution to the methodology of economics, charged him with making disguised value judgments while at the same time alleging objectivity. While there was no doubting Veblen's contribution to economics in general, his critique of orthodox economic method has been the subject of debate. By the late 1930s liberals recognized Veblen's probable influence on some New Dealers and also urged realization of the degree to which Veblen's work paralleled that of John Maynard Keynes (1939.18). Indeed, the influential economist John Kenneth Galbraith claims that he was profoundly influenced in the 1930s by his reading of Veblen (1981.5).

Several of Veblen's liberal critics have suggested that his diagnosis of the ills of capitalism was based on an uncritical admiration for technicians and engineers, pointing in the direction of technocracy or some variant of technocratic elitism. It is claimed that Veblen's ideas, if implemented, would lead to rule by a soviet of technicians, owing to his misunderstanding of the self-serving nature of the engineering profession. Ironically, traces of the animism that he detected in the thinking of others were present in his belief that engineers should assume control of production. Writers like Daniel Bell thus claim that there is a spiritual link between Veblen's ideas and the technocratic movement of the 1930s (1963.2).

Another favorite theme of Veblen's liberal critics was that his quasi-anarchist dislike of established institutions was extremist and utopian in character. Some, like David Riesman, believed that Veblen had little positive to say about institutions for his study of the university, for example, focused obsessively on top administrators and trustees. His proposal for the abolition of both was viewed as institutionally unfeasible (1953.17).

Liberal interpreters of Veblen recognized that an important contribution of The Theory of the Leisure Class was its emphasis on the role of consumption as a symbol of social status. In their view, however, a main fault of the book was its failure to understand the function of consumption as an expression of basic cultural values. Further, Veblen pinpointed only the invidious aspects of conspicuous consumption and not the positive ones. Thus, his theory of consumption, while insightful, was badly flawed since it failed to adequately appreciate the positive aspects of consumer behavior under the conditions imposed by advanced industrial society.

Veblen was critical of classical and neoclassical economic thought for he believed these theories were irrelevant to the solution of economic problems. Crucial for Veblen in this respect was the ultimate extinction of capitalism, although he differed from Marx in neither prescribing action nor predicting what was to follow the demise of capitalistic society. Two dominant themes in Veblen's analysis were the goal of maximum production and hostility toward institutionally supported inequality. An important distinction for Veblen, though liberals thought he exaggerated its significance, was that between business and industry. Industry was the factor in modern civilization that brought about growth, whereas business was concerned with profit and property rights. Veblen pointed out that the "invisible hand" was no longer effective in dealing with modern monopoly, allowing great profits for business at the expense of the community. But his theory of economic stagnation was generally considered by liberals to be inadequate because he lacked a theory of aggregate demand. He believed that monopoly and depression were linked but failed to adequately tie them together.

Veblen did not distinguish between economics and politics. For him, business interests dominated both industry and politics and that domination resulted in a stagnant economy. Liberals often criticized Veblen for not realizing that social legislation and government control of business would serve to indefinitely stabilize the system. Thus Veblen's emphasis on the conflicts in modern society unjustifiably discounted the virtues of welfare reform, while it was in this emphasis that the basics for his analysis lay.

Introduction

<u>The</u> <u>Radical</u> Critics

Veblen's radical and Marxist interpreters focused on themes of
contemporary significance in his work. In the 1920s their attention
was riveted by what appeared to the radical mind to be the prime
deficiencies of the American capitalist order: its waste of resources on luxury items and its indulgence in an orgy of status
emulation and conspicuous consumption. Also, his satirical wit and
irony was appreciated, like that of contemporaries such as Sinclair
Lewis and H.L. Mencken, as part of an exposé of conformist leisure
class morals and foibles. In the 1930s, however, the Marxist focus
shifted to Veblen's study of business cycles and the roots of economic instability, exploitation of the working class, and responsibility of corporations for the depression debacle. His strident
attacks on the bourgeois order struck a response in the radical heart
although not all Marxists responded to his message with enthusiasm.

By the late 1930s, with the rise of fascism, Veblen's predictions
regarding a resurgence of authoritarianism in Germany and Japan
attracted attention for their obvious relevance to understanding
those two political systems. In the 1940s and 1950s their focus was
on Veblen's work on the linkage between imperialism, colonialism, and
war as Marxists grappled first with the Second World War and later
with the Cold War. Those writing for the <u>Monthly</u> <u>Review</u> during this
period saw validity in Veblen's theories explaining American foreign
policy and Cold War politics (1957.28). Still, only a few years
later the New Left paid little attention to him. Even though Marxism
made considerable inroads in New Left circles in the 1960s and early
1970s the characteristic stance of radical intellectuals was to
ignore Veblen (1978.18). It is probable that during this period many
young radical economists had not read a word of <u>The</u> <u>Theory</u> <u>of</u> <u>the</u>
<u>Leisure</u> <u>Class</u>. Indeed, it was only in the mid-1970s that the Marxian
New Left "rediscovered" Veblen and began to pay attention to his work
(1982.2).

Marxists also criticized Veblen because his theory of crisis and
depression, though bearing a strong resemblance to the Marxian theory, was not sufficiently systematic (1957.27). Marxists often con-
demned Veblen for offering no plausible solutions and having almost
nothing to say of current political issues. They believe he was,
unfortunately, silent regarding the role of unskilled workers and the
general population in such a new social order. Also, Veblen's view
of the future was typically vague, cynical, or pessimistic. He
rejected not only business civilization but also the Socialist alternative and had no viable third possibility to offer. Finally, many
Marxists argued that while Veblen's espousal of the empirical study
of institutions provided the inspiration and set the stage for the
important school of institutionalism, his avowed followers, the institutionalists, having shed his radicalism, are often bound to him
only by their devotion to factual study and quantitative methods.

Radical interpreters of Veblen often suggest there were two
Veblens. One was the disinterested liberal, reluctant to take sides,
while the other, the revolutionary Veblen, emerged more clearly
during and after the First World War. In this vein, critics noted

that while there is little in his later work that Veblen did not deal
with earlier, his later writings do tend to take the form of concrete
application and propaganda, moving away from the abstraction, detachment, and greater impartiality of his earlier work.

In the United States Veblen's influence has probably been greatest in the ranks of the non-Marxian left. Native radicals like C.
Wright Mills have seen in Veblen an indigenous strain of radical
thought with potent implications for the analysis of American capitalism. Although not disposed to rank Veblen with Marx or Weber as a
general theorist, Mills believed that Veblen was "the best critic of
America that America has produced" (1953.13).

Max Lerner, while still in his radical phase, found six ideas in
Veblen that were nevertheless usable. The first was his emphasis on
the rigor and potentialities of the machine process, provided it
could be harnessed to the idea of community serviceability. The
second was the antithesis between business and industry or the
ceremonial-technological dichotomy, as it is now called by institutional economists. A third was the antisocial tendency of business
enterprise. A fourth was Veblen's view of legal and political institutions as the vesting of economic interests or, in contemporary
jargon, a "zero-sum" game in which the wealthy and powerful "win" and
the underlying population "loses." Lerner, too, was impressed by
Veblen's emphasis on the compulsive force of idea patterns and the
inability of the common man to overcome their hold on him. He also
believed Veblen was essentially correct in his belief in the bank-
ruptcy of leisure class values and a culture dominated by them
(1935.14). Indeed, there was much in Lerner's analysis of Veblen
with which others on the far left could agree.

The Conservative Critics

Veblen is sometimes portrayed as a "radical apologist for conservatism." In this vein it is argued that Veblen was "philosophically
an optimist" and sound apologist for the "extrinsic value of the
conservative's role in society." "Immanent but impermanent absolutes" may be used to describe Veblen's concept of principles and
truth for truth was limited to the case or situation-at-hand. Veblen
"saw the institution as a functional social instrument which, though
retrogressive in many instances, represents the means by which society preserves what it believes to be the best principles of individual and social adaptation" (1959.7).

Conservative critics of Veblen, while occasionally impressed by
his satire and irony, have generally disliked his attacks on private
property, institutional religion, existing authority, and leisure
class values. This has been true since The Theory of the Leisure
Class first appeared in 1899. At that time a conservative reviewer
wrote that the most "vicious distinction" made in the book was between pecuniary and industrial economic processes (1899.7). Other
reviewers saw in the book a savage attack on Christian ideals, perhaps mistaking Veblen's assault on religious ceremonialism and waste
as an attempt to repudiate moral altruism. Others claimed that it

was no difficult task to point to immoral business practices in bygone eras, but that while such an analysis might impress the readers of sensational magazines, it contained an unjust portrayal of American business morality.

Perhaps the most elaborate summation of the conservative case against Veblen came from Abram L. Harris, once an admirer of Veblen, who ultimately concluded that Veblen's work was deficient in many respects. Harris criticized Veblen for depicting a state of primitive savagery for which there was no scientific proof and disguising value judgments behind scientific facades. He also claimed that, as an economist, Veblen had ignored the relationship between investment cost and the creation of capital and had falsely connected the entrepreneurial function with mechanical performance of the entrepreneur's role. In this same vein Harris argued that Veblen had not attempted any serious evaluation of the real limitations of competition or its utility as method and policy.

For Harris, Veblen's conception of the basic defects of the system was mistaken. His program of economic reorganization, designed to increase efficiency, lessen inequality, and create greater freedom, would achieve none of these things but would cause greater evils than already existed (1958.19).

Other conservatives, who saw little virtue in Veblen, have complained that he was a cynic who got his major ideas from Karl Marx and updated them to suit his own satirical and bitter purposes. They attacked his attitudes with respect to waste, show, and conspicuous consumption, for in their view these were not social evils. Finally, his efforts to link business enterprise with imperialism and war were disputed by conservatives who instead thought that such phenomena were the result of Communist aggression. in the main, conservatives were bothered by Veblen's animosity toward capitalist institutions, nationalism, patriotism, and private property. In some instances, they also voiced dissatisfaction with his Darwinian-materialist metaphysic.

The Cultural-Aesthetic Critics

Veblen's writing has been the subject of interest to cultural and literary critics ever since publication of The Theory of the Leisure Class. This most famous of Veblen's books was praised by William Dean Howells for its style and characterization. Howells added that the book provided an excellent opportunity to render leisure class activities into fictional accounts (1899.3-4). The book was also warmly received by Stephen MacKenna (1899.5) and Robert Benchly (1919.7) but was savaged by Henry L. Mencken, who lampooned Veblen's style and belittled his ideas (1919.14). Francis Hackett (1917.7) as well as Floyd Dell (1917.5) found valuable insights in Veblen's The Nature of Peace. The novels of Sinclair Lewis and John Dos Passos show strains of Veblenian thought and the latter devoted considerable space to portraying Veblen in his novel, The Big Money (1930.2). Literary critic Alfred Kazin has written that while the satiric element in The Theory of the Leisure Class was "almost pyrotechnical in its elaboration," the "art in his prose has often been exaggerated." Veblen's humor was described as "monstrously grotesque" and he was as much "a victim of his material as he was the master of it" (1942.3). There is also a certain pompousness to Veblen's style, but such was the manner of his era. As another cr_tic put it, "His prose had a deadpan humor that was the intellectual equivalent of Buster Keaton and W.C. Fields" (1973.5).

Critics have been more intrigued by Veblen's prose style and his role as a satirist than perhaps anything else. They contend that The Theory of the Leisure Class deserves to be recognized for its contributions to linguistic theory. Veblenian concepts such as conspicuous waste and invidious distinction provide insights in understanding speech and spelling patterns and the use of obsolescent forms (1960.1). It is contended that Veblen's prose was overwhelmingly Latinate and that he "was a self-conscious stylist" who used alliteration and incongruous word sets to suit his taste (1968.4). While Veblen's prose was a parody of the leisure class, it was probably also a conscious self-parody—a form of satire itself.

Of course, by considering Veblen as a satirist, it is possible to shed more light on his style. In this vein Edgar Johnson claimed that "Literary critics, misled by his purely technical reputation, have for the most part left his work unanalyzed" (1941.3). Lewis Mumford has gone so far as to claim that Veblen was not only the outstanding social scientist in America but also our most important satirist (1935.16).

Veblen's interpreters have often surmised that one of his basic ideas was the class nature of taste. Certain notions of taste among the leisure class were permanent and were based upon the consumption of unproductive goods and services. Veblen was sometimes praised by critics for emphasizing the "pecuniary" motivations of taste but criticized for underemphasizing the class function of leisure (1949.11). Recent writings, however, indicate renewed interest in Veblenian themes. John Brooks (1981.3), Lewis Lapham (1977.12), and Cesar Graña (1967.9) have either updated or shed light upon certain of Veblen's ideas contained in The Theory of the Leisure Class.

Veblen's ideas concerning culture have been warmly received by thinkers such as Lewis Mumford and Norman O. Brown (1959.4), but an imposing dissent from their general opinion has been written by Marxians such as Theodor W. Adorno (1941.1) and Paul Baran (1957.3), both of whom faulted the The Theory of the Leisure Class for its "one-sided" attack on culture. Other Marxists, however, have been more disposed to accept the main features of this book as the critical literature indicates.

Mention should also be made of the opinions of writers such as Quentin Bell (1948.4), who sees Veblen as having made very important contributions to the theory of fashion, and David Riesman who, in spite of his critical attitude toward Veblen, continued the Veblenian mode of sociocultural analysis into the 1950s and 1960s. In the field of rhetoric and criticism, Kenneth Burke (1950.3) has assessed Veblen's contributions and one writer asserts that Burke himself was heavily influenced by Veblen (1971.6).

Introduction

A review of this reference guide will show that the writings of Thorstein Veblen brought forth enthusiastic responses from many and diverse fields of interest. Not only did Veblen spark controversy in economics, his primary interest, but in sociology, politics, literature, anthropology, journalism, and other fields as well. The number and quality of the responses to his ideas remain testimony to his insight and originality.

Major Writings of Thorstein Veblen

The Theory of the Leisure Class, 1899.
The Theory of Business Enterprise, 1904.
The Instinct of Workmanship and the State of the Industrial Arts,
   1914. [In text abbreviated to The Instinct of Workmanship.]
Imperial Germany and the Industrial Revolution, 1915.
An Inquiry into the Nature of Peace and the Terms of its
   Perpetuation, 1917. [In text abbreviated to The Nature of
   Peace.]
The Higher Learning in America: A Memorandum on the Conduct of
   Universities by Business Men, 1918. [In text abbreviated to The
   Higher Learning in America.]
The Place of Science in Modern Civilization and Other Essays, 1919.†
   [In text abbreviated to The Place of Science in Modern
   Civilization.] (Reprinted as Veblen on Marx, Race, Science, and
   Economics, 1969).
The Vested Interests and the State of the Industrial Arts, 1919.
   (Title changed in 1920 to The Vested Interests and the Common
   Man). †
The Engineers and the Price System, 1921.
Absentee Ownership and Business Enterprise in Recent Times: The Case
   of America, 1923. [In text abbreviated to Absentee Ownership and
   Business Enterprise in Recent Times.]
Essays in Our Changing Order (Edited with an introduction by Leon
   Ardzrooni, 1934).†
Thorstein Veblen: Essays, Reviews, and Reports, Previously
   Uncollected Writings (Edited with an introduction by Joseph
   Dorfman, 1973.)†

†These books are compilations of articles, reviews, or reports
written by Veblen. For a complete bibliography of Veblen's writings,
the reader is advised to consult together Thorstein Veblen and His
America (1966.4) by Joseph Dorfman and his edition of Thorstein
Veblen: Essays, Reviews, and Reports, Previously Uncollected
Writings (1973.8).

Writings about Thorstein Veblen, 1891-1982

1891

1 [GUNTON, GEORGE]. Review of "Some Neglected Points in the Theory of Socialism." Social Economist [Gunton's Magazine] 2 (November):61-62.
    Finds Veblen's views on socialism to be vague and idealistic. Defends emulation against Veblen's critique; without it people would relapse into idleness.

1899

1 ANON. Review of The Theory of the Leisure Class. Popular Science Monthly 55 (August):557-58.
    Summarizes the main points of the book.

2 CUMMINGS, JOHN. "The Theory of the Leisure Class." Journal of Political Economy 7 (September):425-55.
    A critique of Veblen based upon the general assumptions that underlie justification of vested interests. Finds Veblen's ethnology less than convincing and rejects his contention that the wealthy leisure class retards development while simultaneously striving to preserve obsolescence. Retorts that if the captain of industry is a social parasite, then so is the laborer. Disagrees with Veblen that accumulated wealth constitutes confiscation of the earnings of others; accumulated wealth is accumulated earnings. In general, finds Veblen's history to be "histrionic," his theory of predation factually unjustifiable, his theory of property as "booty" unfair, and his attack on business partially incorrect. "It is the cleverness itself, the sophistry consistently maintained that bears witness to a more or less conscious intent on the part of the author, and itself elicits criticism. The author of The Theory of the Leisure Class is clearly a master of sophistical dialectic."

3 HOWELLS, W[ILLIAM] D[EAN]. "An Opportunity for American Fiction [First Paper]." Literature, n.s. no. 16 (28 April): pp. 361-62.

Reviews The Theory of the Leisure Class. Praises Veblen's "clear method," "graphic and easy style," and "delightful accuracy of characterisation." Sees the work as an inspiration for a novelist who wishes to detail the foibles of the leisure class. Reprinted: 1973.13.

4 _____. "An Opportunity for American Fiction [Second Paper]." Literature, n.s. no. 17 (5 May): pp. 385-86.
After a brief summary of The Theory of the Leisure Class writes that "Mr. Veblen has brought to its study the methods and habits of scientific inquiry. To translate these into dramatic terms would form the unequalled triumph of the novelist who had the seeing eye and the thinking mind, not to mention the feeling heart." Reprinted: 1973.14.

5 [MacKENNA, STEPHEN]. "The Luxury of Lazihead." Criterion, no. 479 (25 March): pp. 26-27.
Reviews The Theory of the Leisure Class. Praises the book for its "lively reading," "humor" and "shrewd observation." An "immensely educating" book, "it deserves to be widely read and lovingly set on the nearer shelves." Reprinted: 1973.16.

6 WELLS, B.W. Review of The Theory of the Leisure Class. Sewanee Review 7 (July):369-74.
Characterizes Veblen's book as one of the "most curious" to be reviewed this season. The work contains satire, "irony, and much of it is a vicious attack on Christian ideals. It is not worth reading for instruction, in spite of its assumption of economic terminology; but there is an element of truth in its satire and there is a taking incisiveness in some of its epigrammatic statements."

7 WELLS, D. COLLIN. Review of The Theory of the Leisure Class. Yale Review, o.s. 8 (August):213-18.
Finds the title of the book pretentious. The work is characterized by insufficient economic data and a paucity of necessary definitions of key terms. Faults Veblen's anthropology and writes that the "most vicious distinction made in the book is that between pecuniary and industrial economic institutions. . . ." Veblen's use of the English language is described as "scientific? jargon from which no clear meaning can be extracted."

1900

1 HENDERSON, CHARLES. "Social Discussion and Reform." Dial 28 (January):436-40.
Reviews The Theory of the Leisure Class. Asserts that Veblen "proceeds with the cool temper of pure intelligence . . . his style is chilled steel: hard, cold and sharp. Its light is dry and frosty." The book avoids the word "socialism," yet the tenets of that doctrine certainly "gleam" through. Though the

book does not sufficiently define the concept of "usefulness," it should be read by those who will either not read it or throw it "aside in anger and contempt."

2　LINDSAY, SAMUEL McCUNE. "The Economic Principle Underlying Human Institutions." Annals of the American Academy of Political and Social Science 15 (March):282-86.
　　Reviews The Theory of the Leisure Class. Charges that Veblen attempts to explain modern institutions by using data taken "largely from the disputable facts of primitive society without sufficient evidence that he has made good use of the best material as far as it goes. . . ." Veblen is also to be faulted for writing that animistic habits of thought result in "a lowering of . . . effective intelligence" in the believer. Veblen's book has not succeeded in explaining the topics it alleges to; it is a "cynical comment on modern life" and is not a satisfactory account of the leisure class.

3　WARD, LESTER F. Review of The Theory of the Leisure Class. American Journal of Sociology 5 (May):829-37.
　　Comments that if anything, Veblen's book contains too much truth and is bound to upset some readers. The subject dealt with is clearly and consistently handled. The focus is on economic matters and Veblen should not be attacked for not detailing the positive contributions made by the leisure class. Veblen effectively distinguishes pecuniary value from intrinsic value and links the former to barbaric residues from an earlier stage of predation. He also shows the difference between acquiring the most by the least effort and producing the most. The leisure class does little of value--its function is exploitation. Praises Veblen's theory of fashion as "largely true." Veblen's style is "plain and unmistakable" and he is credited with introducing a plethora of satiric and penetrating expressions. The book is to be praised. Reprinted: 1967.18; 1973.23.

1901

1　DAY, A.M. Review of The Theory of the Leisure Class. Political Science Quarterly 16 (June):366-69.
　　Claims that readers may dissent in part or even wholly from such a radical thesis as Veblen puts forth. Veblen fails to clearly define the parameters of the leisure class and his "estimates of the force and value of various motives and perhaps most of all, his neglect to explain why his, rather than another's 'dispassionate common sense' should decide for us whether a given expenditure results in a net 'gain in comfort or in the fullness of life.'" States that Veblen's attempts to measure the function of a given social institution by its effects on economic welfare must fail. While Veblen has not presented the theory of the leisure class, there are stinging truths to be found on every page which are worthy of stimulation.

2   SIMONS, A.M. Review of "Industrial and Pecuniary Employ-
     ments." International Socialist Review 1 (May):739-40.
          Considers the work a masterpiece. "It takes all the pet
     phrases of the classical economists of the colleges and uses them
     to make their teaching ridiculous. How any of the professors who
     listened to this talk could go back to their classes and continue
     their work with sober faces is hard to comprehend."

                              1904

1   COLBY, F.M. Review of The Theory of Business Enterprise.
     Bookman 20 (November):255-57.
          Finds there is much that is suggestive to both specialists
     and laymen despite the fact that Veblen has a way of making
     "plain everyday matters look rather queer; . . . when he touches
     on broader sociological themes, he is probably mad. . . ."

2   [GUNTON, GEORGE]. Review of The Theory of Business Enter-
     prise. Gunton's Magazine 27 (November):517-19.
          Veblen's book is "true to its title." Veblen is worried
     about the effect of the machine process on culture. His pessi-
     mism notwithstanding, there are benefits which result from indus-
     trialization, for example, industrial insurance. Veblen provides
     scant evidence to support his claim that business enterprise will
     decay and disappear. Veblen's pessimism is at the same time his
     chief weakness, "the book is a careful discussion of the business
     enterprise, and abounds in wholesome suggestions. . . ."

3   SIMONS, A[LGIE] M. "The Theory of Business Enterprise."
     International Socialist Review 5 (December):348-55.
          Reviews The Theory of Business Enterprise. Finds Veblen's
     book to be shrewd and insightful, although sarcastic and cynical.
     Perhaps the strongest part of the book is its analysis of the
     effect of the machine process on contemporary culture. The
     weakest portion is Veblen's theory of crises that result from
     credit operations.

4   TUFTS, J[AMES] H[AYDEN]. Review of The Theory of Business
     Enterprise. Psychological Bulletin 1 (15 June):398-403.
          Praises the book for its insights into the psychology of
     business practices. Notes the "cool, scientific dissection of
     current processes, standards and ideals. . . ." While there are
     other works purporting to explain business enterprise, none can
     compare in interest with Veblen's analysis. Reprinted: 1973.22.

5   WERGELAND, A[GNES] M. Review of The Theory of Business Enter-
     prise. Journal of Political Economy 13 (December):115-17.
          Claims that Veblen's latest book is less entertaining than
     The Theory of the Leisure Class and is burdened with language
     which may befuddle the lay reader. Also asserts that the book
     will perplex good Republicans. "It may be pertinent to ask what

                               4

shall become of the individual consumer when prices are regulated
by a monopoly, which, as experience shows, does not tend to lower
prices, even if it does help to cheapen production." Praises
Veblen's analysis of business thinking and his awareness of the
absence of thrift amongst industrial workers. A scholarly and
well-informed book.

1905

1   ANON. "Veblen's Business Enterprise." Nation 81
     (13 July):37-38.
          Veblen's "oracular style" notwithstanding, it is difficult
     to find anything original in The Theory of Business Enterprise.
     Veblen's theory may impress the "half-educated," and it is no
     difficult task to point to immoral business practices in bygone
     eras. "Such a theory as is here set forth may impress the
     readers of sensational magazines; but it is a travesty of
     economics, and an unjust aspersion of our business morality."

2   CARVER, THOMAS NIXON. Review of The Theory of Business Enter-
     prise. Political Science Quarterly 20 (March):141-43.
          Admits that Veblen is difficult to understand and offers a
     hypothesis as to what he is driving at. Veblen puts forth an
     analysis of the "large businessman" and an economic interpreta-
     tion of history. His assertion that the big business entrepre-
     neur is an acquirer rather than a producer of wealth is no doubt
     correct.

3   DANIELS, WINTHROP M. Review of The Theory of Business Enter-
     prise. Atlantic Monthly 95 (April):557-59.
          Contends that the book contains glimpses "of the cosmic
     irony of Ibsen and the nihilistic doctrines of Nietzsche."
     Veblen's fascination with the morbid aspects of economic proces-
     ses blinds him, however, to their wholesome sides. "Veblen has a
     preternaturally vivid insight into the pathological side of busi-
     ness and society; and he follows remorselessly the poisoned tract
     which his scalpel has discovered."

4   DIXON, FRANK HAIGH. Review of The Theory of Business Enter-
     prise. Yale Review, o.s. 14 (May):96-99.
          Questions whether Veblen has carried the distinction be-
     tween industrial and pecuniary employments too far. Nonetheless
     Veblen has performed a real service if he has compelled us for a
     moment "to look at modern industrial life from the point of view
     of the businessman instead of the producer and consumer."

5   DUNCAN, JOHN C. Review of The Theory of Business Enterprise.
     Annals of the American Academy of Political and Social Science
     25 (May):198.
          States that Veblen overemphasized the influence of the
     machine process on the modern "matter-of-fact attitude of mind."

It is difficult to follow Veblen when he suggests that "business enterprise will cause man to give up his spiritual beliefs. . . ."

6   LaMONT, ROBERT RIVES. "Veblen, the Revolutionist." Inter-
     national Socialist Review 5 (June):726-39.
          Argues that the main features of Veblen's economic theory
     are "nothing more than Marxian exegesis." Recognizes Veblen as
     "the very greatest intellect that has been applied to economic
     and social questions since Marx and Engels" but still sees him as
     operating within a framework laid down by those earlier thinkers.

7   WALLING, WILLIAM ENGLISH. "An American Socialism." Inter-
     national Socialist Review 5 (April):577-84.
          Points out some major differences between the socialist
     views of Veblen and Marx. In Veblen's mind, it is the business-
     man rather than the great capitalist who stands as the enemy of
     society. Veblen's businessman believes in himself and is a
     sincere fellow, while Marx's capitalist is a cynic. Marx and
     Veblen agree that businessmen are useless to society. A signifi-
     cant difference between Marx and Veblen has to do with the advent
     of socialism. Marx and his followers envisage one industry after
     coming under democratic control. But Veblen has witnessed a
     trend toward trusts, monopolies, and mergers; so what Marx and
     his followers predicted is not occurring in America. Veblen more
     than Marx recognized the importance of environment in human
     progress. With respect to class struggle, Marx sees it in terms
     of conflict of interests while Veblen stresses a conflict of
     minds (habits of thought). Veblen's view suggests that attitudes
     might be harder to mold or change than Marx thought. Although
     Veblen thinks that evolutionary economics will bring socialism to
     the United States, he refrains from adopting a position on public
     ownership and does not even attempt a tight definition of
     socialism.

1906

1   HEATH, J.St.G. Review of The Theory of Business Enterprise.
     Economic Review 16 (October):492-97.
          Finds the book to be "a most remarkable and valuable con-
     tribution to economic literature . . . a daring attack upon the
     absurdity of modern methods of production." Veblen draws back
     from offering solutions to the problems he illuminates in such an
     original and bold fashion.

2   STUART, HENRY W. Review of "The Place of Science in Modern
     Civilization." Journal of Philosophy, Psychology, and
     Scientific Method 3 (July):385-87.
          Summarizes the article and claims that Veblen makes an
     "interesting" and "important" contribution to the discussion of
     the relationship of pragmatism to science.

1909

1   FISHER, IRVING. "Capital and Interest." Political Science
    Quarterly 24 (September):504-16.
         Replies to Veblen's critical reviews of his work. States
    that Veblen faults him for not confining his study to "pecuniary"
    concepts and for not basing his analysis of interest rates on a
    historical analysis of private property and industrial organiza-
    tion. Veblen's characterization of him as a "classifier" con-
    fuses classification with analysis. Denies Veblen's accusation
    that he relies upon Benthamite hedonistic calculus. "His criti-
    cisms are almost all generalities on methodology and concepts,
    and for the most part they disregard the special conclusions
    which differentiate my books from others on his index
    expurgatorius."

1914

1   ANON. "The Industrial Situation and Society." Review of
    Reviews 49 (May):637.
         Finds The Instinct of Workmanship to be a "suggestive
    essay."

2   HOLLINGSWORTH, H.L. Review of The Instinct of Workmanship.
    Psychological Bulletin 11 (15 November):441-42.
         Argues that Veblen tends to mistake "convenient historical
    description for adequate psychological explanation, and to confuse
    the conceptualized forms of behavior with its causal mechanism."

3   MITCHELL, WESLEY C. "Human Behavior and Economics: A Survey
    of Recent Literature." Quarterly Journal of Economics 29
    (November):1-47.
         Analyzes Veblen's concept of the "instinct of workmanship"
    and defends it against critics. Argues that Veblen was fully
    aware of the fact that instinct was a suspect category in biology
    and psychology and qualified his use of the term. Relates the
    instinct of workmanship to the use of technology.

4   WEATHERLY, ULYSSES G. Review of The Instinct of Workmanship.
    American Economic Review 4 (December):860-61.
         Notes Veblen's concept of culture lag and criticizes him
    for being "too remote and impersonal" and for never letting the
    reader know whether his conclusions are actually those the author
    intends him to draw. Nonetheless, this is a stimulating essay on
    the psychology and sociology of work.

1915

1   ANON. "Mr. Veblen's Interesting Theory to Account for the
    Rapidity of Economic Growth in the Empire." New York Times
    Book Review, 18 July, p. 258.

Reviews Imperial Germany and the Industrial Revolution.
"Though sometimes too wordy and often needlessly technical in its
language, this book contains much vigorous, original thinking and
its main conclusions command assent."

2   ANON. Review of Imperial Germany and the Industrial Revolution. Booklist 12 (November):68.
     Notes the elaborate comparison made between the economic
and political systems of Germany and England.

3   ANON. Review of Imperial Germany and the Industrial Revolution. Dial 59 (14 October):331-32.
     Suggests that little is gained by Veblen's discussion of
the Baltic peoples of the Stone Age. Nonetheless, the book is as
successful as Veblen's earlier efforts.

4   ANON. Review of Imperial Germany and the Industrial Revolution. Nation 101 (2 September):292.
     Summarizes German industrial development. Veblen is both
economist and sociologist and combines the two.

5   DOWNEY, E.H. Review of The Instinct of Workmanship. Journal
of Political Economy 23 (January):78-80.
     This volume follows in the spirit of Veblen's earlier works
though stylistically and satirically less brilliant. A "substantial contribution."

6   FREEMAN, R.E. Review of Imperial Germany and the Industrial
Revolution. Journal of Political Economy 23 (October):852-54.
     Summarizes Veblen's book and concludes, "If the reader has
developed a taste for the author's characteristically cumbrous
verbiage, he will find Imperial Germany and the Industrial Revo-
ution excellent in every respect."

7   GEDDES, PATRICK. Cities in Evolution. London: Williams and
Norgate, pp. 117-18. Reprint. New York: Howard Fertig,
1968.
     Claims that Veblen was the first to provide a keen analysis
of the diverse tendencies of the machine and commercial processes.
Veblen recognizes the unremitting force of the machine and its
impact on society. "Thus in his own way he practically expresses
and explains that birth of the neotechnic age from the paleo-
technic, which is a central thesis of the present volume."

8   HAYES, EDWARD C. Review of The Instinct of Workmanship.
American Journal of Sociology 20 (March):706-8.
     Claims that Veblen "recognizes the importance of inborn
propensities. . . ." One may wish to raise questions concerning
the nature of instincts or the relationship between institutions
and habits. The book is "thoroughly characterized by the sociological point of view. . . ."

9   WALLAS, GRAHAM. "Veblen's Imperial Germany and the Industrial
     Revolution." Quarterly Journal of Economics 30
     (November):179-87.
          Claims that Veblen overestimates the importance of the
     neolithic period in forming the "human nature of the North
     European hybrid peoples." Even though Veblen affects an air of
     detachment, his contempt for the German imperial system is evi-
     dent. Approves of Veblen's demonstration of how latecomers to
     industrialization eventually eclipse their predecessors. Would
     prefer that Veblen's next book not be marred by "irony and reti-
     cence" and that he write directly and propose some alternatives
     to the institutions he attacks.

10   WEYL, WALTER E. "The Dynastic State." New Republic 4
     (24 July):317.
          Commends Veblen's Imperial Germany and the Industrial Revo-
     ution. Nonetheless Veblen's aloofness leaves the reader with a
     feeling of frustration. Does not the German system contain
     something valuable or permanent? To what does Germany owe its
     discipline? Veblen should supply some answers to questions such
     as these.

                              1916

1   BOGART, ERNEST L. Review of Imperial Germany and the Indus-
     trial Revolution. Mississippi Valley Historical Review 3
     (September):229-30.
          Praises the book for its keen analysis, incisive criti-
     cisms, and timely and unique economic interpretation. "The book
     is broader than its title."

2   FAY, SIDNEY B. Review of Imperial Germany and the Industrial
     Revolution. American Economic Review 6 (June):353-56.
          Veblen offers few facts "but advances many interesting
     propositions." Summarizes his explanation of Germany's rapid
     industrialization.

3   JOHNSON, ALVIN S. Review of The Instinct of Workmanship.
     Political Science Quarterly 21 (December):631-33.
          Charges that Veblen is a master at locating traces of
     teleology in the writings of others but falls prey to it himself.
     Provides a brief analysis of Veblen's theory of workmanship.

4   SUTHERLAND, E.H. Review of Imperial Germany and the Indus-
     trial Revolution. American Journal of Sociology 21 (November):
     555-57.
          Veblen does much more than describe German culture and
     institutions; he offers an explanation. Praises Veblen's in-
     sights but criticizes his "usual cumbrous" style.

                               9

<u>1917</u>

1   ANON. Review of <u>The Nature of Peace</u>. <u>Nation</u> 105 (5 July):
    14-15.
        Disagrees with Veblen's complete denunciation of patri-
otism--surely it must mean something more than "invidious prestige." The most interesting aspect of the book is the concrete
and specific conditions that Veblen sets down for the attainment
of peace.

2   ANON. Review of <u>The Nature of Peace</u>. <u>North American Review</u>
    206 (October):633-35.
        Contends that Veblen's conclusions regarding the possibil-
ity of peace are cynical and gloomy, and there is a "bitter
criticism" of the social order. Feels that there must be "an
implied fallacy" in Veblen's dark vision. But then, his "analysis is clarifying and his warnings are well-timed."

3   ANON. Review of <u>The Nature of Peace</u>. <u>Springfield Republican</u>,
    3 June, p. 17.
        Suggests that Veblen's book is an elaborate case for
socialism. Interesting as it is, "it hardly fails to outline the
framework of peace." There is "no lack of candor" in this book.

4   ANON. Review of <u>The Nature of Peace</u>. <u>Times Literary
    Supplement</u> (London), 9 August, p. 383.
        "This is the work of an American Economist of some note in
the university world. . . . We have seldom read a book written
in a style so repellently ponderous."

5   DELL, FLOYD. Review of <u>The Nature of Peace</u>. <u>Masses</u> 9
    (July):40-41.
        Refers to Veblen as the "most brilliant and perhaps the
most profound of American scholars." Notes that Veblen's work
will damage the cherished beliefs of both pacifists and mili-
tarists. Thinks, but is not certain, that Veblen is on the side
of those who would destroy Germany.

6   FRAINA, LOUIS C. "Socialists and War." <u>Class Struggle</u> 1
    (July-August):75-99.
        Finds a "great deal of truth" in Veblen's analysis in
<u>Imperial Germany and the Industrial Revolution</u>, but not the
"fundamental truth." Argues, contrary to Veblen, that German
autocracy prevails not because of its own power, but rather
because the autocracy has compromised with "Imperialistic capitalism." This article is part of a debate with Robert Rives
LaMont in the same issue, see 1917.10.

7   HACKETT, FRANCIS. Review of <u>The Nature of Peace</u>. <u>New
    Republic</u> 11 (26 May):113-14.
        Veblen is not well known and is extremely difficult to read
and understand. This is "the most momentous work in English on

the encompassment of lasting peace." Veblen is credited with
pinpointing the warlike tendencies of nations such as Germany and
Japan. The "Brahms-like quality" of Veblen's writing ensures
that he will not gain a wide reading audience. Reprinted:
1918.2; 1973.12.

8   HANDMAN, MAX SYLVIUS. "Some Fundamentals of Peace." Dial 62
     (14 June):514-15.
         Summarizes The Nature of Peace and commends Veblen's
     "scientific objectivity" in his investigations.

9   HOXIE, ROBERT FRANKLIN. Trade Unionism in the United States.
     New York: D. Appleton & Co., pp. 365-70.
         Compares Veblen's theory with socialism. Sees Veblen's
     theory as overly deterministic and pessimistic.

10   LaMONT, ROBERT RIVES. "Socialists and War." Class Struggle 1
     (July-August):59-75.
         Relies upon Veblen's Imperial Germany and the Industrial
     Revolution to support his pessimistic conclusions regarding
     Socialists and their support for World War I. This article is
     part of a debate with Louis Fraina in the same issue, see 1917.6.

11   LASKER, BRUNO. Review of The Nature of Peace. Survey 38
     (22 September):554.
         Claims that Veblen "is perfectly open-minded in his
     approach" to the problem of achieving peace. The book will do
     much to stimulate readers.

12   MacELWEE, R.S. Review of Imperial Germany and the Industrial
     Revolution. Political Science Quarterly 32 (June):336-37.
         "This is a most suggestive work. . . ." Claims that while
     there exist many "misconceptions or misstatements of fact," it is
     well worth the trouble to read. States that Veblen does not pay
     sufficient attention to the fact of political unification as a
     precondition for Germany's drive to economic development and
     industrialization.

13   MAROT, HELEN. Review of The Nature of Peace. Political
     Science Quarterly 32 (September):590-94.
         Suggests that Veblen's book will please American patriots
     in spite of the fact that Veblen has nothing positive to say
     about patriotism in general.

14   R., D.S. "On the Nature and Uses of Patriotism during the
     Price System." Radical Review 1 (October):193-96.
         Reviews The Nature of Peace. Notes that Veblen does
     not use the expression "capitalism" in his book, but, rather the
     expression "price system." Quetions Veblen's premise that
     machine discipline will do away with not only illiteracy but
     also faith. However, Veblen's general conclusions appear to be
     correct.

<u>1918</u>

1   BEARD, CHARLES. "The Hire Learning in America." <u>Dial</u> 65
    (14 December):553-55.
        Reviews <u>The Higher Learning in America</u>. Accepts much of
    what Veblen says but demurs over the issue of how the modern
    university is to be financed. Veblen's suggestion that trustees
    and presidents of universities be scrapped is unrealistic.

2   HACKETT, FRANCIS. "The Cost of Peace." In <u>Horizons:</u> <u>A Book</u>
    <u>of Criticism</u>. New York: B.W. Huebsch, pp. 245-52.
        Reprint of 1917.7. Reprinted: 1973.12.

3   HOWERTH, I.W. Review of <u>The Nature of Peace</u>. <u>American</u>
    <u>Journal of Sociology</u> 23 (November):408-12.
        Chides Veblen for being too "cool" and detached and also
    for taking a "fling" at the pacifists who, in Veblen's view, have
    accomplished little or nothing. Otherwise the book is "thor-
    oughly worthwhile."

4   MEAD, GEORGE H. Review of <u>The Nature of Peace</u>. <u>Journal of</u>
    <u>Political Economy</u>. 26 (June):752-62.
        Veblen's "formulas are too simple and abstract to do jus-
    tice either to social movements or to the psychology of the
    individual." Takes the position that Veblen overemphasized the
    exploitive function of the propertied class and finds Veblen's
    proposals to end war unsatisfactory.

<u>1919</u>

1   ANON. "Our Commercialized Universities." <u>Nation</u> 108
    (22 February):286-88.
        Summarizes Veblen's attack on American universities in
    <u>The Higher Learning in America</u>. Sympathizes yet feels that
    Veblen may be wrong in arguing that professors should pursue
    knowledge and research only. "Versatility is not a lost gift."

2   ANON. "Prof. Veblen's New Book." <u>Springfield Republican</u>,
    14 July, p. 6.
        Reviews <u>The Vested Interests and the State of the Indus-
    trial Arts</u>, calling it "characteristically brilliant. . . ."
    Notes that Veblen refuses to use the expression "capitalism" in
    his criticism of the present economic system.

3   ANON. Review of <u>The Higher Learning in America</u>. <u>American</u>
    <u>Historical Review</u> 24 (July):714-15.
        Agrees that the state of affairs in the running of univer-
    sities by businessmen is as bad as Veblen charges. Feels, how-
    ever, that Veblen is wrong in believing that the university's
    mission is to conduct research rather than teach students and
    claims that Veblen exaggerates the degree of stimulation which

graduate students provide for their instructors. "But Mr. Veblen's essay is profitable reading--especially for trustees."

4   ANON. Review of The Higher Learning in America. North American Review 209 (19 March):417-20.
     Writes "that The Higher Learning in America bears all the marks of being one of those rare books which contain such truth as seldom finds its way into print. . . ." Feels that Veblen's book will have the effect of bringing about a "different state of affairs" in university matters. Reprinted: 1973.1.

5   ANON. Review of The Vested Interests and the State of the Industrial Arts. Booklist 16 (November):44.
     Writes that Veblen applies his usual keen analysis to explain how capital can control wages and limit production in an age when the machine has become so important.

6   ANON. "Vested Interests versus Humanity." New York Times Book Review, 5 October, p. 525.
     Reviews The Vested Interests and the State of the Industrial Arts. Sees Veblen as "chief" of a handful of "serious" thinkers who, dissatisfied with the state of the world, aim to change it.

7   BENCHLY, ROBERT C. "The Dullest Book of the Month." Vanity Fair 12 (April):39.
     A tongue-in-cheek review of The Theory of the Leisure Class which was selected because "Dr. Veblen has recently been the storm-center of a soviet uprising among the young ladies of New York who compose the Junior League." Considers the book on the whole to be a good work, hastily done. "In the hands of a more serious-minded student it might have been developed to greater lengths." Finds it interesting that only those with leisure would be able to read the book. Reprinted: 1973.3.

8   DUFFUS, ROBERT L. "Two Iconoclasts: Veblen and Vanderlip." Dial 67 (26 July):62-64.
     Considers Veblen's views on the sabotage of production by businessmen. Rates Veblen a socialist but not as dogmatic as Lenin or Marx.

9   DUPRAT, G.L. Review of The Higher Learning in America. Revue international de sociologie [International review of sociology] 27 (June):311-12.
     Summarizes Veblen's critique of the American university. Notes Veblen's pessimism regarding the possibility of freeing higher learning from business domination.

10   HAMILTON, WALTON H. "Veblenian Common Sense." New Republic 20 (26 November):16-17.

Reviews The Vested Interests and the State of the Industrial Arts. What Veblen says here he has said in his previous
works. The book should be read by those who sit in industrial
conferences.

11 J., W. "A Work for Thinkers." New York Call, 20 April,
    p. 10.
        Reviews The Nature of Peace. A masterpiece by a master.
Not a book for the casual reader, it might well "puzzle an igno-
ramus like William Howard Taft and other promoters of 'Leagues
for International Peace.'"

12 LASKI, HAROLD J. "The Higher Learning in America." New
    Republic 17 (11 January):317-18.
        States that "Veblen's criticisms are always pointed and
often profound." Feels that Veblen is wide of the mark in his
attack on graduate and law schools, which serve a decent purpose.

13 MATHEWS, BRANDER. "Mr. Veblen's Gas Attack on Our Colleges
    and Universities." New York Times, 16 March, pp. 125, 127-28.
        Reviews The Higher Learning in America. Charges Veblen
with poor craftsmanship, "illiteracy," and awkward style. Evinces
"surprise" that Veblen had not only graduated from college but
held a Ph.D. Argues further that Veblen's attack on university
administrators is based on ignorance of higher education. Claims
that "this book is unusual in its bad manners and perhaps, I
should say, its bad morals."

14 MENCKEN, HENRY L. "Professor Veblen and the Cow." Smart Set
    59 (May):138-44.
        Reviews The Theory of the Leisure Class. Lampoons Veblen's
use of language and belittles his ideas. The only thing that is
new in Veblen's books "is the astoundingly grandiose and rococo
manner of their statement--the almost unbelievable tediousness
and flatulence of the learned schoolmaster's prose. . . . The
result is a style that affects the higher cerebral centers like a
constant roll of subway expresses." Finds The Theory of the
Leisure Class to be simply socialism and water. Veblen's charges
in The Higher Learning in America are found to be exceedingly
correct, but only too obvious. He has a way of making obvious
things look profound. Revised and reprinted: 1919.15. Excerpted and reprinted: 1949.13; 1960.3; 1965.8.

15 _____. "Professor Veblen." In Prejudices: First Series.
    New York: Alfred A. Knopf, pp. 59-82.
        Minor stylistic revision of 1919.14. Excerpted and
reprinted: 1949.13; 1960.3; 1965.8.

16 PARKER, LOCKIE. "Veblen on the Vested Interests." Reedy's
    Mirror 28 (11 December):872-73.
        Reviews The Vested Interests and the State of the Indus-
trial Arts. Finds it interesting that the more conservative

periodicals are taking an interest in Veblen. Does not think
that Veblen's language is "weird" and states that Veblen has
always been careful in defining his terms. Although there is
not much in this volume that Veblen has not dealt with in earlier
writings, one notices that this work moves toward "concrete
application and propaganda, and away from the abstraction,
detachment and greater impartiality of his early work."

17   ROCHE-AGUSSOL, MAURICE. Étude bibliographique des sources de
      la psychologie economique [Bibliographical study of the
      sources of economic psychology]. Montpellier: R.V. Darsac,
      pp. 89-92.
          Brief description of Veblen's critique of the orthodox
      tradition in economics.

18   S., H. "Thorstein Veblen, Iconoclast." New York Call,
      5 October, p. 515.
          Reviews The Vested Interests and the State of the Indus-
      trial Arts. Veblen's aloof style will not appeal to the common
      man; it is uninviting. So his ideas will have to be passed on by
      other intellectuals. Veblen's criticism is rich and powerful.

                              1920

1   ANON. "Mr. Veblen's Economics." Springfield Republican,
      18 March, p. 539.
          Reviews The Place of Science in Modern Civilization. The
      study is provocative and comprehensive in spite of Veblen's
      involved style and ponderous vocabulary. "Is it too much to hope
      that some of his followers will translate this book into English
      readable to economic laymen?"

2   ANON. Review of The Engineers and the Price System. Review
      of Reviews 64 (August):23.
          Brief comment on the importance of technicians and the
      remote possibility of a revolutionary overturn in the United
      States.

3   ANON. Review of The Place of Science in Modern Civilization.
      Survey 44 (5 June):352.
          States that Veblen's delvings into anthropology and natural
      philosophy "are evidence of a range of interests, which by its
      extent, explains the originality of his thinking on topics fall-
      ing more immediately within the scope of the student of
      economics."

4   DEUTSCH, BABETTE. "Neo-Darwinian Economics." Dial 69
      (20 July):79-82.
          Reviews The Place of Science in Modern Civilization.
      Emphasizes the genetic or evolutionary approach taken by Veblen.

Refers to "passages that rouse impatience because of the author's very carelessness of pragmatism." Veblen's work is eminently Darwinian.

5   KNIGHT, FRANK H. Review of The Place of Science in Modern
    Civilization. Journal of Political Economy 28 (June):518-20.
        Accuses Veblen of knocking down idols only to replace them
with his own. Veblen is a keen critic but not a clear or constructive thinker. The most serious error in Veblen's philosophy
is his distinction between pecuniary and industrial employments.
Nonetheless the work is stimulating and worth study.

6   LeR[OSSIGNOL], J[AMES] E[DWARD]. Review of The Vested Inter-
    ests and the State of the Industrial Arts. Mississippi Valley
    Historical Review 7 (June):66.
        Complains that a brilliant satirist like Veblen finds it
easy to ridicule capitalism and the kept classes. Thinks that
Veblen's position is an orthodox Marxian one holding that industrial evolution "will create its own system of make-believe. . . ."

7   OVERSTREET, HARRY A. "The Place of Science." Nation 111
    (28 August):250.
        Reviews The Place of Science in Modern Civilization. Calls
special attention to Veblen's analyses of the preconceptions of
economics and socialism. This is "Veblen at his scientific
best."

8   ____. "Vested Interests." Nation 110 (31 January):150.
        Reviews The Vested Interests and the State of the Indus-
trial Arts. Notes the "bitterness" and "withering sarcasm" in
the book and Veblen's emphasis on the detrimental effect of old
ideas on current methods of production and distribution.

9   THORNDIKE, EDWARD L. "Psychological Notes on the Motives for
    Thrift." Annals of the American Academy of Political and
    Social Science 35 (January):212-18.
        Suggests that the best illustration of the desire for
objective approval can be found in "Veblen's brilliant analysis
of the economic activities of the leisure class." Perhaps a
display of thrift by the upper class would have the effect of
spurring emulative behavior on the part of the rest of society.

10 WILENSKY, NATHAN W. "The Interpreter Interpreted." New York
    Call, 16 May, p. 10.
        Reviews The Place of Science in Modern Civilization and
concludes that Veblen says nothing in this book that he has not
said before. The work lacks Veblen's usual witty style and
epithets. Veblen offers an acceptable theory of socialism for
"closet intellectuals; they can now accept socialistic principles
without the stigma attached to the term, and yet offer it as the
expression of their own befuddled liberalism."

1921

1   ANON. Review of The Engineers and the Price System. Booklist
    18 (December):72.
         Veblen discusses with clarity and without technical ver-
    biage the causes of sabotage, the evils of absentee ownership,
    and other questions.

2   ANON. Review of The Engineers and the Price System. Dial 71
    (21 November):614.
         Views Veblen's proposal that a soviet of technicians rule
    the United States with less than obvious enthusiasm. "One feels
    that the thinker has been swallowed alive by the propagandist."

3   ANON. Review of The Engineers and the Price System.
    Wisconsin Library Bulletin 17 (December):207.
         The book will attract attention, especially after the
    report of the Hoover Commission on industrial waste. Although
    the book is composed of articles published in Dial in 1919, the
    ideas are fundamental and not dated.

4   HALBWACHS, MAURICE. "Le facteur instinctif dans l'art
    industriel" [The instinctive factor in the industrial arts].
    Revue philosophique [Philosophical review] 91
    (March-April):214-33.
         Describes and assesses Veblen's theory of instincts, in
    particular the instinct of workmanship. Sees Veblen as a pene-
    trating thinker and observer of modern life. His theory of the
    instinct of workmanship is significant in understanding the evo-
    lution and nature of the industrial economy.

5   HAMILTON, WALTON H. Review of The Place of Science in Modern
    Civilization. American Economic Review 11 (June):268-71.
         Praises Veblen's critical evaluation of economic theories
    in general and suggests that this criticism plays an important
    constructive role as well. "The present danger is that his work
    will be appraised in terms that are indefinite and cosmic."

6   JOHNSON, ALVIN. Review of The Place of Science in Modern
    Civilization. Political Quarterly 36 (March):129-32.
         Veblen indicted orthodox economics in order to demonstrate
    the barrenness of the present order. Yet would Veblen not "fall
    back upon the good old taxonomic economics . . . for an answer to
    present day practical economic problems?" Veblen's theory should
    enrich orthodox economics and not call for its abandonment.

7   KNIGHT, FRANK H. Risk, Uncertainty, and Profit. Boston and
    New York: Houghton Mifflin Co., pp. 28, 188, 234. Reprint.
    New York: Kelly and Millman, 1957.
         Disagrees with Veblen's contentions that capital restricts
    access to technical knowledge and that business engages in sabo-
    tage in order to control prices.

8   MUMFORD, LEWIS. "If Engineers Were Kings." Freeman 4
    (23 November):261-62.
        Claims that Veblen's latest books, The Vested Interests and
    the State of the Industrial Arts and The Engineers and the Price
    System are different from his earlier writings and reveal more
    clearly his prejudices and dislikes. "Because we lack any common
    humane standards, the Utopia of Engineers, even at its best, is
    likely to be little better than the Mohammedan paradise of busi-
    ness." The problem lies in determining what is to be produced
    and how it is to be distributed.

                                1922

1   SINCLAIR, UPTON. The Goose-Step: A Study of American Educa-
    tion. Pasadena, Calif.: the author, pp. 163-64, 243, 297,
    308, 375, 434.
        Relates several incidents involving Veblen and his sojourn
    through American universities. Describes how Nicholas Murray
    Butler of Columbia University turned over to Brander Mathews the
    job of writing an unfavorable review of Veblen's The Higher
    Learning in America.

                                1924

1   ANON. Review of Absentee Ownership and Business Enterprise in
    Recent Times. Booklist 20 (March):201-2.
        "With beautiful clarity the author makes an objective,
    theoretical analysis and formulation of the main drift of the
    economic situation of today, applying his philosophy particularly
    to business as practiced in the United States. A searching
    inquiry into modern economic tendencies that is provocative of
    thought to the American citizen."

2   AYRES, CLARENCE E. Review of Absentee Ownership and Business
    Enterprise in Recent Times. International Journal of Ethics
    35 (October):101-2.
        Calls attention to Veblen's irony and his emphasis on the
    conflict between old mores and norms and the facts of the contem-
    porary machine age.

3   BERNARD, LUTHER LEE. Instinct. New York: Henry Holt & Co.,
    pp. 79-80, 131-32, 325, 354, 416, 451.
        Analyzes Veblen's theory of instincts and finds it to be
    more in accord with popular usage rather than scientifically
    precise language. Argues that Veblen's theory does violence to
    both the facts of neurology and the Mendelian theory.

4   CLARK, JOHN M. Review of Absentee Ownership and Business
    Enterprise in Recent Times. American Economic Review 14
    (June):289-93.

Suggests that Veblen's greater outspokenness in this volume
will lay him open to more criticism than he received as a result
of his earlier writings. Despite the alleged objectivity of the
book, it "is in fact highly selective and highly colored." Advances the criticism that Veblen in places is guilty of unsound
conclusions, e.g., that consolidations "generally succeed in
taxing the consumer enough to pay returns on inflated capitalization." In terms of literary quality, "probably the best thing he
has done." Scientifically speaking, "less than the height of his
achievement."

5   FRANK, LAWRENCE K. Review of Absentee Ownership and Business
     Enterprise in Recent Times. Political Science Quarterly 29
     (September):509–12.
     Asks whether it may be possible that the unearned income
which the few receive as a result of new tools and machinery
could benefit the underlying population in terms of pensions and
insurance.

6   GAUS, JOHN M. "Thorstein Veblen's Absentee Ownership."
     Springfield Republican, 10 August, p. 603.
     Veblen's Absentee Ownership and Business Enterprise in
Recent Times more than his other books provides a complete system
of economics. Importunes Veblen to abandon his dispassionate
style "and let your particular brand of eagle scream."

7   JAFFE, WILLIAM. Les théories économiques et sociales
     de Thorstein Veblen [The economic and social theories of
     Thorstein Veblen]. Paris: Marcel Grand, 187 pp.
     Submitted as a doctoral dissertation at the University of
Paris, this book introduces Veblen's ideas to French readers. It
provides historical background and assesses Veblen's political
economy, criticisms of orthodox economics, psychological theories, distinction between industry and business, and his analysis
of corporation finance. Faults Veblen for lack of systematic
organization and concrete proposals to remedy the institutions he
so vehemently attacks.

8   MacDONALD, WILLIAM. "Present Course of Business Enterprise in
     an Analysis." New York Times Book Review, 13 April, p. 14.
     A favorable review of Absentee Ownership and Business Enter-
prise in Recent Times but finds Veblen too dogmatic, learned, and
at times pessimistic.

9   MUSSEY, HENRY R. "Economics of the Madhouse." Nation 118
     (4 June):652–53.
     Reviews Absentee Ownership and Business Enterprise in
Recent Times and briefly compares Veblen's theory with that of
Marx. Although Veblen has much to say of value, he goes too far
in suggesting that the underlying population is exploited by
absentee owners.

19

10   TODD, ARTHUR J. Review of Absentee Ownership and Business
      Enterprise in Recent Times. American Journal of Sociology 29
      (March):619-20.
           Considers the book to be an astute economic analysis with
      leftist tendencies. Claims, however, that Veblen marshals facts
      in such a way as to support his thesis. Veblen's rather pessi-
      mistic depiction of the economic and social situation is not
      entirely correct.

                                  1925

1   ANON. "The Cynic in Economics." Times Literary Supplement
      (London), 2 April, pp. 224-30.
           Complains that Veblen is a cynic who gets his major ideas
      from Marx and updates them to suit his own satirical and bitter
      purposes.

2   BOUTHOL, GASTON. "Les théories économiques et sociales de
      M. Thorstein Veblen" [The economic and social theories of
      Thorstein Veblen]. Revue international de sociologie [Inter-
      national review of sociology] 33 (September-October):482-91.
           Describes Veblen's critique of classical economics and his
      instinct of workmanship theory, the latter of which bears a
      resemblance to ideas put forth by Rousseau. Veblen's distinction
      between industrial and pecuniary interests is given extensive
      treatment and his writings on economics are deemed to be incon-
      testably original. The only disappointing thing about Veblen is
      his refusal to offer practical proposals to remedy the problems
      he pinpoints so effectively.

3   BRANFORD, VICTOR. "Thorstein Veblen." Sociological Review,
      o.s. 17 (January):65-68.
           Summarizes Veblen's major ideas. Claims that while Veblen
      is primarily an economist, he has mastered psychology and anthro-
      pology as well. Veblen's psychology is of that approach now
      termed behaviorist. Finds it remarkable that an economist rather
      than a sociologist should provide such a supreme description of
      the characteristic processes of Western civilization.

4   HOLLANDER, L.M. Review of Veblen's translation of The
      Laxdaela Saga. Scandinavian Studies and Notes 8
      (November):258-59.
           Notes some peccadillos in Veblen's translation but finds it
      spirited and admirable. "It should be placed in every collection
      of Scandinavian books."

5   LASKI, HAROLD J. Review of The Theory of the Leisure Class
      and Absentee Ownership and Business Enterprise in Recent
      Times. Economica, no. 13 (March), pp. 95-96.
           Finds Veblen to be penetrating and incisive, with a gift
      for ironic statement. Faults him for his indirect approach and

relates some of his major themes to Mandeville, Tawney, and
Butler.

6   REYNAUD, H. Review of <u>Les theories économiques et sociales de</u>
    <u>Thorstein Veblen</u>, by William Jaffe. <u>Economic Journal</u> 35
    (September):446-48.
        In the course of the review, makes the following points
    about Veblen: that he is by no means a dispassionate writer;
    that he owes much to Marx and Sombart in his economic theories;
    that his instinct of workmanship is an adaptation of William
    James's "instinct of constructiveness"; that he has no proposals
    for reform and that "the average reader needs a walk in the sun
    to clear his head of sulphuric acid fumes between every two
    volumes." Finds Veblen's most original idea to be the distinc-
    tion between production and finance or between community inter-
    ests and those of big business. See 1924.7.

7   _____. Review of <u>The Theory of the Leisure Class</u>. <u>Economic</u>
    <u>Journal</u> 35 (September):445-46.
        Suggests that "A Theory of the Leisure Class" would be a
    more appropriate title for the book since Veblen has nothing
    positive to say about the leisure class nor why the lower classes
    tolerate its existence. "The whole treatment of the subject, and
    even more the style in which it is written, must make it most
    acceptable to the exponents of the class war."

8   VEBLEN, ANDREW A. <u>Veblen Genealogy</u>. San Diego: the
    author, 156 pp.
        Subtitle reads: "An account of the Norwegian ancestry of
    the Veblen family in America which was founded by Thomas Anderson
    Veblen and his wife Kari Bunde Veblen."

9   YOUNG, ALLYN A. "The Trend of Economics, as Seen by Some
    American Economists." <u>Quarterly Journal of Economics</u> 39
    (February):155-83.
        Maintains that while Veblen is a man of genius, he is more
    an impressionist or artist than scientist. Accuses Veblen of
    illogical statements and adroit fumblings.

1926

1   ANON. Publisher's Note to <u>The Theory of the Leisure Class</u>.
    New York: Vanguard Press, unpaginated.
        Describes Veblen in part as follows: "Urbanity of manners,
    executive ability and an innate gift of shedding light upon
    difficult economic complexities, made him a lecturer and editor
    of enduring popularity in the field of political economy. His
    life story as a university teacher is a long record of skillful,
    even-tempered resistance against encroachments upon academic
    freedom." As to the book: "American capitalism has established
    a larger number of boors of actual or potential leisure than can

be found anywhere else on the face of the habitable globe. The Theory of the Leisure Class is a thoroughly readable inquiry into their mode of life, their views and habits of expenditure, enlivened by an undercurrent of polite sarcasm that forms the main characteristic of Veblen's writings."

2　FOX, R.M. "Thorstein Veblen." Nineteenth Century 100 (November): 684-96.
　　　　Outlines Veblen's major ideas. Stresses Veblen's utilitarian view of life but finds his "abstraction of a perfectly adjusted industrial mechanism" a bit impracticable.

3　SLICHTER, SUMNER H. Review of Absentee Ownership and Business Enterprise in Recent Times. Yale Review 15 (April):614-18.
　　　　Contends that Veblen's book "does not explain why industry cannot profitably sell its potential output, and it suggests no remedies for the situation."

1927

1　CLARK, JOHN M. "Recent Developments in Economics." In Recent Developments in the Social Sciences. Edited by Edward C. Hayes. Philadelphia: J.B. Lippincott Co., pp. 213-306.
　　　　Addresses Veblen's place in American economics. Covers his criticism of marginal economics and his reversal of orthodox economic abstractions. Argues that Veblen's "taxonomy ranges from a sheer tool of polemics to the necessary framework of dynamic inquiry." While Veblen's insights are keen and challenging, they are not themselves amenable to scientific demonstration. Veblen's restatement of Marxism is commended, and criticisms of his work by others are noted.

2　EDIE, LIONEL. "Some Positive Contributions of the Institutional Concept." Quarterly Journal of Economics 41 (May): 405-40.
　　　　Devoted mainly to the school of institutional economics. Credits Veblen with being one of the first to recognize the significance of the pecuniary concept and the fact that private interest does not necessarily coincide with public benefit. Notes Veblen's influence on W.C. Mitchell.

3　FETTER, FRANK A. "Amerika [America]." In Die Wirtschaftstheorie der Gegenwart: Gesamtbild der Forschung in den einzelnen Ländern [Contemporary economic theory: summary of research in the various countries]. Edited by Hans Meyer with Frank A. Fetter and Richard Reisch. Vienna: Verlag von Julius Springer, pp. 31-60.
　　　　Describes Veblen's contributions to economic theory, stressing his critique of marginal utility theory and his contribution to the institutional theory of economics. Notes his

relationship to, and influence on, such thinkers as W.C.
Mitchell, W.H. Hamilton, Paul Douglas, H.J. Davenport, and
others.

4 FLUGGE, EVA. "Institutionalismus" [Institutionalism].
   Jahrbucher für Nationalökonomie und Statistik [Yearbook for
   national economy and statistics], 3d ser. 71:337-56.
       Discusses Veblen's place in the institutionalist movement
   in economics. Compares the role of American institutionalism
   with that of the German historical school.

5 HOMAN, PAUL [T.]. "Thorstein Veblen." In American Masters of
   Social Science. Edited by Howard W. Odum. New York: Henry
   Holt & Co., pp. 231-70.
       Claims that Veblen is not merely a critic of orthodox
   economic theory; he supplies an institutional theory based on
   human instincts and habits of thought. A great deal of Veblen's
   best work involves his analysis of business enterprise as it
   operates in the context of the machine age. Questions whether
   the evolutionary or genetic approach favored by Veblen in economics and sociology is applicable to fields such as physics, chem-
   istry, or botany. Veblen also fails to supply a canon of welfare
   and cannot be rated very highly as a scientist either. His
   greatest contribution lies in his ability to raise questions,
   influence others, and stimulate interest in social matters.
   Abridged and reprinted: 1928.3; 1968.10.

                            1928

1 ANON. Review of Contemporary Economic Thought, by Paul T.
   Homan. Nation 127 (3 October):326.
       "As a contribution to the history of economic theory it is
   as novel and commendable as the writing of Veblen and Hobson in
   the field of economic theory."

2 HOMAN, PAUL T. "Issues in Economic Theory: An Attempt to
   Clarify." Quarterly Journal of Economics 42 (May):333-65.
       Argues that Veblen exaggerated the importance of evolution
   with respect to economic study. Veblen was guilty of grossness
   and absurdity in framing his indictment of orthodox economics.

3 _____. "Thorstein Veblen." In Contemporary Economic Thought.
   New York: Harper & Row, pp. 105-92. Reprint. Freeport, New
   York: Books for Libraries Press, 1968.
       Abridged version of 1927.5.

4 TUGWELL, REXFORD G. Review of Contemporary Economic Thought,
   by Paul T. Homan. New Republic 54 (16 May):397-98.
       Argues that Veblen's reaction to traditional economics was
   perhaps engendered in the Northwest when business practices were

under heavy fire. Veblen no doubt had a purpose, in spite of the scientific mask he donned.

5   WILCOX, CLAIR. Review of Contemporary Economic Thought, by Paul T. Homan. Annals of the American Academy of Political and Social Science 139 (September):213-14.
         Describes Veblen as the "radical philosopher, the prejudiced critic, the satirist who, behind his scientific prose, does not scruple to handle facts with violence that he may the more vehemently condemn the competitive order."

1929

1   ANON. "Thorstein Veblen." Nation 129 (14 August):157.
         Memorializes Veblen. Cites the impact of The Theory of the Leisure Class and points to Veblen's "mordant wit, his extraordinary gift of phrase-making and his uncanny power of discovering wholly new meanings in old facts. . . ." Examines Veblen's "fruitful" distinction between industry and business and his emphasis on the notion of use and wont.

2   ANON. "Veblen, Noted Economist, Dead." San Francisco Chronicle, 6 August, p. 5.
         Reports that Veblen was regarded by some "as the most important economist, the most brilliant scholar and the Bernard Shaw of America."

3   CLARK, JOHN M. "Thorstein Bundy [sic] Veblen." American Economic Review 19 (December):742-45.
         Memorializes Veblen and provides a brief biographical sketch. Evaluates Veblen's significant contributions and claims that he "left his mark." Reprinted: 1973.6.

4   HAZLITT, HENRY. "Thorstein Veblen." Century 119 (Fall):8-10.
         Memorializes Veblen, stating that he was one of America's most original and influential economic thinkers. Notes Veblen's satirical skill and his tendency to commit excesses. The Theory of the Leisure Class is his most popular and best book. Contends that H.L. Mencken's criticism of Veblen is off base; that the latter's use of language, like the former's, was "largely employed with ironic intent."

5   HOBSON, JOHN A. "Thorstein Veblen." Sociological Review, o.s. 21 (October):342-45.
         Sees Veblen as America's most considerable economic thinker. Yet it makes better sense to speak of Veblen as a sociologist rather than as an economist. Veblen's was an acute and penetrating mind and he provides "a far more convincing exposure of capitalist theory than is contained in any of the Marxian or other avowedly socialistic treatises." Veblen deserves to be more widely recognized in both America and Britain.

6   INNIS, HAROLD A. "A Bibliography of Thorstein Veblen."
    Southwestern Political and Social Science Quarterly 10
    (June):56-68.
        Provides a brief biography of Veblen. Considers his work
on race. Contends that Veblen was influenced by German economic
historians and that his work constitutes "a consistent whole and
springs from a post Civil War environment." Credits Veblen with
having a liberating effect on the study of economics. Reprinted:
1956.5. Abridged and reprinted: 1979.10.

7   MITCHELL, WESLEY C. "Thorstein Veblen, 1857-1929." Economic
    Journal 39 (December):646-50.
        Memorializes Veblen. Surveys his life accomplishments and
notes the English lack of interest in his works. Refers to
Darwin's influence on Veblen and the latter's oblique manner of
attacking economic puzzles. States that the best general introduction to Veblen is his Theory of the Leisure Class. Reprinted:
1973.18.

8   _____. "Thorstein Veblen, 1857-1929." New Republic 60
    (4 September):66-68.
        Memorializes Veblen. Surveys his life and career, calling
attention to Veblen's quizzical style, aloofness, and interest in
the evolution of human institutions. Veblen's criticism of economic theory and his reconstruction of it are based on the genetic method. Veblen was fascinated with the difference between
making money and making goods which he saw as an underlying
social problem that could lead to class conflict. Veblen
"remains the most interesting economist of his generation, and
the one who is provoking most thought in others." Reprinted:
1973.19.

1930

1   ANON. "Obituary Records of Graduates Deceased during the Year
    Ending July 1, 1930." Yale University Bulletin, pp. 307-8.
        Obituary recording Veblen's career accomplishments and
other biographical information.

2   Dos PASSOS, JOHN. "The Bitter Drink." In U.S.A.: The Big
    Money. New York: Harcourt, Brace & Co., pp. 93-105.
        Concisely illustrates Veblen's life and influences. Veblen
was continually hoping that "the working-class would take over
the machine of production before monopoly pushed the western
nations down into the dark again." He was continually frus-
trated, both in his life and work. "He suffered from women
trouble and the constitutional inability to say yes and an unnat-
ural tendency to feel with the working-class instead of with the
profiters." Most of all, it is "the sharp clear prism of his
mind," which is to be remembered and admired. Reprinted several
times in different collections.

3   FOX, R.M. "Thorstein Veblen." New Statesman 35
    (13 September):706-7.
        Summarizes the main themes found in Veblen's work. "Like
    most original thinkers, he will probably be known far more widely
    after his death than during his lifetime. . . ."

4   FREEMAN, MAURICE. "The Economic Philosophy of Thorstein Bundy
    [sic] Veblen." Master's thesis, Ohio State University.
        A general account of some major elements of Veblen's works.
    Provides a personal history of Veblen; relates his ideas to
    others; presents his theories of human nature and technology, his
    criticism of orthodox economics, his contributions to the insti-
    tutional approach, and his ideas regarding business and social
    change. Contends that Veblen's prolix and Latinate style has
    made it difficult for many to appreciate his penetrating
    insights.

5   MITCHELL, WESLEY C. "Research in the Social Sciences." In
    The New Social Science. Edited by Leonard D. White. Chicago:
    University of Chicago Press, pp. 4-15.
        Assesses Veblen's disturbing effect on social science re-
    search. Finds it difficult to pigeonhole Veblen--he is econo-
    mist, anthropologist, sociologist, social psychologist, and
    political scientist in turn. He and John Dewey were powerful
    forces in turning social science research in a new direction.
    Reprinted: 1937.8.

6   SAIDLA, LEO E., and WARREN E. GIBBS. Science and the Scien-
    tific Mind. New York: McGraw-Hill Book Co., pp. 46-47.
        Veblen is better understood as a sociologist even
    though he is one of the most considerable American thinkers in
    economics. Veblen's contribution lies in the fact he "has inter-
    preted society historically and philosophically in connection
    with an analysis of the instincts, interests, and activities of
    men . . . he has pointed the way for a more comprehensive inter-
    relation of the sciences in building the new civilization."

                                1931

1   LERNER, MAX. "Veblen and the Wasteland." New Freeman 3
    (25 February):565-67.
        Sees Veblen's chief contribution as his summary rejection
    of a late nineteenth-century neatly ordered world view. Building
    on the distinction between technology and business, Veblen beat
    a steady tune on a society founded on pecuniary principles. "His
    thought, judged cynical and pessimistic by the generation that
    saw the publication of The Theory of the Leisure Class, struck an
    accord with the mood of the generation that read T.S. Eliot. In
    a sense Veblen anticipated the dissatisfaction of the Post-War
    critics with society. Veblen has suffered the most consummate
    compliment that can be paid to any thinker: in a few decades his

ironies have become the basic material of economic discussion."
Reprinted: 1939.11.

2   MacIVER, ROBERT M. Society: Its Structure and Changes. New
    York: Ray Long and Richard R. Smith, pp. 493-99.
        Classifies Veblen as a technological determinist and ana-
    lyzes that bias in detail.

3   MASERO, ARTURO. "Un Americano non edonista" [An American non-
    hedonist]. Economica [Economics], n.s. 7, no. 2:151-72.
        Summarizes Veblen's major ideas and highlights his opposi-
    tion to the hedonistic assumptions of the classical and neo-
    classical economists.

4   MUMFORD, LEWIS. "Thorstein Veblen." New Republic 67
    (5 August):314-16.
        An appreciation of Veblen the man and his work. Claims
    that no more than a few perfunctory appreciations of Veblen would
    be found in the economics and sociology journals soon after his
    death. Perhaps the chief reason for this neglect was the fact
    that Veblen was much more than an economic theorist--he was "one
    of the half-dozen important figures in scholarship that America
    had produced since the Civil War. . . ." Veblen was also a great
    sociologist and great satirist. He was not so naive as to be-
    lieve that the Industrial Revolution began with the steam engine;
    he found the roots of the revolution in earlier times. Excerpted
    and reprinted: 1975.11.

5   TEGGART, RICHARD VICTOR. "Thorstein B. Veblen: A Critical
    Study of His Ideas in Relation to Movements of Economic
    Thought in America." Ph.D. dissertation, University of
    California, Berkeley.
        Revised and published, see 1932.8.

6   VEBLEN, FLORENCE. "Thorstein Veblen: Reminiscences of His
    Brother Orson." Social Forces 10 (December):187-95.
        A biographical sketch of Veblen. Claims that the Veblen
    family did not experience poverty; Veblen's father Thomas was
    quite "well-to-do." Details young Thorstein's interest in flora
    and fauna and his curious attitude in general.

                                1932

1   ANDERSON, KARL L. "Thorstein Veblen's Economics." Ph.D.
    dissertation, Harvard University.
        Sees Veblen's importance in the fact that he was a
    "deranger" of orthodox economics and discusses his criticism of
    its psychological assumptions and static character. Claims that
    there is a system or unity to Veblen's thought, exemplified in
    his skepticism and evolutionary or gradualist approach to econom-
    ics. Defends orthodox economics and business in general against

what he feels is Veblen's one-sided analysis. In spite of his
guise of science, Veblen exhibits a normative bias against the
business enterprise. Feels also that Veblen's own psychological
theories are imprecise and that his theory of history is unsatis-
factory in its abstract and general character. Charges that
Veblen postulated a "golden age" by which he criticizes contemporary institutions. Nonetheless, Veblen's criticism of economic
psychology was important; he was not so far removed from "real"
economics as sometimes alleged, and his influence on thinkers
such as W.C. Mitchell and others is demonstrable, although his
followers have interpreted his ideas more narrowly than Veblen
might have desired. Veblen was the "prophet" of the institutional movement. See also 1933.1.

2 CHAMBERLAIN, JOHN. Farewell to Reform: The Rise, Life, and
   Decay of the Progressive Mind in America. New York:
   Liveright, pp. 154, 197, 199-200, 202-3, 215-21, 307, 318, 320.
        Provides a brief sketch of Veblen's life and contributions.
   Refers to his obscure literary style and his distinction between
   business and industry. Praises Veblen's ability as a phrasemaker
   and economic-distinction maker. Feels that at heart Veblen was a
   syndicalist. "Few were to do him reverence at his death. But
   now he shines like a star of the first magnitude."

3 DORFMAN, JOSEPH. "Introduction to a Previously Unpublished
   Paper on the I.W.W. by Thorstein Veblen." Journal of Political Economy 40 (December):796-97.
        Provides background information on Veblen's 1918 proposal
   that the I.W.W. (Industrial Workers of the World) be utilized to
   harvest grain. "In striking contrast to his published work, but
   like all his unpublished papers submitted to official or semi-
   official bodies, this memorandum is written in a simple, straightforward style."

4 _____. "The 'Satire' of Thorstein Veblen's Theory of the
   Leisure Class." Political Science Quarterly 47
   (September):363-409.
        Although Veblen was greatly influenced by Spencer, he uses
   the latter's material to satirize and reverse his position.
   Compares, at some length, the free-contract ideas of Spencer with
   Veblen's attack on the same. Topics such as economics, religion,
   dress, dogs, and trophies are examined in light of both Spencer-
   ian and Veblenian theories. Avers that "The Theory of the
   Leisure Class is a ruthless dissection of the modern economic
   order and of the traditional economic theory. . . ."

5 _____. "Two Unpublished Papers of Thorstein Veblen on the
   Nature of Peace." Political Science Quarterly 47 (June):185.
        Introduces two previously unpublished papers by Veblen.
   Notes that Veblen was not invited to join the staff requested by
   President Wilson to conduct an inquiry in order to help him with

his peace plans. Veblen submitted two papers written in a
straightforward style, unlike so much of his writings, anyway.

6   HARRIS, ABRAM L. "Types of Institutionalism." Journal of
     Political Economy 40 (December):721-49.
         Attempts to define and classify the various "institution-
     alist" economists. Veblen is deemed to be more akin to Marx
     (class-struggle theory) than to Mitchell (quantitative-statistical
     institutionalism). Veblen's chief objections to neoclassicism
     were its assumptions of "hedonistic psychology and natural law"
     that helped to buttress the status quo. His evolutionary
     approach, with its borrowings from anthropology and biology, are
     contrasted with the equilibrium theories of the neoclassical
     school. Veblen's economics goes beyond the traditional types to
     study "social structure as shaped by material conditions. . . ."
     Modern capitalism is seen by Veblen as a combination of two
     conflicting elements--the pecuniary business types and producers
     or engineers. The latter express themselves through the machine
     process while the former are typified by profit seeking. Veblen
     actually stands closer to Marx than to other types of institu-
     tionalists. The "only visible tie between institutionalism of
     the Veblen variety and quantitative analysis is their common
     departure from the concept of equilibrium and their common shift
     of interest from the theory of value and distribution in class-
     ical and neoclassical works."

7   HOMAN, PAUL T. "An Appraisal of Institutional Economics."
     American Economic Review 22 (March):10-18.
         Claims that other economists have done little to continue
     and develop Veblen's evolutionary approach to economics. Insti-
     tutional economics is difficult to define, yet the figure of
     Veblen stands as one element in the school. Sees little or no
     value in continuing to search for the meaning of institutional-
     ism. See also 1933.13.

8   TEGGART, RICHARD VICTOR. Thorstein Veblen: A Chapter in
     American Economic Thought. Berkeley: University of
     California Press, 126 pp.
         Explores the background of economic theory prior to Veblen
     and the intellectual influences reflected in his life and work.
     Treats both the critical and constructive aspects of Veblen's
     writings. Argues that Veblen can be properly understood only in
     the context of a wave of interest in "interventionism." While
     cloaked under the guise of science, Veblen's writings are
     actually a "subtle form of dialectic." Claims that Veblen was
     dependent upon German idealist philosophy and the historical
     school, the "biological dicta" of Darwinism, the materialist
     "bias" of Marx, and the cultural evolutionism of nineteenth-
     century British anthropology. Criticizes The Theory of the
     Leisure Class for its unverified conjectures, outmoded anthro-
     pology, and invidious distinctions. Veblen's ideas concerning
     business cycles are also criticized, as is his "psychogenetic"

approach to industry and workmanship. Discusses Veblen's influence on subsequent writers and notes his flirtation with "syndicalism in his later writings." Veblen "expounded a complete philosophy of change and transformation, extending his efforts to include both a philosophy of history and a sociology founded upon the materialist interpretation." Revision of 1931.5.

1933

1   ANDERSON, KARL L. "The Unity of Veblen's Theoretical System." Quarterly Journal of Economics 47 (August):598-626.
     Veblen's theory remains something of a "mystery"; it has never been "judged in a true perspective." Claims that Veblen has a system. Treats his critique of traditional economics and the psychological postulates underpinning his own approach, including the "instinct of workmanship," the "parental bent," and "idle curiosity." Considers Veblen's broad historical stages and points to certain difficulties in his formulation, for example, of how peaceful peoples suddenly become warlike. States that Veblen's views on business enterprise are a "continuation of his general evolutionary method and that his economic theory bears a closer relationship to orthodox theory than hitherto realized." Criticizes Veblen's psychological theory for being in part suspect and his treatment of history for being incomplete. Concludes that social institutions cannot be comprehended with the compass of a simple formula. See also 1932.1.

2   ANON. "Thorstein Veblen." Springfield Republican, 14 January, p. 6.
     Notes Veblen's relationship to technocracy and his invention of new terms. Refers to Richard Victor Teggart's book, Thorstein Veblen: A Chapter in American Economic Thought, and questions why Teggart did not classify Veblen as a sociologist rather than an economist. States that Veblen's influence in the twentieth century coincides with capitalist excesses.

3   ARDZROONI, LEON. "Veblen and Technocracy." Living Age 344 (March):39-40.
     Discusses The Engineers and the Price System. Describes Veblen's participation in the New School for Social Research and his relationship with Howard Scott. Argues that Veblen's ideas on technocracy were formulated prior to his contact with Scott or the New School. Outlines Veblen's plan for a soviet of technicians. Points out two paths that must be followed: informing the public and creating a consciousness among the technicians. Suggests that present-day technocracy offers no remedy for social problems nor does it accomplish the goals of Veblen's soviet of technicians, for modern technocracy is oppressive and exploitive.

4   ATKINS, J.K. "Thorstein Veblen--Father of Technocracy." Technocracy Review 1 (February):16-19, 41.

Claims that Veblen was the intellectual father of the technocracy movement. Explains Veblen's proposals, particularly his prescription for rule by engineers and his dislike of wasteful and parasitic absentee ownership.

5   BATES, ERNEST SUTHERLAND. "Thorstein Veblen." Scribner's Magazine 94 (December):355-60.
Veblen is one of the few original thinkers to appear on the American scene. His writing is still fresh today--unlike that of many of his contemporaries--no one reads Roosevelt, Wilson, or Croly. Recounts Veblen's successes and failures, his life and times. The chief influences on Veblen were "Darwin, Spencer, Tylor, and above all, Karl Marx." Reviews Veblen's major book. "He could not shake the walls of Jericho, but he silences its defenders. He bridled economic theory and made it ready to perform human service. He was a profound critic of American culture."

6   BRICKELL, HERSCHEL. "The Literary Landscape." North American Review 235 (March):279-88.
Writes that The Engineers and the Price System "is good, sensible reading."

7   COLEMAN, McALISTER. "Veblen Comes Back." World Tomorrow 16 (11 January):35-36.
Praises Veblen's dissection of capitalism. Veblen was rejected by American Socialists because he dared to criticize Marx. Nonetheless, "his influence upon the new economics has been enormous and vitalizing." It would have been beneficial for Veblen to modify his criticism of Marxism.

8   DORFMAN, JOSEPH. "An Unpublished Memorandum of Thorstein Veblen on Government Regulation of the Food Supply." South western Social Science Quarterly 13 (March):372.
Introduces Veblen's memorandum on price schedules for foods when he was employed by the Statistical Division of the Food Administration.

9   _____. "An Unpublished Project of Thorstein Veblen for an Ethnological Inquiry." American Journal of Sociology 39 (September):237.
Introduces Veblen's grant proposal to study the Cretan and Baltic civilizations. Nothing came of the proposal.

10   HOMAN, PAUL T. Review of Thorstein Veblen: A Chapter in American Economic Thought, by Richard Victor Teggart. American Economic Review 23 (September):480-81.
Notes the negative attitude toward Veblen in the book. Writes that Teggart does not "make any constructive contribution to the problem with which Veblen was centrally concerned, the relation of technical economic doctrines both to the facts of

social organization and to the impinging areas of sociological thought." See 1932.8.

11   PARRISH, WAYNE W. An Outline of Technocracy. New York: Farrar and Rinehart, pp. 25-31.
        Concedes that there are some resemblances between the technocracy movement and the ideas put forth in The Engineers and the Price System but stresses the difference and concludes that Veblen was in no significant sense an apostle of the technocracy movement.

12   RIORDAN, JOHN. "Engineers as a Vested Interest." Commonweal 17 (12 April):666.
        Reviews The Engineers and the Price System. Sees Veblen's proposal of rule by engineers as just another vested interest. How would they be checked? The main economic question is not production, but rather distribution. Claims that "this master of corrosive irony should have a wide public."

13   SCOTT, D.R. "Veblen Not an Institutional Economist." American Economic Review 23 (June):274-77.
        Responds to Paul Homan's critical article in the same review (1932.7). Objects to Homan's "implication that Veblen's work was fundamentally antirational. . . ." Claims that "Veblen was fond of contrasting methods of economics with those of the physical and biological sciences." As to the often-voiced complaint that Veblen had no constructive system, states that Veblen simply felt that "economic systems made by economists had no validity." It must also be remembered that Veblen came to economics from philosophy and that philosophical knowledge at that time had not arrived at the conception of the intangible nature of the physical world. "To call him [Veblen] an institutional economist would emphasize an incidental aspect of his work rather than characterize its essential features." See 1932.7.

14   WILSON, EDMUND. "The Great Revelation." New Republic 74 (22 February):50-51.
        Writes that technocracy can be traced back to Veblen's works. Credits Veblen and the technocrats with emphasizing "the importance of the engineers--something traditional Marxism had largely neglected."

                                        1934

1   ANON. Review of Essays in Our Changing Order. Management Review 23 (October):318.
        "A final volume of papers, written over a period of thirty years, by a man who is now recognized--five years after his death--as one of America's acute economic thinkers."

2   ANON. Review of Essays in Our Changing Order. Wisconsin
     Library Bulletin 30 (December):238.
         Writes that Veblen "had a profound influence on the thought
     of our day and . . . was probably responsible for many of the
     theories now being tried out in practice."

3   ANON. "Veblen's Joke." Review of Reviews 90 (October):11.
         Reviews Essays in Our Changing Order. "It is one of the
     prize ironies of existence that the ideas of Thorstein Veblen,
     which reaped for him a harvest of abuse in his day, should now
     exercise so much influence upon current economic thought."

4   ARDZROONI, LEON, ed. Introduction to Essays in Our Changing
     Order. New York: Viking Press, pp. v-xv. Reprint. New
     York: Augustus M. Kelley, 1964.
         Veblen's importance has to do with his contributions to
     social science and his influence on his times. Claims that
     Veblen had considerable polemical ability along with powers of
     prophetic insight. Defends Veblen against various critics and
     offers an explanation of his literary style. Veblen was way
     "ahead of his time. . . ."

5   CHASE, STUART. Foreword to The Theory of the Leisure Class.
     New York: Modern Library, pp. v-xv.
         Describes his meeting with Veblen and provides a brief
     survey of Veblen's major works. Claims that The Theory of the
     Leisure Class "will probably remain Veblen's most popular book."
     Pays special attention to the notion of conspicuous consumption.
     "The collapse of orthodox economic doctrine during the years of
     the world depression has vindicated the keenly analytic and
     prophetic writings of Thorstein Veblen. The new point of view
     and method elaborated by him riddled the whole structure of
     economics as a pseudo-social science and created instead an
     entirely original set of economic categories, based on changing
     industrial conditions rather than an inflexible system formulated
     from so-called eternal principles."

6   COMMONS, JOHN R. Institutional Economics. Vol. 2. New York:
     Macmillan Co., pp. 4-5, 115, 228-29, 649-80.
         Asserts that Veblen was the first thinker to build upon the
     modern concept of intangible property. He did not, however,
     investigate Supreme Court decisions dealing with intangible prop-
     erty. Veblen's analysis arrives at a theory of exploitation and
     pecuniary gain, while the Supreme Court decisions arrive at a
     theory of reasonable value. Discusses Veblen's theory of the
     instinct of workmanship and calls him the founder of programs
     that would elevate the engineer rather than the capitalist to the
     head of the social process. Veblen's distinction between busi-
     ness and industry is treated, and a theoretical relationship
     between Veblen and Henry Ford is also drawn.

7   COREY, LEWIS [pseud. of Louis Fraina]. "Veblen and Marx."
    Nation 139 (26 December):745-46.
        Reviews Essays in Our Changing Order. Calls Veblen "the
    greatest American thinker in the social sciences." Veblen is
    best at superstructural analysis, and his treatment of the con-
    flict between business and industry is "brilliant." Veblen is
    weaker in his analysis of the substructure and weaker yet when he
    castigates Marx as a "romantic." Yet Veblen sheds much light on
    the problem of bureaucracy and his "analysis of the instinct of
    workmanship has much to contribute to the theory and creation of
    a labor culture."

8   DEUTSCH, BABETTE. "Veblen--Freud and Darwin of Economics."
    New York Herald Tribune Books, 9 December, p. 5.
        Reviews Essays in Our Changing Order, edited by Leon
    Ardzrooni and Thorstein Veblen and His America, by Joseph
    Dorfman. Summarizes Veblen's experiences and some of his major
    ideas. States that Veblen could write simply when he desired.
    Stresses his critical abilities, owing something perhaps to his
    studies of Kant. "One of Veblen's admirers called him 'the Freud
    of economics.' But it would be true to call him the Darwin of
    his own field. He did in a sense discover the basic needs of a
    normal society by studying the fantasies of a sick one. But his
    chief contribution was an understanding of social evolution."
    See 1934.9.

9   DORFMAN, JOSEPH. Thorstein Veblen and His America. New York:
    Viking Press, 556 pp.
        A comprehensive biography of Veblen, treating him from the
    standpoint of the socioeconomic and intellectual currents of his
    time. The various influences on Veblen are covered, as well as
    his impact on the course of American history. Attention is given
    to Veblen's personal life, his academic career, and his efforts
    to get his ideas into print. Writes that Veblen "remains a
    figure of mystery and his views an object of controversy. In the
    hope that an inquiry into Veblen's life history might throw some
    light on the meaning of his work, this study was undertaken."
    Appendix contains several letters from Veblen to his friend,
    J. Franklin Jameson. Thorstein Veblen and His America was
    submitted to Columbia University as Dorfman's Ph.D. dissertation.
    Reprinted with some corrections and additions in Veblen's bibli-
    ography and new appendices: 1966.4.

10 DUFFUS, ROBERT L. "An Analyst of Modern Society." New York
    Times Book Review, 2 December, pp. 5, 38.
        Reviews Thorstein Veblen and His America by Joseph Dorfman
    (1934.9). Remarks that Veblen probably considered his life to be
    a failure. Nevertheless his thinking will outlast that of any
    sociologist or economist of his generation. Veblen had a fond-
    ness for the "instinct" of workmanship but came to hold a pessi-
    mistic attitude toward modern society. Argues that Veblen was no

Communist and was certainly not a technocrat of the Howard Scott variety.

11 _____. "Thorstein Veblen's Social Vision." New York Times Book Review, 30 September, pp. 4-17.
     Reviews Essays in Our Changing Order edited by Leon Ardzrooni. Credits the editor for a careful and intelligent effort. Claims that while Veblen's writing might at times be "technical" and "abstruse" it was never "obscure" or "dull." Veblen often coined newer expressions and phrases because "plain terms" often seemed "too heavily charged with prior assumptions." Veblen also write with "an exquisite sense of humor, which some of his critics seem never to have discerned." Man, according to Veblen, was not "temperamentally averse to labor." Only with the ascendence of predatory cultures does labor become "indecorous." While Veblen avoids the mistake of sentimentally glorifying poverty and the downtrodden in and of themselves, he nonetheless believed in the basic dignity of human nature. "The song he sung was of natural man. . . ."

12 HARRIS, ABRAM L. "Economic Evolution: Dialectical and Darwinian." Journal of Political Economy 42 (February):34-79.
     Compares the economic theories of Marx and Veblen with emphasis on the role of technology in their respective systems. Differences between the two are treated. Argues that Veblen's concept of technology is not to be simply equated with the mechanical arts--its also includes the "non-mechanical arts of plant and animal breeding." Veblen's concept of technology is close to Marx's concept of "modes of production." Claims that Veblen's theory of "occupational habituation plays a role analogous to Marx's class struggle" but Veblen downplays class conflict. Veblen's theory of human nature also leads him to different conclusions from those of Marx regarding the relationship of "human nature and material conditions." Veblen's views regarding racial endowment and its impact on industrial growth are also analyzed. The Darwinian postulates underlying Veblen's approach are compared to Marx's Hegelian postulates. "Veblen is no more successful than Marx in formulating a scientific and objective explanation of history--assuming, of course, that such an explanation is possible. Like Marx, he sought to develop certain standards for evaluating economic practices under current institutions. Unlike Marx, his social judgements lack the political passion which impels men upon the adoption of them to seek their realization through concerted action against the established order."

13 MUMFORD, LEWIS. Technics and Civilization. New York: Harcourt, Brace & Co., pp. 25, 55, 96, 226, 284, 317, 354, 366, 401, 472, 475.
     After referring to several of Veblen's major contributions, claims that after "Marx, Veblen shares with Sombart the distinction of being the foremost sociological economist." Claims that

Veblen made a unique contribution to the theory of modern technics. Writes that "Only second to the profound debt I owe Geddes
is that which I must acknowledge to two other men: Victor
Branford and Thorstein Veblen."

14   P., I.M. "Turns with a Bookworm." New York Herald Tribune
     Books, 9 December, p. 23.
        Reviews Thorstein Veblen and His America by Joseph Dorfman
     (1934.9). Younger serious thinkers may get steamed up over
     Veblen but not this reviewer. He cannot figure out why someone
     who looked more "like a walrus than a walrus itself could appeal
     to so many women. Professor Veblen also made several financial
     ventures. . . . He invested his money in a raisin farm, run by
     one of his disciples. . . . Need we say more? Obviously such an
     experience would make almost anyone write about the impending
     Collapse of Capitalism." And so on.

                              1935

1   AMLIE, THOMAS R. "Thorstein Veblen Today." Common Sense 4
     (April):14-16.
        Praises Veblen's powers of analysis and prediction.
     Assesses Veblen's analysis of property, change, technology, and
     resources. Comments favorably on Veblen's scepticism regarding
     oranized labor and his appreciation of the role of the independ-
     ent farmer. Veblen's great contribution "is to be found in the
     fact that he gave us an exact analysis of things as they are."
     Had Veblen not died in 1929, he would have provided a blueprint
     for action during the Great Depression.

2   ANON. "Thorstein Veblen." Fortune 11 (February):162.
        Veblen is achieving fame in these depression years owing to
     his prophetic insights into absentee ownership and the conflict
     between pecuniary and industrial interests.

3   BALZER, J.F. "Thorstein Veblen and His America." Northfield
     Minnesota News, 7 June, p. 2.
        Veblen refused to participate in the life of the community
     where he spent his youth. In spite of his "matter of fact"
     attitude toward those things he observed, there appears to be
     "implcit in Veblen's writings a deep faith in democracy." Feels
     that too often Veblen's analytical attempts are "interpreted as
     attack."

4   BUEHRER, EDWIN T. "Thorstein Veblen Speaks Again." Christian
     Century 52 (2 January):17.
        Remarks that Veblen was one of America's "best informed"
     economists and one of the "most profound thinkers of the imme-
     diate past generation." Notes Veblen's concern with the "de-
     structive forces that inhere in our capitalistic society."

Nevertheless, Veblen failed, as did many radicals of his era, to provide prescriptions for the ills they diagnosed.

5   CHRISTOPHERSEN, H.O. "En norsk-amerikansk videnskapsman-- Thorstein Veblen" [A Norwegian-American scientist--Thorstein Veblen]. Aften posten [Oslo], 10 July, page unknown.
    In Norwegian. Reviews Thorstein Veblen and His America by Joseph Dorfman. Argues that Norway could use more people like Thorstein Veblen.

6   CLARK, EUNICE. Review of Thorstein Veblen and His America, by Joseph Dorfman. Common Sense 4 (January):26.
    Veblen was a student of the author's grandfather, John Bates Clark, at Carleton College. Notes the role played by Clark in Veblen's intellectual development. Highlights Veblen's major achievements, especially hs views regarding the impact of the machine process. Veblen's popularity was inhibited by his "precise" and "unusual" style.

7   FALNES, OSCAR J. "Thorstein Veblen." American Scandinavian Review 23 (March):24-33.
    A biographical treatment "based largely upon data in the book by Mr. Dorfman (Thorstein Veblen and His America)." Emphasizes Veblen's Norwegian heritage and his lifelong interest in matters Scandinavian.

8   G., R.B.P. "The Influence of a Man from Norway." Boston Evening Transcript, 2 January, pt. 4, p. 2.
    Claims that Veblen has exerted a significant influence on our times.

9   H., W.J. Review of Essays in Our Changing Order. Saturday Review of Literature 11 (12 January):424.
    Notes that "Veblen emphasized the national direction of the economic system. This viewpoint is widely held today. Once more to quote Veblen's words: 'It is not an appeal to local self-help; it is an appeal to Caesar.'"

10 HAGA, CLIFFORD I. "Now Here's a Book." Minnesota Techno-Log 15 (March):125.
    "Veblen knew science, used it, wrote it--and criticized it, neither wooing it with symbols nor surrendering to it with that yearning which drives less-balanced minds to seek some neat, vest-pocket panacea."

11 HOBSON, J[OHN] A. "A Great American Thinker." New Statesman and Nation 12 (19 October):564.
    Regrets that Veblen is not more widely known in England. Considers the "core" of Veblen's thought to be a "devastating criticism and indictment of capitalism in its central pecuniary fortress."

37

12   KNIGHT, FRANK H. The Ethics of Competition and Other Essays.
      New York: Harper & Brothers, pp. 21, 29, 43, 51, 99, 128.
      Reprint. Freeport, New York: Books for Libraries Press,
      1969.
            Critical references to Veblen's dichotomy between the pecu-
      niary and industrial interests, his dislike of advertising, and
      his prescription for rule by engineers.

13   LERNER, MAX. "Was Veblen a Coward?" New Republic 83
      (26 June):196.
            Lerner responds to Sinclair by writing that if Veblen "had
      been concerned mainly to save his own skin, he could have done
      what the other college professors did: stifle every impulse
      toward criticism, and celebrate the glories of capitalist society
      and individualist business enterprise. The distinction I was
      trying to draw was between cowardice and protective coloration."
      See 1935.14, 20.

14   _____. What Is Usable in Veblen?" New Republic 83
      (15 May):7-10.
            The lack of prescriptive elements in Veblen's system not-
      withstanding, there are six ideas that are still usable. They
      are: (1) the rigor and potentialities of the machine process;
      (2) the antithesis between industry and business; (3) the anti-
      social tendency of business enterprise; (4) the legal and polit-
      ical institutions as the vesting of economic interests; (5) the
      compulsive force of idea patterns, and (6) the bankruptcy of
      leisure class (business class) values and a culture dominated by
      them. Veblen's greatest weakness was his "lack of direction."
      Comments on Veblen's oblique style as a device for protecting
      himself against charges of advocating Marxism. Had he lived
      through the depression years, Veblen would have objected to the
      rhetoric and plans of the New Deal. Reprinted: 1936.14;
      1939.12. See also 1935.13, 20.

15   MITCHELL, WESLEY C. "Commons on Institutional Economics."
      American Economic Review 25 (December): 635-52.
            Submits that Commons misunderstands Veblen, in particular
      with respect to Veblen's conception of science and purpose.
      Reprinted: 1937.7.

16   MUMFORD, LEWIS. "A Stick of Dynamite Wrapped like Candy."
      Saturday Review of Literature 11 (12 January):417, 421-22.
            Claims Veblen to be not only the outstanding social scien-
      tist in America but also our most important satirist. "The
      foremost analyst, after Marx, of the social contradictions in our
      economic order, he was regarded as a dilettante by professional
      economists who had not a modicum of either his factual knowledge
      or his historic insight." If Marx erred in overemphasizing the
      dialectical nature of social change, then Veblen erred in attrib-
      uting too great a force to the effects of the machine process on
      the minds and habits of individuals.

17   PARKES, H[ENRY] B[AMFORD]. "The Life of Veblen." Nation 141
     (14 August):194-95.
          "Veblen approached modern society with the detachment of an
     anthropologist studying a tribe of cannibals." Notes that Veblen
     dissected capitalism while other economists were paying homage to
     the "captains of industry." Only Marx has done a comparable job
     in exposing the "criminal absurdities" of the system. Unlike
     Marx, however, Veblen had little faith in the revolutionary
     potential of the working class; rather, he favored the idea of
     governance by technicians.

18   PARSONS, TALCOTT. "Sociological Elements in Economic
     Thought." Quarterly Journal of Economics 49 (May):414-53.
          Contrasts the orthodox and institutional schools of eco-
     nomics and Veblen's role in the development of the latter.
     Describes the main elements of Veblen's theory and his criticisms
     of the hedonistic psychology of orthodox economics. While some
     aspects of Veblen's thought approximate Marx's, the former sees
     the working class as essentially passive. For "Veblen empiricism
     has borne the curious fruit that the science of economics has
     become a complete philosophy of history emphasizing everything in
     human life. . . ." One also finds in Veblen elements of a
     "psychological antiintellectualism." The relationship therein is
     related to behaviorism.

19   PIROU, GAETAN. Les nouveaux courants de la théorie économique
     aux États-Unis [New currents of economic theory in the United
     States]. Vol. 1. Paris: Éditions Domat-Montchrestien,
     pp. 13-85.
          A general introduction to Veblen's major ideas. Provides
     biographical information and describes Veblen's critique of the
     classical economists, the marginalists, the historical school,
     and the Marxists. Stresses Veblen's essentially philosophical
     analysis, along with its satire and sarcasm. Also covered are
     Veblenian concepts such as the instinct of workmanship and the
     parental bent, as well as Veblen's theory of barbarian residues
     in modern society. Attention is given to Veblen's ideas concern-
     ing business versus industry, credit, and depressions. Notes
     Veblen's influence on figures such as W.C. Mitchell, who elabo-
     rated a descriptive theory of business cycles. Veblen is also
     cited for his critique of capitalism and his influence on some
     technocratic writers. Several pages are devoted to this last
     topic.

20   SINCLAIR, UPTON. "Was Veblen a Coward?" New Republic 83
     (26 June):196.
          Responding to an article on Veblen by Max Lerner in the
     same periodical, Sinclair asks: "I am wondering if in the first
     sentence the word 'never' is not a typographical error? If the
     actions described do not constitute 'cowardice' then will someone
     please tell me what is or could be cowardice in a college profes-
     sor?" See 1935.13-14.

21 WILD, JOSEPH. "Thorstein Veblen: Interpreter of the Leisure
    Class." Millgate 31 (October):27-30.
        Reintroduces Veblen to English readers by summarizing The
    Theory of the Leisure Class. The current depression demonstrates
    the validity of Veblen's theories. "In Thorstein Veblen we can
    promise instruction, the pleasure of sustained irony, and, once
    the peculiar style of the author is overcome, the fascination
    which follows from a rational explanation of the oddities of
    human nature."

                                    1936

1   ANON. Review of Veblen, by John A. Hobson. Times Literary
    Supplement (London), 30 October, p. 794.
        Refers to Veblen as "the distinguished American sociolo-
    gist" who, with bitter humor and irony, pinpointed the predatory
    characteristics of capitalism. See 1936.10.

2   ANON. Review of What Veblen Taught, edited by Wesley C.
    Mitchell. Booklist 32 (April):223.
        Refers to Veblen as "this influential economist."

3   ANON. Review of What Veblen Taught, edited by Wesley C.
    Mitchell. Wisconsin Library Bulletin 32 (April):47.
        Writes that Veblen was "perhaps the most influential eco-
    nomic thinker of our time."

4   BAIN, READ. Review of Thorstein Veblen and His America by
    Joseph Dorfman and What Veblen Taught, edited by Wesley C.
    Mitchell. American Economic Review 26 (June):485-87.
        Questions the degree of Veblen's originality. Argues that
    two of Veblen's famous ideas, the concept of conspicuous consump-
    tion and the distinction between business and industry, are
    restatements of ideas originated by Karl Marx and John Rae. See
    1934.9.

5   BELL, EDWARD W. "Veblen and Henry George." Nation 142
    (20 May):659.
        A letter to the editor responding to an article by Max
    Lerner in the same periodical. Shares Lerner's enthusiasm for
    Veblen but desires to indicate Veblen's debt to such thinkers as
    Henry George (vested interest) and John Dewey. Asks for a study
    comparing George and Veblen. see 1936.12.

6   DILLARD, IRVING. "Veblen Seven Years after His Death." St.
    Louis Post-Dispatch, 9 March, pt. 3, p. 2c.
        Sees Veblen as "an acute critic" of our society, a thinker
    "who saw and wrote ahead of his time."

7   GINZBERG, ELI. "The Artist in Economics." Saturday Review of
    Literature 14 (13 June):12.

Veblen's logic may indeed be weak and his factual data questionable, but his analyses of social class and modern industrial society, his critique of economic theory, and his dissections of capitalism, status emulation, and statecraft are a work of genius.

8   HANEY, LEWIS H. "Veblen and Institutionalism." In History of Economic Thought. 3d ed. New York: Macmillan Co., pp. 740-53.
    Provides a summary tour of some Veblenian ideas, noting contributions. Concludes with a set of critical questions and comments. Finds many institutionalist concepts to be abstract, vague. Appears to be particularly bothered by the negativism, emphasis on change, and evolution in Veblen and other institutionalists.

9   HERSKOVITS, MELVILLE. "The Significance of Thorstein Veblen for Anthropology." American Anthropologist 38 (April-June):351-53.
    Maintains that Veblen's "significance for anthropology has been greatly overlooked." Employing an approach to data that was "almost ethnological," Veblen had little concern for "social laws" as such but was more interested in evolution or process. While some of his assumptions "might be untenable, his conclusions were brilliantly valid." Veblen's "instinct of workmanship" and his concern with technology's impact on culture are "impeccable."

10   HOBSON, JOHN A. Veblen. London: Chapman and Hall, 227 pp. Reprint. New York: Augustus M. Kelley, 1971.
    After providing some biographical information, goes on to discuss Veblen's attitude toward economics, Karl Marx, and socialism. Though he often disagrees with Marx, it is obvious that Veblen feels that he was a great and original thinker. Covers Veblen's ideas concerning the social implications of business practices, the economics of education, and politics. Portrays him as a brilliant and penetrating mind. In spite of his apparent detachment, Veblen was not devoid of sympathy for the downtrodden and exploited. Veblen is singularly American in his treatment of the impact of economics upon social institutions and certainly ranks as one of the great sociologists of the present day.

11   HOOK, SIDNEY. "On Rereading Veblen." New Republic 87 (17 June):182.
    Blessed with a gift of objectivity, Veblen was capable of providing "fruitful insights." While one may agree with Veblen concerning the existence of social conflict, it is the case that he has not sufficiently demonstrated the historic or dialectical interaction between positive and negative social institutions.

Although Veblen overemphasizes the impact of technology and relegates politics to an epiphenomenal position, "only those congenitally blind will fail to see better because of him."

12 LERNER, MAX. "Gateway to Veblen's World." Nation 142 (11 March):321-22.
    Suggests that there are two Veblens—one the disinterested liberal, reluctant to take sides; the other, the revolutionary Veblen, implicit in the first writings but emerging more clearly during the Great War. Veblen is highly relevant to the present— he would seek the roots of fascism not only in the current power struggle but also in "the entire history of the predatory barbarian tradition." He is not unintelligible: "the manner of writing is one that was beautifully calculated to achieve the purpose of this thought . . . any anthology of American prose in the future of American literature will ignore Veblen at its peril." Reprinted: 1939.9. See also 1936.5.

13 _____. "Veblen, Thorstein Bunde." In Dictionary of American Biography. Edited by Dumas Malone. Vol. 19. New York: Charles Scribner's Sons, pp. 241-44.
    Provides a considerable biography of Veblen, emphasizing his academic experience and publications. Claims that Veblen's work "was perhaps the most considerable and creative body of social thought that America has produced." Largely unaffected by American writers, Veblen was to some degree responsible for the "trend toward social control in an age dominated by business enterprise." Reprinted with additions: 1939.10. Revised and reprinted: 1977.14.

14 _____. "What Is Usable in Veblen?" In The New Republic Anthology. Edited by Groff Conklin. New York: Dodge Publishing Co., pp. 496-504.
    Reprint of 1935.14. Reprinted: 1939.12.

15 LINDEMAN, EDUARD C. "Veblen at First Hand." Survey Graphic 25 (November):630-31.
    Sees Veblen's style as "quixotic," "catchy," and "pragmatic." "The content of his thought, on the other hand, ran counter to the favorite wishes and desires of our privileged groups. Consequently, Veblen assumed a dual role: he pleased the sharp-minded critics and frightened the privileged."

16 MARSHALL, T.H. "The Service of Mammon." New Statesman and Nation 12 (17 October):598.
    Claims that "Veblen was a man with a message." The common theme in Veblen's work is his "endeavor to expose the queer, insensate and often suicidal behavior to which men are driven in the service of mammon." Sociology owes a debt to Veblen.

17 MITCHELL, WESLEY C., ed. "Thorstein Veblen." In What Veblen Taught. New York: Viking Press, pp. vii-xlix.

Provides a biographical sketch of Veblen and surveys his work. Notes the influence of Charles Darwin, William James, and others. Suggests that Veblen is "too modern to be wholly intelligible to those of his contemporaries who are most neatly abreast of their time." Reprinted: 1937.9. Excerpted: 1952.9.

18 MOFFAT, J.E. Review of What Veblen Taught, edited by Wesley C. Mitchell. American Economic Review 26 (June):302.
"The appearance of this book furnishes additional evidence of the growing interest in the work of Thorstein Veblen."

19 REDMAN, BEN RAY. "Veblen." New York Herald Tribune Books, 12 April, p. 14.
Notes the steady growth of interest in Veblen's ideas since his death in 1929.. Veblen was an "economist whose pollinating thought has blown far and wide with fruitful results."

20 WOLFE, A.B. "Institutional Reasonableness and Value." Philosophical Review 45 (March):192-206.
Assesses Veblen's contribution to institutional economics. Veblen, considered the founder of institutionalism, helped clear away "the fog of natural law" that surrounded nineteenth-century economics. Stresses Veblen's evolutionary economic approach but cautions that the "as-if" economic approach need not be discarded. Veblen should be credited with introducing the distinctions between wealth and property and tangible and intangible property.

21 WRIGHT, JOHN G. "Thorstein Veblen, Sociologist." New International 2 (January):21-23.
Criticizes Veblen from a Marxian point of view. Veblen's work can serve "only as a basis for liberalism because his theoretical approach is founded on preconceptions and not laws." Veblen's views diverge only superficially from his predecessor Spencer; both were Darwinians. Veblen also and incorrectly attributed social change to men's minds or habits of thought. Although Veblen's criticism of the existing system indicates his dissatisfaction, his pessimism regarding the future reveals his essentially conservative bent.

1937

1 ANON. Review of Veblen, by John A. Hobson. Nature 139 (13 February):268.
Claims that Veblen's sociological analysis is little more than sublimation of his personal experiences. His anthropology is superficial and lacks understanding. See 1936.10.

2 BRODERSEN, ARVID. "Thorstein Veblen som sociolog" [Thorstein Veblen as sociologist]. Statsøkonomisk tidskrift [Journal of political economy] (Denmark) 1:30-70.

Analyzes Veblen's social theory. Demonstrates the influence of Darwin, Spencer, Kant, and Schopenhauer on Veblen's thought. Argues that Veblen provides many penetrating insights into modern society. Emphasizes Veblen's work on the German problem and the nature of peace.

3   COREY, LEWIS [pseud. of Louis Fraina]. "Veblen and Marxism."
    Marxist Quarterly 1 (January–March):162–68.
        Argues that Veblen is the greatest American thinker in
    the social sciences. He has often been misunderstood and is
    certainly not to blame for those who vulgarize his thought.
    Discusses Veblen's criticism of Marxism and points out the dif-
    ferences between him and Marx. "Unlike Marx, Veblen neglected
    the factors of consciousness and purposive struggle in human
    history, despite his emphasis on the psychological approach to
    the study of culture." Although Veblen is brilliant in his
    discussion of the conflict between pecuniary and industrial
    interests, his prophecy of the decay of capitalism does not
    necessarily follow from his postulates. Veblen's strong point
    is his superstructural or cultural analysis. His theory of
    workmanship also deserves praise. "All that is vital in
    Thorstein Veblen may fulfill itself in Marxism and socialism."

4   FOSSATI, ERALDO. New Deal: il nuovo ordine economico di
    F.D. Roosevelt [New Deal: The New Deal economics of F.D.
    Roosevelt]. Padua: Cedam, pp. 290–92.
        Claims that the institutional economics of Thorstein Veblen
    played an instrumental role in the New Deal of Franklin Delano
    Roosevelt.

5   HOBSON, JOHN [A.] "The Economics of Thorstein Veblen."
    Political Science Quarterly 52 (March):139–44.
        In one sense Veblen was a "disorderly thinker and writer,"
    but nevertheless he was one of the few original thinkers of his
    time. Veblen's chief claim to fame is not his well-known distinc-
    tion between the engineers and the price system, but rather "his
    insistence upon interpreting social institutions and their values
    in terms of an instinct-habit psychology. . . ." Claims that
    Veblen never directly attacked the problem of maldistribution of
    income.

6   HORNE, ROMAN I. Review of What Veblen Taught, edited by
    Wesley C. Mitchell. Social Education 1 (January):68–70.
        Stresses Veblen's distinction between business and indus-
    try. Feels that The Theory of Business Enterprise is his most
    notable contribution to economic theory. Finds it curious that
    "Veblen's own life seems to have followed on a small scale the
    pattern he drew for cultural change."

7   MITCHELL, WESLEY C. "Commons on Institutional Economics." In
    The Backward Art of Spending Money and Other Essays. New York

and London: McGraw-Hill Book Co., pp. 313-41. Reprint. New
York: Augustus M. Kelley, 1950.
    Reprint of 1935.15.

8   . "Research in the Social Sciences." In The Backward
Art of Spending Money and Other Essays. New York and London:
McGraw-Hill Book Co., pp. 72-82. Reprint. New York:
Augustus M. Kelley, 1950.
    Reprint of 1930.5.

9   . "Thorstein Veblen." In The Backward Art of Spending
Money and Other Essays. New York and London: McGraw-Hill
Book Co., pp. 279-312. Reprint. New York: Augustus M.
Kelley, 1950.
    Reprint of 1936.17. Excerpted: 1952.9.

10   STORY, RUSSELL M. Review of Veblen, by John A. Hobson.
American Political Science Review 31 (June):572.
    Praises Veblen's impressive analyses of social phenomena.
States that Veblen has made significant contributions to the
field of political science and should be more widely recognized.
See 1936.10.

11   TUCKERMAN, GUSTAVUS. Review of Veblen, by John A. Hobson.
American Economic Review 27 (December):773-75.
    Believes that Hobson misses several important points in
Veblen's theory. Veblen certainly did not believe in teleology,
although one might get the contrary impression in Hobson's book.
"The general impression which this book gives is that Veblen's
thought lacks the depth, cohesiveness and persuasiveness which
were in fact its most characteristic features." See 1936.10.

                                 1938

1   ANON. "A Note on the Work of Thorstein Veblen." In Introduction to Technocracy, by Howard Scott and others. New York:
Technocracy, pp. 53-54.
    States that, in spite of the fact that Scott had been
introduced to Veblen and their respective ideas bear some similarities, the systems of thought that each produced were independent of one another. Technocratic ideas cannot be expressed
in Veblenian terms, nor can Veblenian ideas be expressed in
technocratic terms.

2   CUTLER, ADDISON. "The Ebb of Institutional Economics."
Science and Society 2 (Fall):448-70.
    Calls attention to Veblen's critique of orthodox economics
in which he "failed to recognize the progressive features of the
classicists." Veblen was also guilty of faulty class analysis in
elevating the role of engineers over that of unskilled workers.

Nevertheless Veblen is to be credited for pinpointing the basic
contradictions of capitalism.

3   FERGUSON, JOHN M. Landmarks of Economic Thought. New York:
     Longmans, Green, & Co., pp. 250-55, 259, 262, 268.
         Feels that Veblen, as one of America's most influential
     economists, has unfortunately not received the recognition he
     deserves. Notes Veblen's tendency to investigate areas not nor-
     mally considered to be within the province of economics, but
     nevertheless one always sees that Veblen's writings are at bottom
     concerned with economic questions. Argues that Veblen's most
     significant work is The Theory of Business Enterprise and that
     his was more a critique of economics than a reconstruction.

4   HOMAN, PAUL T. "The Institutional School." In Encyclopedia
     of the Social Sciences. Edited by Edwin R.A. Seligman.
     Vol. 5. New York: Macmillan Co., pp. 387-95.
         Discusses Veblen's ideas in the context of the institution-
     alist school of economics. Asserts that much of Veblen's thought
     is a mixture of the historical school and the ideology of Marx.

5   JOHNSON, ALVIN [S.]. "Veblen, Thorstein Bunde." In
     Encyclopedia of the Social Sciences. Edited by Edwin R.A.
     Seligman. Vol. 15. New York: Macmillan Co., pp. 234-35.
         Provides a brief biography of Veblen and surveys his con-
     tributions to economics and social theory. States that Veblen
     was skeptical of capitalism's long term survival but was not
     explicit about an economic alternative lest it be a system in
     which production and distribution lay largely in the hands of
     "engineers." Veblen has exerted "an important influence on phi-
     losophers, sociologists and historians. . . ."

                                  1939

1   ANON. Review of Imperial Germany and the Industrial Revolu-
     tion. New York Herald Tribune Books, 28 May, p. 14.
         Notes that after World War I "Veblen dropped out of the
     news and his books went out of print, but since 1929 there has
     been renewed interest in his writings." The technocracy episode,
     the depression, and the rise of Nazi Germany have sent readers
     back to Veblen.

2   ANON. Review of Imperial Germany and the Industrial Revolu-
     tion. North American Review 248 (Autumn):203.
         Described as an "excellent book," it is just as true of
     Germany under Hitler as it was of Germany at the time of World
     War I.

3   BAIN, READ. Review of Imperial Germany and the Industrial
     Revolution. American Sociological Review 4 (October):732-34.

Angrily denounces the "stupendous stupidity of college administrators" for not seeing to it that Veblen was rewarded with a decent and secure university post. Rejects the contention that Veblen was merely an "ironic satirist." "If Imperial Germany is satire, I am ready for psychotherapy." This book should be read, not reviewed.

4   DORFMAN, JOSEPH. Introduction to Imperial Germany and the Industrial Revolution. New York: Viking Press, pp. xi-xxi.
    Believes that this book, in "one particular respect," is the "finest drama" that Veblen ever wrote. Notes the mixed reaction to it and points out that its scope goes well beyond Germany to include the cases of Japan, England, and the United States. Suggests that the satirical style Veblen employed in The Theory of the Leisure Class, which was praised by William Dean Howells, cost him dearly--for he did not then receive the recognition due him as an astute analyst of economics and modernization. Veblen's distinction between business and industry lies at the heart of his explanations of the rapid growth of certain dynastic nations. He also noted that certain nations pay a "penalty" for industrial innovation and can be overtaken by latecomers to the process.

5   GINZBERG, ERI. "Slow to Change." Saturday Review of Literature 20 (15 July):13-14.
    Reviews Imperial Germany and the Industrial Revolution. It is still the "best guide to the most terrifying country in Christiandom." In spite of the book's merits, Veblen overemphasizes technology at the expense of "biography and accident."

6   GRUCHY, ALLAN G. "The Concept of National Planning in Institutional Economics." Southern Economic Journal 6 (October):121-44.
    Claims that earlier institutional economists, including Veblen, had little faith in the "reordering" of capitalism in order to eliminate the conflict of competing interests. Suggests that later institutionalists believe it is possible to revamp capitalism in order to bring about reform.

7   HAMILTON, WALTON H. "Veblen on the Munich Pact." New Republic 100 (30 August):107-8.
    Reviews the reprinting of Imperial Germany and the Industrial Revolution. Writes that Veblen remains aloof and "refuses to be trapped into striking a balance, arguing merits or taking sides." Consequently the book was banned by the Postmaster General in the United States and was not well received in Germany either.

8   KOHN, HANS. "A Significant Book Reissued." Survey Graphic 28 (September):549.

Rates <u>Imperial</u> <u>Germany</u> <u>and</u> <u>the</u> <u>Industrial</u> <u>Revolution</u> "a book of great perspicacity. . . ." Praises Veblen's treatment of the connections leading to German's warring tendencies.

9　LERNER, MAX. "Gateway to Veblen's World." In <u>Ideas</u> <u>Are</u> <u>Weapons</u>. New York: Viking Press, pp. 138-41.
　　　Reprint of 1936.12.

10　　　　. "Thorstein Veblen." In <u>Ideas</u> <u>Are</u> <u>Weapons</u>. New York: Viking Press, pp. 117-23.
　　　Slightly expanded reprint of 1936.13. Revised and reprinted: 1977.14.

11　　　　. "Veblen and the Wasteland." In <u>Ideas</u> <u>Are</u> <u>Weapons</u>. New York: Viking Press, pp. 123-29.
　　　Reprint of 1931.1.

12　　　　. "What Is Usable in Veblen?" In <u>Ideas</u> <u>Are</u> <u>Weapons</u>. New York: Viking Press, pp. 129-38.
　　　Reprint of 1935.14; 1936.14.

13　LEVY, MARION J. "The Vision of Veblen." <u>Harvard</u> <u>Guardian</u> 4 (October):17-22.
　　　Argues that Veblen's break with the folklore of "his day was perhaps the most complete of any writer of his field and time." Investigates Veblen's critique of orthodox economics, his insistence upon an evolutionary approach emphasizing the human being, and his views concerning business enterprise and the machine process. Credits Veblen for envisaging the rise of fascist forces in world politics. "The heresies of Veblen now appear to us as truths which we were unwilling to have as truth."

14　PIROU, GAETAN. <u>Les</u> <u>nouveaux</u> <u>courants</u> <u>de</u> <u>la</u> <u>théorie</u> <u>économique</u> aux <u>États-Unis</u> [New currents of economic theory in the United States]. Vol. 2. Paris: Éditions Domat-Montchrestien, pp. 154-57, 205-10, 216.
　　　Describes the relationship between Veblen and John R. Commons and the latter's critique of the former. Attention is also given to Wesley C. Mitchell's and Abram Harris's views toward Veblen.

15　SCHUSTER, GEORGE N. "Schuster on Veblen." <u>Commonweal</u> 30 (16 June):219-20.
　　　Reviews <u>Imperial</u> <u>Germany</u> <u>and</u> <u>the</u> <u>Industrial</u> <u>Revolution</u>. So much of what Veblen wrote in 1915 is true today "that one is disarmed by the intelligence and luminousness of Veblen's intuitions." Disagrees, however, with Veblen's diagnosis of German racial traits.

16　SIMS, LeROY NEWELL. <u>The</u> <u>Problem</u> <u>of</u> <u>Social</u> <u>Change</u>. New York: Thomas Y. Crowell, pp. 300-302.

Places Veblen in the camp of technological determinism.
Veblen was not concerned with the determinants of social change,
only the consequences.

17 TUGWELL, REXFORD G. "Veblen and 'Business Enterprise.'" In
    Books That Changed Our Minds. Edited by Malcolm Cowley and
    Bernard Smith. New York: Doubleday, pp. 91-107.
        Provides a background sketch of Veblen and his works.
    Mentions the impact of Darwinian thought on Veblen. In The
    Theory of Business Enterprise Veblen demonstrates how the machine
    process exacts a certain discipline and serves to undercut the
    system of vested rights. Emphasizes Veblen's isolated personal-
    ity and unhappiness.

18 VINING, RUTLEDGE. "Suggestions of Keynes in the Writings of
    Veblen." Journal of Political Economy 47 (October):692-704.
        Relates Veblen's recognition of overproduction to Keynes's
    concept of effective demand. Suggests that Veblen's writing on
    the interest rate "approximates a Keynesian discussion." Veblen
    also wrote on the "unstable schedule of the marginal efficiency
    of capital" that Keynes described. Finally, Veblen advocated
    an equilibrium theory of unemployment to be found in Keynes.
    "Veblen was a major heretic--in the sense in which Keynes uses
    the word--and on this score is entitled to equal rank with
    Mandeville, Malthus, Gesell, and Hobson."

19 WOLFE, A.B. "Thoughts on Perusal of Wesley Mitchell's Col-
    lected Essays." Journal of Political Economy 47 (February):
    1-29.
        Discusses the influence of Veblen's evolutionary theory on
    Mitchell's system of thought. Emphasis is on genetic development
    and the importance of factual data in control of economic proces-
    ses. Reprinted with a new title: 1952.15.

1940

1 BOGARDUS, EMORY S. The Development of Social Thought. New
   York: Longmans, Green & Co., pp. 373-75.
       Surveys several Veblenian concepts including the "canons"
   of pecuniary emulation, conspicuous consumption, leisure class
   conservatism, pecuniary efficiency, bellicoseness, pecuniary
   education, and machine process thinking. Veblen's concept of the
   instinct of workmanship is also explained. "Economic and industrial conflict in its subtle social psychological aspects was
   brilliantly analyzed by Thorstein Veblen. . . ."

2 GABRIEL, RALPH HENRY. The Course of American Democratic
   Thought. New York: Ronald Press, pp. 145, 188, 298, 304-6.
       Surveys Veblen's critique of American capitalism.

3 LEVY, MARION J. "The Veblenian Structure and Its Critics."
Master's thesis, University of Texas.
Divides Veblen's work into three main parts to give it more
coherence. These include his analysis of the scope and method of
economic science, his theory of the evolution of institutions,
and his actual economic analysis of modern capitalism, subdivided
into (a) consumption and (b) the industrial process and business
enterprise. Follows with an inquiry into the validity of the
criticism to which Veblen's work has been subjected and claims
that this criticism generally falls into one of three categories:
(1) what is beside the point or false, (2) what is based on a
difference of value systems, and (3) what concerns itself with
empirical disproof of specific points in the Veblenian system.
Suggests that three areas where Veblen is most vulnerable to
criticism are his mode of documentation, which is not sufficiently empirical but rests on casual observation; his analysis
of the effect of the machine process on labor force, which exag-
gerates its socializing and secularizing effects; and his theory
of chronic depression, in which he fails to work out the incidence of underconsumption. Argues in Veblen's defense that on a
methodological or theoretical level no criticism that invalidates
Veblen's structure has been successfully brought against it.
Praises Veblen for his criticisms of the naive hedonism, amateur-
ish metaphysics, and homiletics of the orthodox tradition in
economics. Believes that institutional economics as a whole has
used Veblen's attack on neoclassical methodology and orthodox
value and distribution theory but owes little else to him.

4 MUKERJEE, RADHAKAMAL. The Institutional Theory of Economics.
London: Macmillan & Co., pp. 31, 116-18, 141-44.
Stresses Veblen's contributions to a dynamic theory of
economics and his introduction of biological and psychological
concepts into economics. Compares Veblen's theory with those of
Marshall and Marx. "Thus it is not Marx but Veblen who is right
in the analysis of the mechanics of social change. . . ."

5 PAGE, CHARLES HUNT. Class and American Sociology: From Ward
to Ross. New York: Dial Press, pp. xiii, 9, 19, 24-25, 48-
49, 61, 99, 110, 118, 122, 130, 135, 137, 200, 220, 225-26,
249.
Thorstein Veblen ranks as one of the major theorists, if not
the major theorist of social class, in early American sociology.
Of all the early sociologists, he wrote the "most penetrating
analysis of plutocratic control" of American society. Veblen's
influence is extended to such figures as Albion Small, Lester
Ward, and E.A. Ross. Veblen's ideas, such as conspicuous consumption and emulation and the distinction between business and
industry, were utilized in works by eminent American sociolgists.

6 SPILMAN, LEONA. "A Comparison of Veblen's and Commons' Institutionalism." Ph.D. dissertation, University of Wisconsin.

States that the purpose of her dissertation is to present
and interpret methods used by Veblen and Commons as they wrote
about their economic views or as they actively engaged in economic investigations. These two eminent American pioneers were
selected because both are grouped together as "institutionalists," and their views are often treated alike by economists.
Argues that "the result of classifying Veblen and Commons together may cause as much confusion as throwing an alchemist and
a goldminer into the same category." Also believes that Veblen
was much more of an "arm-chair philosopher" than investigator and
consequently based his theories on secondary material. Veblen is
also criticized for attempting to answer the unanswerable--that
is, how to grasp life processes--and for attempting to separate
the inseparable because business and legal activity are not
processes separate from the industrial process. Believes that
for these and other reasons, Commons' work has more policy relevance than Veblen's and his liberal ameliorist approach is to be
preferred to Veblen's destructive, negativistic radicalism.

7   WALLACE, HENRY A. "Veblen's 'Imperial Germany and The
     Industrial Revolution.'" Political Science Quarterly 55
     (October):435-45.
          A sympathetic and detailed review. Speculates that one of
the reasons Veblen wrote this book was to take another swipe "at
one of his pet abhorrences, the American businessman." Notes
that in spite of his small farm background, Veblen was led to the
conclusion that technology dictated large-scale industrialization--
small, competitive business enterprise would not be efficacious.
Argues that the book provides an excellent study of the forces
that have led to the rise of Nazism.

1941

1   ADORNO, THEODOR W. "Veblen's Attack on Culture." Studies in
     Philosophy and Social Science 9, no. 3:389-413.
          Contends that Veblen is less of an outsider to American
culture than one might think at first glance. Veblen relies not
only upon Darwin, but also the German historical school and
American pragmatism. Critiques Veblen's aesthetic theory and
relates it to functionalism; claims that Veblen was a primitivist
who sought a return to a golden age, that he disliked capitalism
more for its waste than its exploitation, and that his writings
contain traces of anti-intellectualism and anti-intermediarism.
Proposes that there is an attitude of melancholia behind Veblen's
progressive facade, and his pragmatism stands in the path of a
greater awareness of future possibilities. "To adapt oneself to
what is possible today no longer means adapting oneself at all.
It means realizing the objective potentiality." Translated and
reprinted in German: 1955.1. Reprinted in English: 1967.1.
For comment, see 1980.15.

*2   DAVIS, ARTHUR K. "Thorstein Veblen's Social Theory." Ph.D.
     dissertation, Harvard University.
        Source: Comprehensive Dissertation Index, 1861-1972 (Ann
     Arbor: University Microfilms, 1973), no. 26, p. 775. See also
     1944.9-10; 1945.1.

3   JOHNSON, EDGAR. "Veblen: Man From Mars." New Republic 105
     (28 July):121-23.
        Considers Veblen as the satirist, analyzing and shedding
     light on his style. "Literary critics, misled by his purely
     technical reputation, have for the most part left his work unan-
     alyzed; and when H.L. Mencken once attempted it, he came the
     ludicrous cropper of reading Veblen's stylistic ironies as mere
     professional verbosity." Veblen has the "detachment of a Martian
     observer." Claims that "Sinclair Lewis often seems to be nothing
     but dramatized Veblen." Veblen has a very real ability to star-
     tle with his use of "sardonic paradoxes."

4   MARCUSE, HERBERT. "Some Social Implications of Modern
     Technology." Studies in Philosophy and Social Science 9,
     no. 3:414-39.
        "Veblen was among the first to derive the new matter-of-
     factness from the machine process, from which it spread over the
     whole society." Notes that early on he noticed the tendency of
     organized labor itself to become conservative.

5   WEILLER, HERMAN E. "The Vision of Thorstein Veblen." New
     Europe 1 (November):321-23.
        Praises Veblen's The Nature of Peace as prophetic. Argues
     that at the time of World War I he recognized the "German prob-
     lem" and offered a solution. The current behavior of Nazi
     Germany confirms Veblen's analysis as set forth years before.
     Asserts that he has made a lasting contribution.

                                1942

1   ANON. "Veblen, Thorstein Bunde." In Twentieth Century
     Authors: A Dictionary of Modern Literature. Edited by
     Stanley J. Kunitz and Howard Haycroft. New York: H.W. Wilson
     Co., pp. 1451-52.
        Provides a biographical sketch of Veblen, emphasizing his
     eccentricities and difficulties. Considers Veblen a magnificent
     thinker who had the courage of his convictions.

2   KAZIN, ALFRED. On Native Grounds. New York: Reynal and
     Hitchcock, pp. 123, 127-28, 130-42, 144, 148, 194, 235, 240,
     344-46, 352, 445.
        Draws upon 1942.3.

3   _____. "Veblen As Artist." Sewanee Review 50 (April):174-83.
        Provides some biographical information on Veblen. Con-
     siders him an "insurgent" but takes pains to distinguish him from

writers of the same time period. Paints Veblen as an "outsider,"
an alienated individual who vented his hatred of capitalist
society in a peculiar literary style. He had a tragic view of
the world and saw "what so few in his generation could ever
see. . . ." In spite of his influence on progressivism, Veblen
despised it, seeing it as essentially reactionary. Places him in
the naturalist camp, and "yet though he had what Dreiser and
Crane and Norris seemed to lack, he was not their equal as an
artist . . . Veblen was an alien to the end, and the torment of
his alienation is forever to be felt in his prose." Revised:
1942.2.

4   ROLL, ERIC. A History of Economic Thought. 2d ed. New York:
     Prentice Hall, pp. 331, 406, 466, 483-500.
         A general analysis of Veblen's economic theory. Assesses
Veblen's critique of orthodox economics, his theory of business
cycles, and his industrial-pecuniary dichotomy. Veblen's greatest achievement, however, was his analysis of pecuniary culture,
for his fundamental dichotomy has but limited power in explaining
matters of pure economics. Compares Veblen with Marx and notes
that the former was more concerned with human motivation.
Veblen's work has its drawbacks but it also bears the stamp of
an imposing mind. More attention given to Veblen in the revised
edition: 1953.18.

5   TRAYWICK, LELAND ELDRIDGE. "Parallelisms in the Economic
     Ideas of Karl Marx and Thorstein Veblen." Ph.D. dissertation,
     University of Illinois.
         After analyzing studies of Veblen by various writers,
Traywick concludes that none of them contains more than hints and
suggestions about the relationship between Marx and Veblen. Consequently, there has been no systematic or rigorous comparison of
the parallels and discontinuities between the two thinkers. Recognizes some differences between Veblen and Marx but claims that
the similarities are more significant. There are two critical
areas in particular where the author stresses fundamental agreement between Veblen and Marx. The first is that of value theory.
Both assume that human labor alone is productive; rent and interest are unearned because capital goods cost nothing but labor.
Related to this is the significance of labor time, the importance
of labor power, and the mutual use of social labor time with its
emphasis on past and present labor. Finally, especially salient
in Veblen is the view that salesmanship is essentially wasteful
and nonproductive. Second, Traywick believes that the parallel
between Marx and Veblen is important in considering the basic
content of their theories of the business cycle of capitalism.
He focuses on the similarity of their belief that production is
for profit, not use; their utilization of the underconsumption
and overproduction theories to explain instability; and their
mutual conviction of the importance of the role played by banks
and the owners of financial and physical capital. He also emphasizes their mutual stress on the role of fraud and sabotage, the

maldistribution of income, the general capitalist tendency for
the rate of profits to decline, and the inevitability of business
crises given the basic structure of the system, and their belief
in the ultimate decline or overthrow of the system. After eval-
uating Veblen's economic theories in light of his criticisms of
Marx and noting the differences between the Marxian and Veblenian
systems, Traywick concludes that both were utopian agitators
rather than scientific analysts of modern capitalism.

1943

1   ANON. "Diagnosing a Reformer." Nation's Business 31
      (October):100-101.
      Reviews The Spirit of Enterprise by Edgar M. Queeny
(1943.5). Characterizes Veblen as an antagonist of competition,
an archvillain of the American free-enterprise system. His
spiteful diatribes against business have succeeded in influencing
a whole generation of students, and his ideas are echoed even in
the halls of government.

2   CURTI, MERLE. The Growth of American Thought. New York and
      London: Harper and Brothers, p. 570.
      States that Veblen believed that men are basically crea-
tures of instinct and habit rather than hedonistic calculators,
that the then existing economics was largely a rationalization of
myths, and that the history of civilization was a more or less
continuous conflict between the predatory and industrious.

3   McCONNELL, JOHN W. The Basic Teachings of the Great Econo-
      mists. New York: New Home Library, pp. 167-70.
      Introduces the reader to Veblen's ideas regarding the in-
stinct of workmanship, pecuniary emulation, and his critique of
orthodox economics.

4   OSHIMA, H.T. "Veblen on Japan." Social Research 10
      (November):487-94.
      Claims that historical events and scholarly research have
validated Veblen's predictions concerning the behavior of the
Japanese Empire. "One is impressed today, in reading Veblen's
comments on Japan, by the keenness of his insight and the accuracy of his prophecies." Details the instances of cultural
borrowing by Japan from Western nations, fitting quite well with
Veblen's theories.

5   QUEENY, EDGAR M. The Spirit of Enterprise. New York:
      Charles Scribner's Sons, pp. 64-73.
      Suggests that Veblen was unable to comprehend the American
mentality because of his foreign parentage and the fact that he
grew up in a colony of recent immigrants. Contends that Veblen
was a "failure in mathematics" but took to the inexact science

and philosophy of economics where he could vent his "bitter and
sarcastic" attitudes toward the American economic system. Contains a general attack on Veblen and his views toward business
enterprise.

1944

1   ANON. "Prophet of the New Deal." <u>Time</u> 43 (31 January):
    99-100.
        Describes the relationship between Veblen and Robert L.
Duffus. Notes his influence on persons such as Tugwell, Soule,
Chase, and others.

2   ANON. Review of <u>The</u> <u>Innocents</u> <u>at</u> <u>Cedro:</u> <u>A</u> <u>Memoir</u> <u>of</u>
    <u>Thorstein</u> <u>Veblen</u> <u>and</u> <u>Some</u> <u>Others</u>, by Robert L. Duffus.
    <u>American</u> <u>Sociological</u> <u>Review</u> 9 (December):716.
        The young Duffus could not "anticipate the event that
Veblen would in time achieve the distinction of changing economics from a dismal science into sociology." See 1944.11.

3   ANON. Review of <u>The</u> <u>Innocents</u> <u>at</u> <u>Cedro:</u> <u>A</u> <u>Memoir</u> <u>of</u>
    <u>Thorstein</u> <u>Veblen</u> <u>and</u> <u>Some</u> <u>Others</u>, by Robert L. Duffus.
    <u>Chicago</u> <u>Sun</u> <u>Book</u> <u>Week</u>, 30 January, p. 2.
        The years 1907-8 saw Veblen "at the peak of his power and
brilliance--and 30 years ahead of his most intelligent contemporaries in his understanding of American industrialism." See
1944.11.

4   ANON. Review of <u>The</u> <u>Innocents</u> <u>at</u> <u>Cedro:</u> <u>A</u> <u>Memoir</u> <u>of</u>
    <u>Thorstein</u> <u>Veblen</u> <u>and</u> <u>Some</u> <u>Others</u>, by Robert L. Duffus.
    <u>Christian</u> <u>Century</u> 61 (1 March):276-77.
        Book provides glimpses into "the life of the great econo-
mist . . . Veblen repays observation from any angle." See
1944.11.

5   ANON. Review of <u>The</u> <u>Innocents</u> <u>at</u> <u>Cedro:</u> <u>A</u> <u>Memoir</u> <u>of</u>
    <u>Thorstein</u> <u>Veblen</u> <u>and</u> <u>Some</u> <u>Others</u>, by Robert L. Duffus.
    <u>Commonweal</u> 39 (18 February):450.
        Considers Veblen to have been a "materialist" and the "evil
product of puritanical utilitarianism." Despite the un-Christian
bias of his point of view, Veblen contributed greatly to our
social self-awareness. See 1944.11.

6   ANON. Review of <u>The</u> <u>Innocents</u> <u>at</u> <u>Cedro:</u> <u>A</u> <u>Memoir</u> <u>of</u>
    <u>Thorstein</u> <u>Veblen</u> <u>and</u> <u>Some</u> <u>Others</u>, by Robert L. Duffus.
    <u>Wisconsin</u> <u>Library</u> <u>Bulletin</u> 40 (June):84.
        "This is a memory of those days, an appealing story in
which, while the professor remains a distant and Olympian figure,
the spirit of youth shines bright and clear." See 1944.11.

7   AYRES, CLARENCE E. The Theory of Economic Progress. Chapel
    Hill: University of North Carolina Press, 317 pp. passim.
         Endorses Veblen's critique of price theory and sees him as
    the first to clearly understand the technological-ceremonial
    dichotomy. Veblen's lead has not been sufficiently followed by
    economists. Veblen's evolutionary approach, influenced by anthro-
    pology, stressed the continuity between past and present. Faults
    Veblen for assuming that the common man is "less addicted to
    ceremonial behavior than his masters," and for not carrying his
    analysis over into policy.

8   BLOOM, SOLOMON F. Review of The Innocents at Cedro: A Memoir
    of Thorstein Veblen and Some Others, by Robert L. Duffus.
    Nation 159 (15 July):76-77.
         In reviewing the book refers to Veblen as "perhaps the
    greatest economist of the Western Hemisphere." See 1944.11.

9   DAVIS, ARTHUR K. "Veblen on the Decline of the Protestant
    Ethic." Social Forces 22 (March):282-86.
         The most important contribution of The Theory of the Lei-
    sure Class is its emphasis on the role of consumption as a symbol
    of social status. The main fault of the book is its "failure to
    perceive the functions of consumption as an expression of the
    basic cultural values." Further, Veblen pinpoints only the invid-
    ious aspects of conspicuous consumption and not the positive
    ones. Veblen's anthropology is actually "conjectural"; it is not
    based on concrete studies of primitive societies. He is compared
    to Max Weber with regard to the Protestant ethic. By stressing
    predation, Veblen "reverses Weber with respect to the honesty and
    righteousness of business effort."

10 _____. "Veblen's Study of Modern Germany." American Socio-
    logical Review 9 (December):603-9.
         Imperial Germany and the Industrial Revolution is "Veblen's
    most substantial achievement." Yet evident in Veblen's work are
    strains of philosophical anarchism manifested in his negative
    attitude toward social institutions. Veblen also devoted "insuf-
    ficient attention to the role of philosophical ideas in formulat-
    ing Germany's ideologies." His account omits the role played by
    the Lutheran ethic in Germany's development, and he could have
    been more specific in showing how feudal agrarian paternalism
    carried over into industry. Veblen's work on Germany is highly
    prophetic, but his treatment of England suffers in comparison.

11 DUFFUS, ROBERT L. The Innocents at Cedro: A Memoir of
    Thorstein Veblen and Some Others. New York: Macmillan Co.,
    163 pp.
         Recounts his experiences with Veblen while he was a stu-
    dent and Veblen a professor at Stanford University. Duffus, his
    brother, father, and a friend, Harry George, shared Veblen's
    cottage at Cedro during the school year 1907-8. According to
    Duffus, Veblen talked little about his own life. Concluded that

he had pride in his Norwegian background and that the effort by
Veblen's parents to cling to their culturally isolated Norwegian
community in Minnesota accounted for much of Veblen's philosophical detachment from American life. Duffus compares Veblen to an
enlightened explorer in a savage country, viewing it critically,
understanding it very well, but not belonging to it. Duffus felt
that his detachment, which accounted for his speaking of so many
respectable persons and institutions as though they belonged in a
zoo, kept him from being emotional about them. Veblen did not
denounce institutions nor was he indignant at strutting figures
of men. They just seemed ridiculous to him. See also 1946.3.

12   H., R.F. Review of The Innocents at Cedro: A Memoir of
      Thorstein Veblen and Some Others, by Robert L. Duffus.
      Springfield Republican, 6 February, p. 7e.
          Describes Veblen as the "iconoclastic economist whose The
      Theory of the Leisure Class is still provoking squeals of dis-
      pleasure from those who suspect they belong to the leisure
      class." See 1944.11.

13   HOFSTADTER, RICHARD. Social Darwinism in American Thought,
      1869-1915. Philadelphia: University of Pennsylvania Press,
      pp. 50, 65, 121-23, 129-36, 145.
          Shows how Veblen fit into the tradition of Darwinist phi-
      losophy. In many important respects Veblen succeeded in turning
      both Spencer's and Sumner's Darwinism in a totally different
      direction--to the left. Claims that "Veblen exposed the intel-
      lectual sterility of prevailing economic theory, and pointed the
      way to an institutional analysis of the facts of economic life."
      Revised: 1955.4.

14   MANLEY, MARIAN C. Review of The Innocents at Cedro: A Memoir
      of Thorstein Veblen and Some Others, by Robert L. Duffus.
      Library Journal 69 (15 January):70.
          A revealing account of "a leading intellectual," the "de-
      tached and remote catalyzer," Thorstein Veblen. See 1944.11.

15   RUSSELL, C. Review of The Innocents at Cedro: A Memoir of
      Thorstein Veblen and Some Others, by Robert L. Duffus. New
      York Times Book Review, 30 January, p. 3.
          Refers to Veblen's "superb intellect." See 1944.11.

16   SILBERSCHMIDT, MAX. Staat und Wirtschaft in der Entwicklung
      der Vereinigten Staaten [State and economy in the development
      of the United States]. Zurich: Schulthess & Co., pp. 29-30.
          Compares Veblen to Marx; not only were both economists,
      they also engaged in critical social analysis. Missing in
      Veblen's work, however, are the Hegelian dynamics and prophetic
      vision of the triumphant new world. Finds Veblen's evolutionary
      views erroneous but notes his influence.

17 STONG, PHILL. Review of The Innocents at Cedro: A Memoir of
    Thorstein Veblen and Some Others, by Robert L. Duffus.
    Saturday Review of Literature 27 (12 February):11.
        Notes Veblen's ability to annoy other economists and the
    very rich. See 1944.11.

1945

1   DAVIS, ARTHUR K. "Sociological Elements in Veblen's Economic
    Theory." Journal of Political Economy 53 (June):132-49.
        Analyzes Veblen's critique of classical economics, the
    sociological elements in his economic theory, and some ethical
    aspects of his thought. He held that classical economics "failed
    to explain concrete reality" and was based on animism or tele-
    ology. While Veblen claimed to be following a Darwinian method-
    ology, his analysis is really akin to Marx's. His key concepts,
    such as "business enterprise," "industry," "leisure class," and
    "technology," however, do not lend themselves "to the formulation
    of precise causal-functional relationships." The sociological
    elements in Veblen's theory--"habits of thought" and "idle curi-
    osity"--are never elaborated into a broader social theory. The
    ethical aspects can be seen in the sociological elements he
    utilizes.

2   HEIMANN, EDUARD. History of Economic Doctrines. New York:
    Oxford University Press, pp. 182-83.
        Finds Veblen to be a truly American economic theorist,
    rightfully compared to Marx. But the streak of contemptuous
    skepticism in Veblen can also be found in fascist thought.
    Veblen "ranks with the great teachers of Historicism in Europe;
    and as a prophet of impending disaster, he is immeasurably supe-
    rior to them."

1946

1   ABBOTT, LEONARD DALTON. Masterworks of Economics. Garden
    City, New York: Doubleday, pp. 9, 711-14.
        Provides a brief biograhical sketch of Veblen and surveys
    the influences on his thought. Claims that Veblen's distinction
    was his creation of "an original set of economic categories based
    on changing industrial conditions. . . ." Veblen continues to
    stimulate interest.

2   AYRES, CLARENCE. Review of Beyond Supply and Demand:
    A Reappraisal of Institutional Economics, by John Gambs.
    Political Science Quarterly 61 (September):437-39.
        Claims that Veblen was a "technological determinist" who
    rejected price theory. Also states that Veblen was from the
    beginning an instrumentalist, which means that he "was an 'Anti-
    Christ' to the same degree and for the same reasons that Dewey is

supposed to be, and is therefore subject to the same determined misunderstanding and obfuscation." See 1946.5.

3   DUFFUS, ROBERT L. "Veblen at Cedro." American Scholar 15 (Fall):462-68.
    Recounts the year he spent with Veblen at Cedro Cottage, Stanford, California, 1907-8. Found it difficult to penetrate Veblen's motives. Feels that Veblen was not really a happy person, but perhaps those days at Cedro were some of the least unhappy for Veblen. See also 1944.11.

4   FANFANI, AMINTORE. Il neovolontarismo economico statunitense [The economic neovoluntarism of the United States]. Milan: Casa Editrice Guiseppe Principato, pp. 6, 8-11, 14, 16-23 passim, 36-37, 421-59, 468.
    Considers Veblen's role in the formation of institutional economics and his relationship to such thinkers as Commons, Mitchell, and Tugwell. Mention is made also of Veblen's influence on the technocracy movement.

5   GAMBS, JOHN S. Beyond Supply and Demand: A Reappraisal of Institutional Economics. Morningside Heights, New York: Columbia University Press, pp. 1-105 passim.
    Assesses the theories of Veblen and later institutional economists. Argues that Veblen's influence can be found in the work of many New Deal economists. Although influenced by him, the later institutionalists constitute no coherent school nor do they approach the world in the way Veblen did. Notes that Veblen's theory was premised on the recognition of coercion in economic affairs, that he was interested in function rather than content, that there are distinct similarities between Veblen and Freud, and that Veblen's philosophy bears a strong similarity to Gestalt theory with its emphasis on the whole. Holds that the "theory of mechanical determinism represents the highwater mark of Veblen's error" and points to his "engineering attitude." Veblen needs to be rewritten, restated, in order that his originality can bear greater fruit.

6   NEFF, FRANK A. Economic Doctrines. Wichita, Kans.: McGuin Publishing Co., pp. 403-7. Second ed. 1950.
    Provides a biographical sketch and emphasizes that Veblen's eccentric style prevented a ready appreciation and understanding of his contributions. States that Veblen was an inspired critic whose influence has been far-reaching.

7   SOULE, GEORGE. "The Need for Social Therapy." New Republic 115 (23 September):356-57.
    Many institutionalists have "been drawn aside to the brilliant propositions of Keynes, which are derived from the tradition rejected by Veblen and which Veblen, if he were alive, would have probably have satirized."

8   SWEEZY, PAUL M. "Veblen: A Cautionary View." New Republic
     114 (25 February):287-88.
         Reviews Veblen's The Nature of Peace. "While history has
     vindicated Veblen's analysis of the role of Germany and Japan" a
     cautious view must be taken of the reasoning underlying the book.
     As brilliant as it often is, Veblen's analysis is one-sided. He
     sees only the negative aspects of nationalism, ignoring its role
     in the bourgeois revolutions of the past and the Socialist revo-
     lutions of the present. Likewise, Veblen's distaste for capi-
     talism precluded a fuller understanding of that phenomenon's
     historical role. Veblen also ignored the process of accumulation
     and failed to develop an adequate theory of employment and busi-
     ness fluctuations. Nevertheless, The Nature of Peace is a great
     book, written by a man who "was greater than his own theories."
     Reprinted: 1953.21.

                                    1947

1   AARON, DANIEL. "Thorstein Veblen: Moralist and Rhetorician."
     Antioch Review 7 (Fall):381-90.
         Veblen's popularity is partly a result of the relevance of
     his social and economic ideas, but his greatest appeal stems from
     his moralism, satire, and rhetoric. Veblen's apparent detachment
     disguises the fact that he was in reality a passionate reformer
     and critic of American social life, especially its business and
     consumer aspects. Veblen was among the first to recognize that
     economic ills were the result of pure business practices, not the
     outcome of a conspiracy. He had little patience for middle class
     prescriptions for social injustices; if anything, he was more
     inclined toward socialism. Nevertheless, he was critical of
     Marx's teleology. Reprinted with substantial revisions: 1951.1.

2   ANON. "Veblen." Fortune 36 (December):132-35, 192, 194, 198,
     201-2.
         A summary statement of Veblen's ideas and his impact upon
     American thinking. Along with bits of biographical information,
     Veblen is depicted as a brilliant, non-Marxist critic of American
     business practices. There are certainly revolutionary implica-
     tions in his work, "but they are masked in a wondrously involved
     and thoroughly delightful style, dead pan, sesquipedalian, mock-
     pedantic, and sometimes uproariously funny, that has won Veblen
     some acclaim as a literary craftsman." Claims that except for
     Marx, no other thinker so negatively influenced the intellectual
     attitudes toward business and capitalist civilization.
     Reprinted: 1955.2.

3   GAMBS, JOHN S. "The Alleged Revolution in Economic Theory."
     Antioch Review 7 (Fall):391-402.
         Assesses the Keynesian revolution and other developments in
     economics with reference to Veblenian criteria. Sees a wide gulf

between the views of "standard" and Veblenian economists. Questions the use of the concept of competitive equilibrium that has for some time been held suspect by Veblenians. Finds recent economic prescriptions wanting when measured in light of Veblenian standards and ideas.

4   GRUCHY, ALLAN G. Modern Economic Thought. New York:
    Prentice-Hall, pp. 1-8, 26-626 passim.
        Discusses Veblen's criticism of orthodox economics, his concept of process, his social psychology, and his theory of institutions. Also covered are Veblen's analyses of modern capitalism and the corporation revolution. His fundamental dichotomy between the industrial and pecuniary types is treated. Argues that unlike Marx, Veblen was not concerned with a theory of surplus exchange value but rather a theory of "surplus product." Finds both optimistic and pessimistic strains in Veblen's thought. Veblen's instinct theory is now dated, as is part of his theory of capitalism. Often his work is sketchy and weak in its factual basis. Further, he was not much interested in policy questions, and a certain utopian strain can be detected in his writings. Veblen's legacy, however, "continues to be a valuable instrument for the interpretation of our evolving economic system."

5   KOLODNY, JULIUS. "An Interpretive Study of the Social, Political, Economic, and Educational Views of Thorstein Veblen."
    Ph.D. dissertation, New York University.
        Describes and assesses Veblen's views regarding economics, politics, history, sociology, education, war, peace, and methodology. Argues that many readers either reject or accept Veblen's ideas in toto--what is needed is a balanced assessment of his views. Considers him to be a profound thinker, one who made significant contributions to economics (the genetic approach); political science (his views on patriotism, peace, and war); sociology (leisure class behavior); psychology; and education. Argues that Veblen had a brilliant understanding of the events of his time. In spite of this, argues that he built no system and wrote no masterpiece. Criticizes Veblen for intruding a normative bias into his avowed objective social science and for his works's frequent weakness on facts. Finds his social theory naive and contradictory at points, especially when he called for a soviet of technicians.

6   MADISON, CHARLES. Critics and Crusaders: A Century of American Protest. New York: Henry Holt & Co., pp. 308-39.
    Second ed. 1959.
        Provides some biographical information and summarizes the ideas contained in Veblen's more well-known books. Argues that his economic thinking is an "extraordinary intellectual achievement" and has had an important impact on economic thought in general. Avers that "Veblen's written work declined markedly after he had left the University of Chicago." Praises The Instinct of Workmanship, however, for achieving the "remarkable

intellectual feat of clarifying the interaction of instinct and
habit, the basic interrelationships between the industrial and
the pecuniary processes, and the effects of the prevailing cultural lag." Surveys Veblen's acute analysis of peace and war,
modernization, and capitalist business practices. Perhaps Veblen
exaggerated the influence of technology on our thought, but his
fundamental thesis is correct.

7   MORRIS, LLOYD. Postscript to Yesterday. New York: Random
     House, pp. 35, 414-21.
        Describes Veblen's contribution to his time. Emphasizes
     his critique of economic and social institutions. Claims that
     Veblen influenced such figures as Charles Beard, James Harvey
     Robinson, and Thurman Arnold.

8   RUGG, HAROLD O. "The Study of Industrial Culture and Society:
     Veblen and After." In Foundations for American Education.
     Yonkers: World Book Co., pp. 259-72.
        States that only now is Veblen's stature as America's first
     social psychologist being recognized. Claims that Veblen was a
     true "radical" who uncovered the foundations of industrialism.
     These foundations were psychological, resting on the irreducible
     drive of men for security, power, and glory. The history of
     modern culture, he said, duplicated those of primitive ones in
     this respect.

9   SMITH, WILLIAM J.J. "The Theoretical Work of Thorstein
     Veblen." Ph.D. dissertation, Duke University.
        Examines Veblen's entire theoretical system, including his
     theory of human nature and social change. Focuses on various
     aspects of Veblen's economic analysis, including his theory of
     consumption, the historical background of modern industrialism,
     and the distinction between business and industrial pursuits.
     Cyclical fluctuations, depression, and monopoly are an important
     part of Veblen's explanation of business cycles. The historical
     background of the conditions of war and peace and future consid-
     erations regarding the maintenance of peace are also surveyed.
     Believes that "it is the unsystematic, discursive character of
     his writing that constitutes one of the chief difficulties in
     always clearly understanding what he meant. Yet, the fact re-
     mains that the different portions of Veblen's analytical work are
     systematically related."

10   WHITE, MORTON G. "The Revolt against Formalism in American
     Social Thought of the Twentieth Century." Journal of the
     History of Ideas 8 (April):131-52.
        Describes similarities in the intellectual origins of
     Charles Beard, John Dewey, Oliver Wendell Holmes, James H.
     Robinson, and Thorstein Veblen and argues that all revolted
     against formalism in cultural analysis. Considers the attempt
     of each to refer to historical facts and include those social
     sciences not the subject of the study at hand as a unique aspect

of these American thinkers. Points to Veblen's integration of economics, anthropology, and sociology. Reviews the historical origins of the reaction against formalism in terms of the influence of preceeding pioneers in social thought. Refers to Charles Darwin, G.W.F. Hegel, and Karl Marx as inspirational. Alludes to the response of Veblen and others to English and Scottish empiricism and devotes detailed attention to their reactions to John Stuart Mill, Adam Smith, David Hume, and Jeremy Bentham. Material from this article with additions appears in 1949.20; 1957.29.

1948

1 ANON. "Conspicuous Radicalism." Time 51 (24 May):112, 114-15.
    Review of The Portable Veblen, edited by Max Lerner. Veblen survives as a thinker because he trusted neither capitalism nor Marxism. His literary style has gained for him the title of "the most impressive satirist of his day."

2 ANON. Review of The Portable Veblen, edited by Max Lerner. New York Herald Tribune Weekly Book Review, 4 July, p. 10.
    Anyone who has read Main Street by Sinclair Lewis should read Veblen's "The Country Town." "They throw a great deal of light back and forth between them."

3 BARNES, HARRY ELMER. Historical Sociology: Its Origins and Development. New York: Philosophical Library, pp. 126-27.
    Calls Veblen the outstanding student of the evolution of capitalism and asserts that he is more sociologist than economist.

4 BELL, QUENTIN. On Human Finery. London: Hogarth Press, pp. 11-12, 15-16, 22, 24, 28-29, 34, 36, 46, 61, 86, 98, 101-2, 114-21, 126-27.
    Argues that Veblen's analysis of conspicuous display is the true manner to approach the issue of dress. Applies Veblen's ideas to changing economic and social conditions. Despite Veblen's generally correct approach, his theory occasionally falters—he does not explain the shifts from simplicity to ornateness and vice versa sufficiently, and his theory does not account for the fact that women begin to dress in feminine fashion only when they attain status on their own.

5 DAVIS, ARTHUR K. Review of The Freudian Psychology and Veblen's Social Theory, by Louis Schneider. Social Forces 27 (October):94-95.
    Disagrees with Schneider's having accepted Veblen's concept of "predatory instinct" in its literal sense. Feels that Veblen actually regarded the concept as a habit rather than an instinct. See 1948.16.

6   DUNCAN, OTIS DUDLEY. Review of The Freudian Psychology and
     Veblen's Social Theory, by Louis Schneider. American Journal
     of Sociology 54 (November):253.
          Claims that the book fails to do justice to the breadth of
     Veblen's contribution to social theory. This may, however, be a
     function of the rather narrow focus of the book--its relation to
     clinical psychology. See 1948.16.

7   FLYNN, JOHN T. The Roosevelt Myth. New York: Devin-Adair
     Co., pp. 155-57.
          Calls Veblen the great pioneer of planning in the United
     States. Paints Veblen as erratically brilliant, a person of bad
     manners, and implies that he was lazy and exploitive. Sees
     Veblen as influencing the course of the New Deal by teaching his
     ideas to men such as Rexford G. Tugwell and Leon Henderson.

8   FRIEDRICH, CARL JOACHIM. Inevitable Peace. Cambridge:
     Harvard University Press, pp. 22, 209, 219-25.
          Assesses Veblen's ideas concerning peace, found chiefly in
     his The Nature of Peace and Imperial Germany and the Industrial
     Revolution. Considers him to be a Socialist with a nineteenth-
     century optimism about human nature. Unlike many of his contem-
     poraries, "Veblen had no illusions about the undemocratic aspect"
     of internal class warfare. Veblen understood the need for elimi-
     nating the militarist element in societies such as Germany's, but
     he entertained no belief that it could actually be accomplished.
     Detects an "anarchist strand" in Veblen's writings because he was
     disinclined to "face the problem" of government. A really pene-
     trating study of Veblen's political theory has yet to be written.

9   GRAMSCI, ANTONIO. Il materialismo storico e la filosofia di
     Benedetto Croce. [Historical materialism and the philosophy
     of Benedetto Croce]. Turin: Guilio Einaudi Editore,
     pp. 113-14.
          Notes the influence of Spencer and Marx on Veblen. Men-
     tions his instinct of workmanship and sees a resemblance between
     Henry Ford and Veblen.

10   LASKI, HAROLD J. The American Democracy: A Commentary and
     Interpretation. New York: Viking Press, pp. 45, 70-71, 165,
     259, 358, 437-41, 445, 474, 567, 610, 613, 749.
          States that Veblen was "perhaps the most distinguished
     speculative mind in the field of social philosophy that America
     has produced since Thomas Jefferson." Credits Veblen for his
     vision and incisive analysis of the business-dominated institu-
     tions of modern society. Veblen's critiques of the tremendous
     waste of resources have been confirmed. "Of the major economists
     who wrote after 1900, only the work of Thorstein Veblen seems
     seriously relevant to contemporary America. . . ."

11   LERNER, MAX, ed. Editor's Introduction to The Portable
     Veblen. New York: Viking Press, pp. 1-49.

Provides biographical background on Veblen and explores the troubles he experienced during his academic odyssey. Details Veblen's devastating critique of received economic doctrine and stresses his ideas concerning machine technology and its impact upon culture. Veblen's views regarding the price system are noted, including his distinction between productive industry and parasitic business and finance. Considers him to be both theorist and reformer. Although Veblen was an admirer of Marx, he nonetheless criticized him on fundamental points. "Veblen's theory that peace requires the abolition of the price system amounts to an equating of socialism with the survival of civilization." Suggests that Veblen was akin to Rousseau in his belief in man's natural goodness. Comments finally on Veblen's style: It is at times quaint, at times "chugging."

12   MERCIER, VIVIAN. Review of The Portable Veblen, edited by Max
      Lerner. Commonweal 48 (July):362.
          "Any one who hasn't read the American Voltaire at all is given a wonderful opportunity to start now." See 1948.11.

13   REDFIELD, ROBERT. "The Art of Social Science." American
      Journal of Sociology 54 (November):181-90.
          Suggests that social science is more than science--it is also art that requires a gifted perception of certain aspects of human nature. This gift or skill provides a fresh outlook and contributes to humanistic endeavor. Considers three major works as exemplifying this artistic ability--De Toqueville's Democracy in America, Sumner's Folkways, and Veblen's The Theory of the Leisure Class. Argues that all three are important for sociology. Veblen is perhaps the least "objective" of the three authors but nevertheless provides a fresh and creative description of society. He focused attention on consumer behavior and pecuniary emulation and demonstrated the importance of these phenomena.

14   REDMAN, BEN RAY. Review of The Portable Veblen, edited by Max
      Lerner. Saturday Review of Literature 31 (10 July):30.
          Veblen performed a "seminal function" of leadershp in providing fruitful insights into social processes and institutions. See 1948.11.

15   ROSENBERG, BERNARD. "Veblen and Marx." Social Research 15
      (March):99-117.
          Compares various ideas of Marx and Veblen. "It appears then that Thorstein Veblen was a thinker in his own right, related to, but only partly dependent upon, Marx. His class concepts resemble those of Marxian sociology in some respects, but they differ in even more significant ones. Primarily, Veblen wavered in the application of technological determinism, and the doubt he thus revealed is an accurate measure of his success." Material from this article appears in 1956.10.

16 SCHNEIDER, LOUIS. The Freudian Psychology and Veblen's Social
    Theory. Morningside Heights, New York: King's Crown Press,
    270 pp.
        Analyzes the connections between Freudian psychology and
    Veblen's social psychological theory. The psychologies of Veblen
    and Freud have different origins. Veblen's was formulated as a
    tool for attacking orthodox economic theory, whereas Freud's
    evolved out of attempts to solve problems of neurotics. Never-
    theless, both theories provide related insights into the nature
    and origin of irrationality and social cohesion. Emphasizes
    Veblen's theories of human nature, reason, irrationality, anar-
    chism, and the leisure class. Concludes with a psychological
    study of Germany. The book was submitted to Columbia University
    as a doctoral dissertation.

1949

1   ANGIOLINI, VITTORIO. "A proposito della recente traduzione di
    un libro del Veblen" [Regarding a recent translation of a book
    by Veblen]. Critica economica [Economic critique] 4
    (February):102-6.
        Criticizes Franco Ferrarotti's translation of The Theory of
    the Leisure Class into Italian. Claims also that Veblen's multi-
    disciplinary approach leads to a superficial analysis of economic
    problems. Disputes the claims that Veblen is largely unknown in
    Italy and forgotten in the United States. See also 1949.2-3, 8-
    9, 17.

2   _____. "A proposito della recente traduzione di un libro del
    Veblen" [Regarding a recent translation of a book by Veblen].
    Critica economica [Economic critique] 4 (April):99-100.
        Continues the polemic over the translation of The Theory of
    the Leisure Class. Sides with Croce in vehemently attacking
    Veblen's work. See 1949.6. See also 1949.1, 3, 8-9, 17.

3   _____. "A proposito della recente traduzione di un libro del
    Veblen" [Regarding a recent translation of a book by Veblen].
    Critica economica [Economic critique] 4 (June):121-22.
        Continues the polemic over the translation of Veblen's The
    Theory of the Leisure Class into Italian. Replies that
    Giolitti's attempt to pass Veblen off as an unknown is tied into
    his "leftist interpretation. Giolitti is a well-known figure in
    the Italian Communist party. See 1949.9. See also 1949.1-2, 8-9,
    17.

*4 BANFI, R. "Alle origini del qualunquismo" [On the origins of
    indifference]. Unità [Unity], 1 February, no pages cited.
        Source: 1974.6, p. 190. Reviews the Italian edition of
    The Theory of the Leisure Class.

5   BJORK, KENNETH. "Thorstein Veblen and St. Olaf College: A
     Group of Letters by Thorbjørn N. Mohn." Norwegian American
     Studies and Records 15:122-30.
          Introduces letters from Mohn to Veblen and others regarding
     the former's decision not to offer Veblen a teaching position at
     St. Olaf College, Northfield, Minnesota, in 1890.

*6   CROCE, BENEDETTO. "La teoria della classe agiata" [The Theory
     of the Leisure Class]. Nuovo corriere della sera [New evening
     courier], 15 January, no pages cited.
          Source: 1973.8, p. 291.

7   DORFMAN, JOSEPH. The Economic Mind in American Civilization,
     1865-1918. Vol. 3. New York: Viking Press, pp. 190, 275,
     382-493 passim.
          Discusses Veblen's background, career, main ideas, and
     influence. Examines the influence of Kant on Veblen and the
     latter's attempt to rest the study of economics on a new foun-
     dation. Veblen utilizes anthropological concepts to provide
     insights into the nature of economic and social activity.
     Stresses Veblen's industrial-financial dichotomy and its impli-
     cations for the study of economics.

8   FERRAROTTI, FRANCO. "A proposito della recente traduzione di
     un libro del Veblen" [Regarding a recent translation of a book
     by Veblen]. Critica economica [Economic critique] 4
     (April):98-99.
          Continues the polemic over Ferrarotti's "leftist" transla-
     tion of The Theory of the Leisure Class. Defends Veblen. See
     1949.1-3, 9, 17.

9   GIOLITTI, ANTONIO. "A proposito della recente traduzione di
     un libro del Veblen" [Regarding a recent translation of a book
     by Veblen]. Critica economica [Economic critique] 4
     (June):117-20.
          Continues the polemic over Ferrarotti's translation of
     Veblen. Giolitti, who wrote the preface to the translation of
     The Theory of the Leisure Class, criticizes Angiolini. See
     1949.1-3, 8, 17.

10   GRIZIOTTI (KRETSCHMANN), JENNY. "Il nuovo indirizzo
     scientifico nell'economia America" [The new scientific
     direction in American economy]. Critica economia
     [Economic critique] 4 (February):36-44.
          Begins with the premise that American economic science
     differs from its Western European counterpart and then analyzes
     the work of Veblen. Deals largely with his ideas concerning
     technology and its impact on the life process. Considers
     Veblen's ideas regarding work as "utopian."

11   HARAP, LOUIS. The Social Roots of the Arts. New York:
     International Publishers, pp. 86-89.

Examines Veblen's ideas concerning the class nature of
taste. Certain notions of taste amongst the leisure class are
permanent and are based upon the consumption of unproductive
goods and services. Veblen emphasizes the "pecuniary" motivations of taste and tends to underemphasize the class function of
leisure.

12   LEPAWSKY, ALBERT. Administration: The Art and Science of
      Organization and Management. New York: Alfred A. Knopf,
      pp. 133-38, 141, 146, 151, 668.
          Notes the relationship of Veblen's ideas to technocracy and
      administration in general.

13   MENCKEN, HENRY L. "Professor Veblen." In Mencken
      Chrestomathy. New York: Alfred A. Knopf, pp. 265-75.
          Excerpted revision of 1919.14. Excerpted from 1919.15.
      See also 1960.3. Reprinted: 1965.8.

14   MERTON, ROBERT K. Social Theory and Social Structure.
      Glencoe, Ill.: Free Press, pp. 58, 63, 69-70, 153-54, 243,
      290, 307, 325, 370, 375.
          Discusses Veblen's contribution to the notion of manifest
      and latent functions, pointing to his concept of conspicuous
      consumption as a prime example. Refers also to his notions of
      trained "incapacity" and "idle curiosity." Reprinted: 1967.15.

15   METZGER, WALTER P. "Ideology and the Intellectual: A Study
      of Thorstein Veblen." Philosophy of Science 16 (April):
      125-33.
          Sees Veblen as the ideologist for the intellectual. As an
      intellectual, he likewise rejected the farmer, small businessman,
      and worker as not possessing the qualities of mind necessary to
      bring about desired changes.

16   MITCHELL, WESLEY C. Lecture Notes on Types of Economic
      Theory. Vol. 2. New York: Augustus M. Kelley, pp. 218-52.
          Notes from lectures delivered by Professor Mitchell at
      Columbia University and taken down stenographically by a student
      in the years 1934-35. Mitchell claims no responsibility for the
      accuracy of the transcript. In the notes Veblen is compared and
      contrasted with Marx, his relationship to the historical school
      is explored, and his Theory of Business Enterprise and other
      works are discussed. Veblen's relationship to orthodox economics
      is treated and some biographical information is provided.

17   PESENTI, ANTONIO. "A proposito della recente traduzione di un
      libro del Veblen" [Regarding a recent translation of a book by
      Veblen]. Critica economica [Economic critique] 4
      (February):107-8.
          Responds to Angiolini. 1949.1-3. See also 1949.8-9.

18   SFORZA, W. CESARINI. "Una analisi sociale: la classe agiata"
     [A social analysis: the leisure class]. Messaggero
     [Messenger (Rome)], 22 April, p. 3.
          Rejects the thesis that Veblen is unknown in Italy and that
     there is a bourgeois conspiracy of silence regarding his writ-
     ings. Claims that Veblen presents a cold and unbiased analysis
     of American economic institutions that is not Marxist at all.
     Compares Veblen to Freud in his unmasking of flawed elements in
     human nature.

19   WERKMEISTER, W.H. "Thorstein Veblen." In A History of
     Philosophical Ideas in America. New York: Ronald Press,
     pp. 252-61.
          Describes Veblen's concept of conspicuous consumption and
     the conditions out of which it grows. The relationship of class
     to property in Veblen's work is discussed.

20   WHITE, MORTON G. Social Thought in America: The Revolt
     against Formalism. New York: Viking Press, 260 pp. passim.
          Incorporates material from 1947.10. Reprinted with new
     preface and epilogue: 1957.29.

21   WILCOX, SAMUEL. "Veblen's Criticisms of the Austrians and the
     Classicists." Ph.D. dissertation, University of Virginia.
          Restates Veblen's critique of the Austrians and classicists
     and asserts that on the whole the Veblenian analysis is a pene-
     trating one. Believes that Veblen was essentially correct in
     arguing that mainstream economics of his day was contaminated
     with uncritical acceptance of natural law, harmony as opposed to
     conflict of interests, a teleological order, a meliorative trend
     in events, the invisible hand, and the imputation of final
     causes. Finds Veblen correct in his indictment of economists for
     their uncritical acceptance of psychological hedonism, their
     narrow focus on normal cases, and their confusion of creation of
     property rights with creation of useful goods and services.
     Veblen also succeeded in showing that the older body of economic
     doctrine was a priori, static and taxonomic, and deductive, unreal-
     istic, scholastically overrefined, and based on an antiquated
     psychology. "If Veblen did nothing else, he exposed the fact
     that the older economic theories were in need of thorough renova-
     tion and reconstruction, and were inadequate to meet the stand-
     ards set by modern scientific ideals of objectivity, realism and
     freedom from metaphysical preconceptions."

                              1950

1   ANON. Review of The Philosophy of Thorstein Veblen, by
     Stanley Matthew Daugert. School and Society 71 (March):173.
          Writes that there are some issues in Veblen's thought that
     await a more complete formulation and criticism. See 1950.5.

2   AYRES, CLARENCE E. Review of The Philosophy of Thorstein
     Veblen, by Stanley Matthew Daugert. Journal of Political
     Economy 58 (October):451-52.
          Writes that a student of his, Richard Sterba, "has con-
     vinced me that the analytical methodology whch is forecast in
     that neglected essay [Kant's Critique of Judgement] can be traced
     through the whole of Veblen's work and is, indeed, his variant of
     Dewey's well known 'continuum' of means and ends. It is the
     principle of cumulative causation, by Pierce out of Kant, that
     found expression in Veblen's theory of technological process
     and so underlies his 'instrumental or technological theory' of
     value." See 1950.5.

3   BURKE, KENNETH. A Rhetoric of Motives. New York: Prentice-
     Hall, pp. 24, 36, 127-32, 224, 263, 305. Reprint. Berkeley
     and Los Angeles: University of California Press, 1969.
          Considers Veblen as a theorist of rhetoric. The termin-
     ology in The Theory of the Leisure Class is too limited in scope
     and his distinction between pecuniary and workmanlike endeavors
     neither comprehensive nor sufficiently pliant. Notes Veblen's
     "satire-masked-as-science." The Theory of the Leisure Class is
     valuable in showing how identification can operate.

4   COMMAGER, HENRY STEELE. The American Mind: An Interpretation
     of American Thought and Character since the 1880's. New
     Haven: Yale University Press, pp. 54, 107, 235-43.
          Treats the main features of Veblen's thought. Argues that
     Veblen was a son of the middle border and his fundamental ideas
     can be traced to the populist sentiments of the region. Veblen
     saw only change where others saw progress. His most important
     contribution was his elaboration of the distinction between busi-
     ness and industry.

5   DAUGERT, STANLEY MATTHEW. The Philosophy of Thorstein Veblen.
     New York: King's Crown Press, Columbia University, 134 pp.
          Analyzes the origin and development of "Veblen's critical
     and theoretical views in philosophical analysis and speculation."
     Argues that Veblen "formulated and developed a philosophy that he
     applied to the analysis of human problems" but that statement is
     not complete. Assesses Veblen's early writings on Immanuel Kant
     and notes the influence of the German philosophers on young
     Veblen. Veblen combines and reconsiders to some extent "Kant's
     telelogy with Spencer's revolutionism, and both of these with the
     genetic psychology of James and Dewey." Feels that Veblen is
     probably more indebted to Spencer than he might have been willing
     to admit. Points to the differences between Veblen's and Marx's
     conceptions of economic determinism and further analyzes Veblen's
     ideas concerning human nature, institutions, human welfare, sci-
     ence, and technology.

6   DOBRIANSKY, LEV E. "The Social Philosophical System of
     Thorstein Veblen." Ph.D. dissertation, New York University.
          Revised and published under a new title; see 1957.11.

7   FERRAROTTI, FRANCO. "La sociologia di Thorstein Veblen" [The
sociology of Thorstein Veblen]. Rivista di filosophia [Review
of philosophy] 41 (October-December):402-19.
    Disagrees with Benedetto Croce's negative appraisal of
Veblen and claims that there is merit in the biting critical
prose of the American. Finds Veblen's works tainted with posi-
tivism, biologism, and lack of appreciation for the dialectical
method. See 1949.6.

8   GORDON, MILTON M. Social Class in American Sociology.
Durham: Duke University Press, p. 7.
    Claims that Veblen "undoubtedly laid the groundwork for a
cultural analysis of class behaviour." There are in his work,
however, signs of a "peculiar psychological interpretation which
attributes a great deal more conscious awareness of the behavior
process to the participating individuals than a strictly cultural
approach would dictate or validate." Observes that Veblen's
distinction between business and production fits into the economic framework of class definition.

9   LASERSON, MAX M. The American Impact on Russia, 1784-1917.
New York: Macmillan Co., pp. 294, 312-13.
    Notes similarities between Veblen and the Russian thinker
Nicholas Chernyshevski. Holds that Chernyshevski may be called a
forerunner of Veblen.

10   LEIBENSTEIN, HARVEY. "Bandwagon, Snob, and Veblen Effects in
the Theory of Consumer's Demand." Quarterly Journal of
Economics 64 (May):183-207.
    Reformulates certain aspects of the static theory of con-
sumer demand. Sees the "Veblen" effect as a nonfunctional external effect on utility. "By the Veblen effect we refer to the
phenomenon of conspicuous consumption; to the extent to which the
demand for a consumer's good is increased because it bears a
higher rather than a lower price." The Veblen effect is distinguished from both the "bandwagon" and "snob" effects.
Reprinted: 1968.12; 1969.7; 1975.8. Incorporated into a
chapter of a book: 1976.13. See also 1978.1.

11   McGILL, V.J. "The Main Trend of Social Philosophy in
America." In Philosophical Thought in France and the United
States. Edited by Marvin Farber. Buffalo: University of
Buffalo Publications in Philosophy, pp. 679-704. Reprint.
Albany: State University of New York Press, 1968.
    While stating that Veblen is an important figure in the
intellectual history of American radicalism, he is criticized for
the following reasons. First, Veblen's theory of crises and
depression, though it bears a strong resemblance to the Marxian
theory, is sketchy and unburdened by economic details. Secondly,
Veblen's criticism of our pecuniary culture does not always go to
the heart of the matter but is nevertheless immensely clarifying.
Third, criticizes Veblen for offering no plausible solutions

while having almost nothing to say of current political issues.
He is unfortunately silent regarding the role of unskilled workers and the general population in a new social order. Fourth,
Veblen's view of the future was typically vague, cynical, or
pessimistic. He rejected not only business civilization but also
the Socialist alternative and had no viable third possibility to
offer.

12   ROSENBERG, BERNARD. "Thorstein Veblen in the Light of Contem-
     porary Social Science." Ph.D. dissertation, New School for
     Social Research, New York.
          Revised and published under a new title, see 1956.10.

13   SMITH, T.V. Review of The Philosophy of Thorstein Veblen, by
     Stanley Matthew Daugert. Ethics 61 (October):89-90.
          "Veblen's theory of intelligence and his estimate of sci-
     ence seem more like Mead, who is barely mentioned in passing,
     than like James and Dewey, who are here emphasized." See 1950.5.

14   SPENGLER, JOSEPH J. "Evolutionism in American Economics,
     1800-1946." In Evolutionary Thought in America. Edited by
     Stow Persons. New Haven: Yale University Press, pp. 202-67.
     Reprint. N.p.: Archon Books, 1968.
          Fixes Veblen's place in the history of American evolu-
     tionary economics. Holds that he was more responsible than any
     other American economist for introducing Darwinian evolutionary
     ideas to economic analysis. Veblen broadened the scope of eco-
     nomics, adding to it a theory of social change and a new psychol-
     ogy. Notes also that Veblen's approach was pervaded by the
     spirit of Marxism, and while aspects of his economic and social
     theories are defective, he did much to weaken the reputation of
     received economics and helped found the new approach called
     "institutionalism."

15   TUGWELL, REXFORD G. "The New Deal: The Progressive Tradi-
     tion." Western Political Quarterly 3 (September):390-427.
          "Veblen's mind was a vivisecting one. Veblen placed the
     modern business culture on the table, forgot the scientific end
     in view, and used the knife with detached, precise precision."
     Relates Veblen's ideas to his Norwegian-farmer background and
     adverts to his hatred of Yankee business practices. Veblen's
     ideas came to have a significant influence on the New Deal.

16   WHITTAKER, EDMUND. Review of The Philosophy of Thorstein
     Veblen, by Stanley Matthew Daugert. Annals of the American
     Academy of Political and Social Science 269 (May):180-81.
          Writes that "friend and foe agree in classifying Thorstein
     Veblen as one of the greatest of American writers in the social
     sciences. . . ." See 1950.5.

1951

1   AARON, DANIEL. Men of Good Hope. New York: Oxford Univer-
     sity Press, pp. 208-42. Reprint. 1961.
        Elaborates on the previous analysis of Veblen and demon-
     strates the relationship between his ideas and those of other
     thinkers. Places him in historical perspective. Substantial
     revision of 1947.1.

2   AYRES, CLARENCE E. "The Co-ordinates of Institutionalism."
     American Economic Review 41 (May):47-55.
        If there is at least one point of agreement about institu-
     tionalism, it is the preeminent influence of Thorstein Veblen.
     It is quite evident that a value theory is implicit in Veblen's
     writings.

3   FERRAROTTI, FRANCO. "Un critico americano di Marx" [An Amer-
     ican critic of Marx]. Rivista di filosofia [Review of phi-
     losophy] 42 (April-June):154-63.
        Differentiates the petty, largely myopic Italian critiques
     of Marx from that of Veblen. Veblen attacks the very ideological
     roots of Marxism and chides Marx for overemphasizing value.
     While sympathetic toward Veblen, feels that he slights historical
     materialism.

4   HARRIS, ABRAM L. "Veblen and the Social Phenomenon of Capi-
     talism." American Economic Review: Papers and Proceedings 41
     (May):66-77.
        Veblen attempts, as did Marx, Sombart, and Weber, to pro-
     vide a genetic explanation of capitalism. Discusses Veblen's
     philosophy of history, built around his theory of instincts; his
     theoretical analysis of capitalism; his views on scientific
     methods in the study of economics; and his program of reform.
     Veblen thought that classical economics was unscientific and
     sought to bring his own conception of science to that field.
     States that Veblen's belief in mechanical efficiency or "tangible
     performance" cannot be a guide to efficiency as it is understood
     by economists. Criticizes Veblen's use of anthropology and as-
     pects of his theory of business enterprise.

5   LIPSET, SEYMOUR MARTIN, and REINHARD BENDIX. "Social Status
     and Social Structure, 1." British Journal of Sociology 2
     (June):150-68.
        Discusses Veblen's theory of conspicuous consumption.
     Notes that Veblen's name does not appear in any of the works of
     Lloyd Warner and associates, although much of their work is an
     elaboration of his ideas.

6   STEINER, ROBERT L., and JOSEPH WEISS. "Veblen Revised in the
     Light of Counter-Snobbery." Journal of Aesthetics and Art
     Criticism 9 (March):263-68.

Argues that Veblen did not foresee the phenomenon of "countersnobbery"; that the old elite would downplay its conspicuous display in order to differentiate itself from the parvenu class. Examples are provided.

1952

1   ATHERTON, LEWIS E. "The Midwestern Country Town: Myth and Reality." Agricultural History 26 (July):73-80.
    Argues that many literary and scholarly depictions of the country town are overdrawn and imbalanced. Figures including Mark Twain, Edgar Lee Masters, Sinclair Lewis, and Thorstein Veblen have pinpointed the limitations of small town culture. Asserts that while some of Veblen's observations in his article "The Country Town" can be supported, he is often guilty of one-sided analysis. Veblen overestimates the degree of business monopoly as he does the storekeepers' guardianship over local social and moral standards.

2   AYRES, CLARENCE E. The Industrial Economy. Boston: Houghton Mifflin Co., pp. 24-28, 46, 58, 390, 393, 395, 402.
    Discusses Veblen's dichotomy between industrial and pecuniary employments, his notion of the instinct of workmanship, and his evolutionary point of view.

3   EUGSTER, CARL. Thorstein Bunde Veblen, 1857-1929. Zurich: Europa Verlag, 116 pp.
    A general introduction to the ideas of Veblen. Concentrates on Veblen the sociologist rather than Veblen the economist. Considers Veblen to be the "Karl Marx of America" in that his scholarly work also voices criticism of social institutions. Argues, however, that the comparison between Marx and Veblen should not be pushed too far. Believes that Veblen's system lacked Hegelian dynamics and the prophetic ability to foresee the inexorable breakthrough of a new world because he was laboring under the misapprehension of evolutionary ideas.

4   GAMBS, JOHN S. Man, Money, and Goods. New York: Columbia University Press, pp. 123-33, 152-74.
    Describes Veblen as the complete dissident economist. Contends that Veblen founded no school, was not interested in price theory, and had no theory of value. Notes that Veblen's system is based on the distinction between making money and making goods, and that he did have a complete theory of business cycles. Finds his work to be pessimistic, utopian, and characterized by a naive faith in machine technology. In spite of the fact that Veblen tended to push useful ideas to ridiculous extremes, he provided a stimulus for a more realistic economic science.

5   GLADE, WILLIAM P. "The Theory of Cultural Lag and the Veblenian Contribution." American Journal of Economics and Sociology 11 (July):427-37.

Attempts to define clearly the concept of cultural lag and
show how Veblen contributed to an understanding of that concept.
Veblen's theory rested on the dichotomy between technology and
ceremonialism. His analysis goes beyond the typical studies of
cultural lag and deals with its underlying aspects.

6   GOLDMAN, ERIC F. Rendezvous with Destiny. New York:
     Alfred A. Knopf, pp. 114-17, 161, 255.
        Comments on Veblen's dour personality and his impact upon
America. After the 1929 crash, Veblen came into his own. "Then
the bumbling, mumbling professor, who had never known what to do
when someone complimented him, was widely hailed as the most
penetrating thinker of American dissidence."

7   JOHNSON, ALVIN. Pioneer's Progress. New York: Viking Press,
     pp. 44, 167, 198, 205-6, 271, 273, 280, 282-83.
        Recalls impressions of Veblen's teaching days at the New
School for Social Research.

8   MITCHELL, LUCY SPRAGUE. "A Personal Sketch." In Wesley Clair
     Mitchell: The Economic Scientist. Edited by Arthur F. Burns.
     New York: National Bureau of Economic Research, pp. 55-106
     passim.
        Provides insights into Veblen's personality and refers to
Wesley C. Mitchell's admiration for Veblen. Claims that Veblen
influenced Mitchell. Enlarged: 1953.14.

9   MITCHELL, WESLEY C. "Mitchell on Veblen." In The Development
     of Economic Thought. Edited by H.W. Spiegel. New York: John
     Wiley and Sons, pp. 378-402.
        Excerpted and reprinted from 1936.17; 1937.9.

10   NEWMAN, PHILLIP CHARLES. The Development of Economic Thought.
     Englewood Cliffs, N.J.: Prentice-Hall, pp. 344-61.
        Surveys Veblen's major ideas. Finds it difficult to clas-
sify Veblen and measure his influence. Although Veblen reminds
one of Marx, he is neither Marxist nor Socialist. Contends that
Veblen is "easily the most original American economist, and he
can be compared only to Pareto and Max Weber in the overwhelming
range of his knowledge."

11   RIESMAN, DAVID. "A Lecture on Veblen." Journal of General
     Education 6 (April):214-33.
        Assesses Veblen's chief theories and attempts to explain
contemporary habits, tastes, and patterns of social behavior
within a Veblenian framework. Praises Veblen's writings on the
issue of women. Wonders if perhaps Veblen's views on the matter-
of-fact rationality that results from machine discipline is open
to some question. Veblen, Marx, and Freud all saw hidden motives
behind everyday behavior that many of us are bound to dismiss as
mere innocent activity. Like Marx, Durkheim, and Weber, Veblen is
interested in industrial civilization and its effects on human
behavior.

12   SOULE, GEORGE H. <u>Ideas of the Great Economists</u>. New York: Viking Press, pp. 181, 184-92, 199. Reprint. New York: Mentor Books, American Library, 1952.

Summarizes Veblen's major ideas and provides some biographical information. Sees Veblen as a powerful and witty critic of business, waste, and orthodox economic doctrine. American economics have never been the same since Veblen wrote.

13   SWEEZY, PAUL M. "The Influence of Marxism on Thorstein Veblen." In <u>Socialism and American Life</u>. Edited by Donald Drew Egbert and Stow Persons. Vol. 1. Princeton: Princeton University Press, pp. 473-77.

Claims that Veblen, one of America's greatest social scientists, was not a Marxist but was influenced by Marx's ideas. Veblen entertained a variety of economic determinisms, as did Marx. Veblen also followed Marx in maintaining the historically transitory nature of class society and the inevitability of socialism. A glance at Veblen's writings belies a strong interest in and sympathy with socialism.

14   WISH, HARVEY. <u>Society and Thought in Modern America</u>. New York: Longmans, Green, & Co., pp. 174, 185, 229, 334, 547.

Much of Veblen's indictment of the captains of industry and the leisure class can be documented, but not all of it. Some of his analysis is exaggerated.

15   WOLFE, A.B. "Views on the Scope and Method in Economics." In <u>Wesley Clair Mitchell: The Economic Scientist</u>. Edited by Arthur F. Burns. New York: National Bureau of Economic Research, pp. 207-34.

Reprint of 1939.19 with a new title.

1953

1   BROOKS, VAN WYCK. <u>The Confident Years, 1885-1915</u>. London: J.M. Dent and Sons, pp. 46-49, 85, 99-100, 112, 118-20, 154, 215, 237, 267, 275, 295-97, 303, 334, 347.

Discusses Veblen's literary efforts in the context of his times. "In Veblen's apparent impassivity there was a note of the peasant cunning that recalled Uncle Remus' Brer Bear when he 'lay low,' as there was something niggardly and churlish in the deadly acid irony with which he stripped human motives to the psychological bone." For many, Veblen appeared (to use William James's expression) as the "unbribed soul."

2   FELLMANN, DAVID. "A Populist Progressive." <u>New Republic</u> 129 (30 November):18-19.

Reviews <u>Thorstein Veblen: A Critical Interpretation</u> by David Riesman (1953.17). "Some of Riesman's most illuminating observations deal with the analysis of his [Veblen's] personality."

3   FEUER, LEWIS. "Thorstein Veblen: The Metaphysics of the
     Interned Immigrant." American Quarterly 5 (Summer):99-112.
          Provides a biographical sketch of Veblen and relates his
     thought to late nineteenth-century thinkers. Veblen's account of
     the intellectual preeminence of the Jews as a result of cultural
     isolation fails to consider the Jewish tradition of scholarship,
     their heritage of social protest, and their rational monotheism.
     Veblen is compared to William James, whose brand of pragmatism
     Veblen criticized. "Veblen was America's first materialist
     metaphysician."

4   HAMILTON, DAVID. Newtonian Classicism and Darwinian Instu-
     tionalism. Albuquerque: University of New Mexico Press,
     138 pp. passim.
          States that institutionalism is best defined as "that eco-
     nomic theory developed by Veblen and those American economists
     who have largely adhered to the outlook and major premises of
     Veblen." Discusses major themes in Veblen's economic theory and
     his contribution to institutionalism. In this regard stresses in
     particular the influence of Darwin. Veblen's psychology is more
     behaviorist than of the instinct variety. Notes his concern with
     the impact of technology on culture. Reprinted with a new title:
     1970.3.

5   _____. "Veblen and Commons: A Case of Theoretical Conver-
     gence." Southwestern Social Science Quarterly 34
     (September):43-50.
          Attempts to refute the charge that the institutionalist
     school of economics is a mere "hodge podge of unrelated hypoth-
     eses and descriptive monographs." "Holism" is one way to cate-
     gorize institutionalism. A case can also be made that Veblen and
     John R. Commons share much in common and can both be designated
     as institutionalists. Both placed great emphasis on the notion
     of collective as opposed to individual action. Both also empha-
     sized the "coercive" nature of economic institutions. States
     that Veblen's "most outstanding" contribution to economic science
     was his distinction between "technological" and "ceremonial"
     behavior. Compares this distinction with Commons's concept of
     bargaining and managerial transactions. Finds similarity as well
     between Veblen's famous business-industry dichotomy and Commons's
     wealth-assets distinction. Veblen and Commons can be profitably
     compared for similarities, and the difference between the two is
     largely one of approach. In Veblen's case, the approach was
     anthropological; in Commons's, it was based on years of research
     in unions, cooperatives, and governmental agencies.

6   HARRIS, ABRAM L. "Veblen as Social Philosopher--A
     Reappraisal." Ethics 63 (April):1-32.
          A lengthy assessment of Veblen's social philosophy. Notes
     the diversity of opinion regarding his theories and proceeds to
     criticize Veblen for: (1) depicting a state of primitive sav-
     agery for which there is no scientific proof; (2) disguising

value judgments behind scientific facades; (3) ignoring the relationship between investment cost and the creation of capital; (4)
falsely connecting the entrepreneurial function with mechanical
performance and decision making; (5) not attempting any serious
evaluation of the real limitations of competition or its utility
as method and policy; (6) entertaining a false conception of Adam
Smith's social philosophy and economic principles; (7) incorrectly linking war with business motivations and political pro-
tection of capitalistic interests instead of with aggressive
nationalism and militant race consciousness; (8) falsely believing that, in industrial use of technology on a large scale, the
cost curve slopes downward indefinitely; (9) making questionable
application of the doctrine of biological evolution to racial
types and culture; (10) overlooking the fact that if each firm in
every industry attempted to follow a policy of replacing all of
its old or recent equipment and methods by the latest technological innovations, utter waste and chaos would be the result; (11)
failing to specifically outline the role the market mechanism and
price system would play in his ideal economy; and (12) not taking
into account the political obstacles confronting the implementa-
tion of his program. Believes that while Veblen made some important contributions as a critic and historian of capitalism, his
conception of the basic defects of the system was mistaken. His
program of economic reorganization, designed to increase efficiency, lessen inequality, and create greater freedom, would
achieve none of these things but would cause greater evils than
already exist. Revised and expanded: 1958.19.

7   HEILBRONER, ROBERT. "Provocative and Provoking." New York
Times Book Review, 27 September, p. 37.
    A review of Thorstein Veblen: A Critical Interpretation by
David Riesman (1953.17). "By all odds Thorstein Bunde Veblen is
the most provocative--and the most provoking--social analyst that
America has produced to date."

8   _____. "The Savage World of Thorstein Veblen." In The
Worldly Philosophers. New York: Simon and Schuster,
pp. 181-213. Reprint. 1961.
    Contends that Veblen was an important economist and social
philosopher. Outlines both his main ideas and biography and
argues that Veblen had neither a happy nor successful life, at
least in the conventional meanings of these terms. Believes that
Veblen's theoretical work is vulnerable to criticism on several
counts. He underestimated the capacity of a democratic system to
correct itself and did not recognize the ability of the system to
curb the abuses and predation of its business classes. Veblen
was also infatuated with the machine process and was not aware
that technological standards of efficiency may be irreconcilable
with democratic humanism. Nevertheless Veblen, in spite of these
deficiencies, was a unique figure in emancipation of the human
mind on account of his iconoclasm and detachment from mainstream
American culture. Reprinted with minor revisions: 1980.8.

9   HIRSCH, FELIX E. Review of Thorstein Veblen: A Critical
     Interpretation, by David Riesman. Library Journal 78
     (15 September):1526-27.
        Writes that "Veblen's influence on American social thought
     has remained intense, and his works, especially his The Theory of
     the Leisure Class, have retained a prominent place on academic
     reading lists . . . Riesman's appraisal brings out the lasting
     qualities of Veblen's noble contribution. . . ." See 1953.17.

10   HOMAN, PAUL T. "Nemesis of the Leisure Class." Saturday
     Review of Literature 36 (28 November):26.
        A review of Thorstein Veblen: A Critical Interpretation by
     David Riesman (1953.17). Suggests that "Riesman is at some pains
     to establish the psychiatric and cultural basis of Veblen's own
     viewpoint." Riesman does not clearly establish what is to be
     made of the Veblenian legacy.

11   HUTCHISON, T.W. A Review of Economic Doctrines, 1870-1929.
     Oxford: Clarendon Press, pp. 262-68, 273, 307, 360, 383-87,
     391, 398, 425.
        Focuses on Veblen's critical essays and some of his main
     socioeconomic ideas. Surveys Veblen's critiques of marginal
     utility analysis and the scheme of self-equilibrating dynamics.
     Believes that Veblen's theory of crises and chronic depression,
     built on the distinction between business and industry, comes
     close to Marx at points. Credits Veblen with insights into
     forces which disrupt the system of "competitive individualism."
     Sees Veblen as a major influence on the "left-wing" economists of
     the 1930s.

12   LINDBLOM, CHARLES E. "Lonely Iconoclast." Yale Review 43
     (December):282-83.
        Reviews Thorstein Veblen: A Critical Interpretation by
     David Riesman (1953.17). Finds Riesman's summary of Veblen's
     thought "sound." Thinks there is less system to Veblen's ideas
     than does Riesman.

13   MILLS, C. WRIGHT. Introduction to The Theory of the Leisure
     Class. New York: Mentor Books, pp. viii-xix.
        "Thorstein Veblen is the best critic of America that Amer-
     ica has produced." Claims that Veblen's style is "hilarious" and
     that his works "smash through the stereotyped world of our rou-
     tine perception. . . ." Provides a biographical sketch of Veblen
     and assesses his major ideas. Argues that Veblen entertained a
     theory of economic scarcity--such that the times in which he
     lived would lead one to believe in. Feels that Veblen "did not
     pay appropriate attention to the relevance of status to power
     because of his theory of history" and that he did not "recognize
     the terrible ambiguity of rationality in modern man and his
     society"--he overestimates the beneficial effects of rationality
     brought about by technology. Nonetheless, Veblen "makes us see
     through the official sham. Above all, he teaches us to be

aware of the crackpot basis of the realism of those practical Men
of Affairs who would lead us to honorific destruction."

14   MITCHELL, LUCY SPRAGUE. Two Lives: The Story of Wesley Clair
       Mitchell and Myself. New York: Simon and Schuster,
       pp. 82-516 passim.
       Enlarged version of 1952.8.

15   REDLICH, FRITZ. Review of Thorstein Bunde Veblen, 1857-1929,
       by Carl Eugster. Journal of Economic History 13 (Summer):
       333-34.
       The reader must be reminded that Veblen was an economist,
not just a sociologist. See 1952.3.

16   RIESMAN, DAVID. "The Social and Psychological Setting of
       Veblen's Economic Theory." Journal of Economic History 13
       (Fall):449-61.
       Relates Veblen's economic theory to his personality as it
was shaped by his boyhood and the social conditions of his time.
The influence on Veblen of such thinkers as Sumner is noted.
Claims to detect certain paradoxes in Veblen's account of social
institutions. Reprinted: 1954.14; 1964.14.

17   . Thorstein Veblen: A Critical Interpretation. New
       York: Charles Scribner's Sons, 221 pp.
       Attempts to explain Veblen's economic and social theories
with reference to his background and personality. Emphasizes the
ambiguity and internal contradictions of Veblen's thought. Such
confusions of thought, compounded by obscurity of expression,
make Veblen impenetrable for many. Believes that Veblen was
unable to bridge the gap between the culture of the humanities
and that of modern science and technology. Much space is devoted
to Veblen's personal life and social background. Argues that
Veblen was incapable of fighting directly for the things he
believed in, could never exorcise his father, had a repressed
inner urge to show off, and unconsciously conspired in his own
exploitation by preferring to remain underpaid and underranked.
Consequently, Veblen behaved aggressively toward those in authority and was abnormally sensitive to constraint. His main weak-
ness as a scholar was that his moralism and parochialism were
hidden from his own view; and as he grew older, he became increas-
ingly less open to new evidence or interested in any that did not
sustain a previously cherished view. Compares Veblen with Henry
Ford and Mark Twain. Contains a list of Veblen's books and a
selective bibliography on Veblen. Reprinted with a new preface:
1960.6. Abridged version of chapter four reprinted: 1954.15-16.

18   ROLL, ERIC. A History of Economic Thought. 3d ed. Englewood
       Cliffs, N.J.: Prentice-Hall, pp. 369, 423, 439-54, 510.
       Revised edition of 1942.4. More attention is given to
Veblen in this edition.

19   ROSENBERG, BERNARD. "A Clarification of Some Veblenian Concepts." American Journal of Economics and Sociology, 12
(January):179-87.
Attempts to clarify several concepts in Veblen's works.
Feels that Veblen's instinct theory has been raised to "propor-
tions of importance" not deserved by commentators on Veblen.
Figures that even Veblen himself overrated the parental bent and
romanticized primitive life. Veblen's image of primitive life
was shaped largely by Morgan and Tylor, but he overlooked the
fact noted by Durkheim that society and religion were from the
beginning "practically identical." Points to a number of blind-
spots in Veblen's functionalism. Material from this article
appears in 1956.10.

20   SCOTT, D.R. "A Recollection of Veblen at Missouri." Missouri
Alumnus, February, pp. 6, 12.
Recounts impressions of Veblen's stay at the University of Missouri. Recalls Veblen's isolation, humor, and
"self-effacement."

21   SWEEZY, PAUL M. The Present as History. New York: Monthly
Review Press, pp. 295-301.
Reprint of 1946.8.

22   TOOL, MARCUS. "The Philosophy of Neo-Institutionalism:
Veblen, Dewey, and Ayres." Ph.D. dissertation, University of
Colorado, Boulder.
The neoinstitutionalist economic theory is ultimately
rooted in the theory of social value held jointly by Thorstein
Veblen, John Dewey, and Clarence Ayres. This theory is analyzed
and applied to show its broader significance. Although there
were intellectual differences between Dewey and Veblen, Ayres has
successfully synthesized the common aspects of their perspective
into a new version of institutional economics.

23   WIRTH, LOUIS. "The Social Sciences." In American Scholarship
in the Twentieth Century. Edited by Merle Curti. Cambridge:
Harvard University Press, p. 51.
Notes Veblen's original contribution, his trenchant critique of the orthodox and abstract economics of his time. Had
Veblen's criticism been taken seriously when it was written, the
older economics might have reconstructed itself earlier than
it did. Veblen's influence on economics was "indirect" and
"retarded."

1954

1   APTHEKER, HERBERT. "Marx and American Scholarship." Masses
and Mainstream 7 (July):42-47.
Veblen was one of a handful of American scholars to recognize and defend the ideas of Marx.

2   ASHE, GEOFFREY. "The Vision of Industrialism." Commonweal 59
     (1 January):338.
         Reviews Thorstein Veblen: A Critical Interpretation by
     David Riesman (1953.17). Attacks the major ideas of Veblen with
     respect to waste, show, and conspicuous consumption. Finds that
     these things are not so bad. The "trouble with Veblenist common
     sense is that it is so negative."

3   BHATTY, I.Z. "Some Aspects of the Writings of Pareto and
     Veblen." Indian Journal of Economics 35 (October):123-30.
         Discusses Pareto's Trattato di sociologia generale and
     Veblen's The Theory of the Leisure Class and The Instinct of
     Workmanship. Compares Pareto's and Veblen's combination of
     economics and sociology. Pareto's concept of social equilibrium
     is contrasted with Veblen's theory of evolutionary determinism.
     Argues that the approaches of Pareto and Veblen provide a broader
     perspective for the study of economic social order. Criticizes
     Pareto's failure to include his own belief in the irrationality
     of human behavior in his economic theories. Criticizes Veblen's
     style and the clarity of his ideas. Considers both Pareto and
     Veblen as significant in the fields of economics and sociology.

4   COATS, A.W. "The Influence of Veblen's Methodology." Journal
     of Political Economy 62 (December):529-37.
         Assesses Veblen's contribution to the methodology of
     economics. Feels that Veblen pushed his criticisms of orthodox
     economics "to unwarrantable extremes." Claims that Veblen's
     evolutionary method is not "demonstrable on rational grounds"
     and his "entire approach represented a naive form of
     Wissenssoziologie. . . ." Veblen is also charged with making
     disguised value judgments while at the same time alleging objec-
     tivity. While there is no doubting Veblen's contributions to
     economics in general, his contribution to scientific method in
     particular "cannot be rated highly."

5   COHEN, MORRIS RAPHAEL. "Veblen and More Recent Economists."
     In American Thought: A Critical Sketch. Glencoe, Ill.: Free
     Press, pp. 95-99.
         Argues that Veblen's theory of evolutionary economics is
     based on a hazy notion of scientific method because Veblen mis-
     understood the concept of Darwinian evolution. In spite of
     certain methodological weaknesses, Veblen's work, in particular
     his proposal of an alternative to the classical laissez-faire
     theory, had a profound effect on American economic thought.

6   DEWEY, ERNEST W. "Thorstein Veblen's General Theory of Valua-
     tion." Ph.D. dissertation, University of Texas, Austin.
         Assesses major aspects of Veblen's philosophical position.
     Treats his concepts of truth, science, progress, society, and
     individual as well as his distinction between ceremonialism and
     technology. Veblen's relation to the Pragmatists is explored and
     his philosophy is compared and contrasted with Marxian material-
     ism. Argues that Veblen understood the "necessity" of the

progression to "universality" in much the same way as did Kant.
Veblen's concept of truth is a correspondence theory, similar to
those of Pierce and Dewey. States that Veblen could never fully
agree to the materialist position held by Marx, although he
shared may of Marx's ideas. Maintains that there is a unity and
consistency in Veblen's thought and that his "categories of
analysis . . . provide a breadth and clarity of approach not
limited to a particular time or particular social system."

7   DEWEY, ERNEST W., and DAVID L. MILLER. "Veblen's Naturalism
    versus Marxian Materialism." Southwestern Social Science
    Quarterly 35 (September):165-74.
        Compares Marx and Veblen with respect to their philosoph-
    ical commitments and surveys the latter's critique of the for-
    mer's approach. "Considering the ferocity of Veblen's attack on
    Marxian doctrine, one could easily ask how it can be said that
    there is any common ground." Claims that Veblen's analysis of
    the business/industrial conflict in America "is a far more accu-
    rate analysis than Marx's concept of sharply drawn classes."

8   FRIDAY, CHARLES B. "Veblen versus Chamberlin on Monopolistic
    Competition." Western Economic Association Proceedings 29:54-57.
        Compares Veblen and E.H. Chamberlin on the notion of
    monopolistic competition. Veblen dealt with the notion first.
    "Indeed, Chamberlin recognized Veblen's pioneer concern with this
    problem and quotes him approvingly. . . ." Although Veblen is
    "distressingly vague" at times, his historical approach sheds
    light on the problem.

9   GLASER, WILLIAM A. "Algie Martin Simons and Marxism in America."
    Mississippi Valley Historical Review 41 (December):419-34.
        Suggests that Veblen's concept of an instinct of workman-
    ship was picked up by the American Marxist Simons.

10 GOLOB, EUGENE O. The "Isms": A History and Evaluation. New
    York: Harper and Brothers, pp. 576-77.
        Argues that Veblen's idolatrous respect for technical effi-
    ciency explains his venemous attacks on business incompetence and
    waste.

11 HARDWICK, ELIZABETH. "Riesman Reconsidered." Partisan Review
    21 (September-October):548-56.
        Takes a hard look at Riesman's sociology and considers his
    interpretation of the lives and works of Veblen and Freud. After
    summarizing Riesman's treatment of Veblen writes, "But this is
    fantastic--Veblen was great and many a man ready to stand up and
    be counted among the eminent is not."

12 MILLER, PERRY, ed. American Thought: Civil War to World War
    I. New York: Holt, Rinehart, and Winston, pp. xlvi-xlix.
        Sees Veblen as spiritually alienated from American culture.
    Argues that The Theory of the Leisure Class stood Herbert Spencer
    on his head and is a profound and fruitful analysis of traditional

twentieth-century society. "In his tortured and angry prose, the
impersonality of a pure scientist joins forces with the bard of
savagery in an alliance against the perversion of human dignity
perpetrated by a profit-seeking, 'barbarian civilization.'"

13   NEWMAN, PHILLIP, ARTHUR D. GAYER, and MILTON SPENCER, eds.
     Source Readings in Economic Thought. New York:
     W.W. Norton & Co., pp. 521-24.
          Sees Veblen as the leading intellectual figure in American
     institutional economics, the best critical economist of his time,
     and a highly competent satirist. Veblen combined Marxism and
     German historicism with Darwinian evolutionism to help found a
     new school of economics. His best economic analysis is to be
     found in The Theory of Business Enterprise.

14   RIESMAN, DAVID. Individualism Reconsidered. New York: Free
     Press, pp. 73, 77-78, 84, 86, 129, 150, 160, 203, 224-25, 227,
     271-85, 300, 390, 443, 462, 472.
          Contains brief references to Veblen's ideas concerning
     social theory as well as a reprint of 1953.16; reprinted again
     as an article, see 1964.14.

15   ____. "Veblen and the Higher Learning." Introduction to The
     Higher Learning in America. Stanford, Calif.: Academic
     Reprints, pp. ix-xx.
          Finds Veblen's criticisms of and suggestions about higher
     education to be "gloriously impractical" yet the book encouraged
     a counterstyle, a sort of reverse snobbery. "The extra need of
     honor given those who don't teach at all, or those who teach
     graduate student males as against those who teach in secondary
     schools. . . ." Claims that Veblen's notion of idle curiosity
     goes far to explain his own "focus of attention." In spite of
     his errors Veblen is "entitled to his place in the history of
     intellectual freedom." This article is an abridged version of
     chapter four of Riesman's Thorstein Veblen: A Critical Interpre-
     tation (1953.17). Reprinted: 1954.16.

16   ____. "Veblen and the Higher Learning." University of
     Chicago Magazine 46 (January):14-18.
          Abridged version of chapter four of 1953.17. Reprinted:
     1954.15.

17   ____. "Veblen's System of Social Science." Explorations,
     no. 2, pp. 84-97.
          Cites Veblen's theory of history and suggests that unlike
     Marx, "Veblen can be commendably undogmatic on this point." For
     Veblen, technology is the catalyst in transitions from stage to
     stage in history. Notes Veblen's concept of culture lag.
     Veblen, his disclaimers notwithstanding, is allied with the
     progressive-thinking rationalists of the nineteenth century.
     Finds difficulties and paradoxes in many of Veblen's ideas--in
     particular, his explanation of German and Japanese behavior pat-
     terns. It is paradoxical that Veblen, who spoke for the "common

man," had little regard for "common sense." Actually, Veblen's
system is postulated on biology as much as it is on history.
Claims that Veblen had little positive to say about institutions;
his study of the institution of higher learning "is for the most
part obsessed" with the top rank administrators and trustees. Yet
Veblen's "irony is as superior to the naturalists' frequent grimness
as Charlie Chaplin's pessimism is superior to that of soap opera."

1955

1   ADORNO, THEODOR W., ed. "Veblen's Angriff auf die Kultur"
    [Veblen's attack on culture]. In Prismen [Prisms]. Berlin:
    Suhrkamp Verlag, pp. 82-111.
         Translation into German and reprint of 1941.1. Reprinted
    in English: 1967.1.

2   ANON. "Veblen." In Outside Readings in Sociology. Edited by
    Edgar A. Schuler et al. New York: Thomas Y. Crowell Co.,
    pp. 461-74.
         Reprint of 1947.2.

3   GRIMES, ALAN PENDLETON. "Thorstein Veblen." In American
    Political Thought. New York: Holt, Rinehart, and Winston,
    pp. 382-85.
         Sees Veblen as the "arch rival" of business and the founder
    of institutional economics. Veblen's starting point was "univer-
    sal skepticism" which he turned on "past values, prejudices, and
    methods." Briefly surveys Veblen's major ideas and his intellec-
    tual legacy.

4   HOFSTADTER, RICHARD. Social Darwinism in American Thought.
    New York: George Braziller, pp. 65, 82, 143-45, 152-56, 159,
    168-69.
         Revised edition of 1944.13. Contains minor additional
    information on Veblen.

5   JAMES, ROBERT LEWIS. "A Test of an Aspect of Veblen's Theory
    regarding Socioeconomic Class Stratification." Ph.D. disser-
    tation, University of Oregon.
         Discusses Veblen's ideas concerning social class stratifi-
    cation and subjects them to empirical testing. Utilizing income
    statistics, concludes that the findings "generally validate"
    Veblen's contention that "there has taken place in recent years a
    continual process of concentration of material income at the
    upper end of the income scale." Attention is given to Veblen's
    theories regarding the value setting role of the upper classes,
    its pecuniary nature, and that class's access to wealth.

6   NOBLE, DAVID W. "Veblen and Progress: The American Climate
    of Opinion." Ethics 65 (July):271-86.
         Relates Veblen to two predecessors who also taught eco-
    nomics--Richard Ely and Simon Patten. Tries to show that Veblen
    viewed science as value-neutral but when he began to write about

American institutions "his philosophy of history and of human psychology shifted radically." Veblen then followed Ely and Patten and other fellow reformers in believing in the "ethics of the natural man." Claims that value preferences can be found in Veblen's work and after World War I he "began to sound even more suspiciously like the Christian philosopher Ely and the Quasi-Christian thinker Patten." States that Veblen combined "ardor and technique" so effectively "that, for a generation, his inter-preters could not help but accept Veblen in his self-appointed role as the ahistorical, self-contained unique thinker, a role which openly contradicted so much of his social theory." See also 1958.27.

7   ROSENBERG, BERNARD. "Thorstein Veblen: Portrait of the Intellectual as a Marginal Man." Social Problems 2 (January):181-87.
         Portrays Veblen as the marginal man: an alienated intel-lectual, stranger to his social environment. Emphasizes the importance of Veblen's essay on "The Intellectual Pre-eminence of the Jews in Modern Europe" as a key to understanding the author himself. Refers to other writings on the topic of the "stranger" in order to more fully describe Veblen's situation. Revised as a chapter in his book, see 1956.10.

8   UNTERMEYER, LOUIS. Makers of the Modern World. New York: Simon and Schuster, pp. 262-69.
         Surveys Veblen's life and major works. Argues that no "American so savagely mocked the prevailing canons of taste and culture or castigated the pleasure of spending money by labeling it a foolish way of purchasing prestige." Shows how Veblen differed from Marx and comments on the "astringent flavor of his wit." Veblen's faults include his overestimation of the engineer and his underestimation of the ability of a democracy to curb its excesses.

1956

1   FERRAROTTI, FRANCO. "Un sociologo e gli sport" [A sociologist and sports]. Centro sociale: inchieste sociale, servizio sociale di gruppo, educazione degli adulti [Social center: social inquiries, group social service, adult education] (Rome) 3, no. 7:28-30.
         Notes that Veblen considers sport as "conspicuous waste." The core of sporting activities is "aggressiveness" and "uselessness."

2   HAMILTON, DAVID. "What is Positive in Veblen?" New Mexico Quarterly 26 (Summer):147-55.
         Questions the negative appraisal of Veblen by Riesman and seeks to identify the positive or constructive contributions that Veblen made. While it is true that certain of Veblen's ideas are

not dated, e.g., his views on unilinear social evolution, instinct
psychology, and the business cycle, there is one major theme in
his writings--the distinction between workmanship and exploit--
that remains timely and valuable. "This dichotomy which Veblen
stressed so much is his grand theme--not the literary histrion-
ics, the irony, the bitterness, the neuroticism, or the many
other things that Mr. Riesman and others of his bent seem to
think they find in Veblen. He was after all, an economist and
not a literary man or a sociologist or a student of character."

3 HARRIS, JANICE W. "Thorstein Veblen's Social Theory." Ph.D.
   dissertation, New School for Social Research, New York.
      Analyzes Veblen's standing in and contributions to the field
of social theory. Notes the lack of consensus regarding Veblen's
stature as a social theorist. Considers his theory of instincts
and defines it in terms of human "potentialities." Veblen is
credited with having made contributions to group theory, role
theory, a rudimentary sociology of knowledge, culture lag, and a
theory of class and status. Those who influenced Veblen and
those he influenced receive treatment. While admitting that
Veblen's writings are incomplete and vague at times, he nonetheless is stimulating and provoking.

4 HODDER, H.J. "The Political Ideas of Thorstein Veblen."
   Canadian Journal of Economics and Political Science 22
   (August):347-57.
      The clearest way to grasp Veblen's political and social
thought is to evaluate it in terms of philosophical anarchism.
An important feature in Veblen's argument is that if archaic
residues were eliminated, "peaceful, productive efficiency would
emerge." Veblen's satire reminds one of Voltaire's and is doubt-
less an overstatement. Evidence of Veblen's anarchism can be
found in his dislike of the control of capitalism by the captains
of industry, the control of universities by trustees and administrators, and his relations with women. Running throughout
Veblen's writing are signs of his dislike for the institutions of
dominance. His faith rests with scientific management of industry.

5 INNIS, HAROLD A. "The Work of Thorstein Veblen." In Essays
   in Canadian Economic History. Edited by Mary Q. Innis.
   Toronto: University of Toronto Press, pp. 17-26.
      Reprint of 1929.6. Abridged and reprinted: 1979.10.

6 LAYTON, EDWIN T., Jr. "The American Engineering Profession
   and the Idea of Social Responsibility." Ph.D. dissertation,
   University of California, Los Angeles, pp. 12-13, 162-64, 173.
      Describes Veblen's attempt to organize technologists to
promote the ideas set forth in his The Engineers and the Price
System. See also 1962.4; 1971.11.

7 LERNER, MAX. Foreword to The Values of Veblen: A Critical
   Reappraisal, by Bernard Rosenberg. Washington, D.C.: Public
   Affairs Press, v-vi.

Considers Veblen a giant to be reckoned with, someone who
has much to say that is still relevant. Notes the inspiration
that Veblen provided for such figures as Alvin Johnson, Wesley
Mitchell, Walton Hamilton, Randolph Bourne, John Dos Passos,
John R. Commons, Charles Beard, Abram Harris, Arthur Davis,
David Riesman, C. Wright Mills, and Bernard Rosenberg.

8   MILLS, C. WRIGHT. The Power Elite. New York: Oxford Univer-
     sity Press, pp. 53, 58-59, 88-91, 108-9, 191.
        Argues that Veblen's ideas concerning the American upper
class remain convincing, notwithstanding the fact that his analysis is often empirically inadequate. The Theory of the Leisure
Class is not the theory of the leisure class, it is a theory of a
particular element of the upper class at a point in time.
Veblen's theory fails to adequately link status to political
power, and he seems to confuse aristocratic and bourgeois traits.

9   OLIVER, JOHN W. History of American Technology. New York:
     Ronald Press, pp. 456-57.
        Describes Veblen as one who "viewed realistically the im-
pact that technology was having upon the entire economy of the
western world."

10   ROSENBERG, BERNARD. The Values of Veblen: A Critical
     Appraisal. Washington, D.C.: Public Affairs Press, 127 pp.
        Depicts Veblen as a marginal man, a stranger alienated from
the mainstream of society, one capable of seeing things that
others could not. Emphasizes Veblen's book, The Higher Learning
in America, and notes its importance for the rest of his philosophy. Veblen is compared favorably with Marx and Weber, and his
theory of emulation is considered to be a plausible explanation
as to why there is no effective Socialist movement in the United
states. Analyzes at length The Theory of the Leisure Class, The
Theory of Business Enterprise, and Veblen's writings on war and
peace. Brilliant as he was, Veblen was guilty of exaggeration,
one-sided analysis and vacillations. Veblen, the great critic of
institutions, is "preeminently the Rationalist." He is at his
best when his skepticism dominates his thinking; he is at his
weakest when his rationalism wins out. Veblen simply wanted
people to be more rational. Revision of 1950.12. Draws upon
1948.15; 1953.19; 1955.7.

                              1957

1   ADLER, SOLOMON. "Imperial Germany and the Industrial Revolu-
     tion." Monthly Review 9 (July-August):76-82.
        Imperial Germany and the Industrial Revolution ranks high
in the corpus of Veblen's works. Veblen was not just a genius
and a satirist--he had a system that enabled him to effectively
explain the development of German capitalism and its aggressive
nature. His concept of "the penalty of being first" showed how

lesser developed countries can borrow the technological advances
of more advanced countries without repeating the latter's mis-
takes. Although Veblen tended to give too much attention to the
by-products of cultural lags, this book is important for its
penetrating analysis and predictive power.

2   ANON. "Leisure Class." Listener 58 (28 November):872.
     Finds it "difficult not to say that this was a somewhat
overrated book." Criticizes Veblen's lack of precision and
style. Calls Veblen's work "puritan" but without the contents of
puritanism.

3   BARAN, PAUL A. "The Theory of the Leisure Class." Monthly
     Review 9 (July-August):83-91.
     The fundamental weakness of this volume is its failure to
spell out the differences and transformations that set historical
periods apart from one another. Consequently, Veblen does not
succeed in comprehending the notion of historical development.
While Veblen correctly stresses that the upper classes exploit
the lower classes, he fails to differentiate the types of upper
classes and the various methods they employ to sustain their
dominant positions. Veblen is also guilty of utilizing a faulty
biological-psychological theory of instincts and his "normative
yardstick" (productivity and frugality) lacks historical validity. Veblen nowhere inquires into the historical reasons why the
petty bourgeoisie deviated from his standard as typified by the
artisan, mechanic, and farmer. Nor does Veblen recognize that
alienation explains why ordinary people are driven to consumption
in the hope of bringing satisfaction to their lives. Rather than
simply calling for an end to consumption and waste, Veblen should
have undertaken an analysis of the extant historical conditions
feeding these phenomena with an eye to transcending both them and
human poverty. Veblen frequently comes close to a full understanding of the social-historical situation, but "had he gone
further, he would have transcended himself and taken the decisive
step to materialism and to dialectic."

4   BOULDING, KENNETH E. "A New Look at Institutionalism." Amer-
     ican Economic Review: Papers and Proceedings 47 (May):1-12.
     Institutionalism is an interlude in the history of economic
thought. Claims that in the long run John R. Commons will come
to be understood as having made a greater contribution than
Veblen. Veblen's greatest impact as been on a discipline he
despised--the law. For an opposing view see 1957.15.

5   BURNHAM, JAMES. Introduction to Veblenism: A New Critique,
     by Lev E. Dobriansky. Washington, D.C.: Public Affairs
     Press, p. v.
     Notes the ambiguity surrounding Veblen and the mixed recep-
tion he has received. Marxists as well as classical economists
reject him, while others attempt to utilize some of his ideas.

6   COWLEY, W.H., and J.B. LON HEFFERLIN. Review of The Higher
     Learning in America. Epitome (Stanford University) no. 1
     (Experimental), (28 May), pp. 1-4.
         Summarizes the main points of the book. Veblen's "biting,
     bitter criticisms" have "powerfully contributed to the success of
     efforts that have been made to mitigate some of the evils he
     exposed."

7   DAVIS, ARTHUR K. "The Postwar Essays." Monthly Review 9
     (July-August):91-98.
         Considers Veblen's The Vested Interests and the State of
     the Industrial Arts, The Engineers and the Price System, and
     Essays in Our Changing Order. Written mostly after Veblen de-
     parted the academic world, these works tend to be more direct and
     outspoken than his previous writings. The Vested Interests and
     the State of the Industrial Arts constitutes a good example of
     the evolutionary approach to social theory. While its emphasis
     on cultural lag is one-sided, it nonetheless provides a supple-
     ment to the "overemphasis common among Marxists on conscious
     exploitation." The Engineers and the Price System with its call
     for a soviet of technicians displays signs of pre-Marxian utopi-
     anism that deserve criticism. In part 3 of Essays in Our Chang-
     ing Order, however, Veblen provides a penetrating and relevant
     account of capitalism's position vis-à-vis the rest of the world.
     Veblen could well be America's greatest social thinker.

8   _____. "Thorstein Veblen and the Culture of Capitalism." In
     American Radicals: Some Problems and Personalities. Edited
     by Harvey Goldberg. New York: Monthly Review Press,
     pp. 279-93.
         Argues that there is no other American sociologist of
     Veblen's stature and his esteem has increased with the passing of
     the years. Veblen shunned all contacts with organized social
     movements. His increasing skepticism about the possibilities of
     positive social change may have reflected his recognition of
     simple tragedy or gave evidence of the cultural malaise or bour-
     geois pessimism that has been manifest in Western literature for
     some time. Nevertheless, Veblen never abandoned his basically
     Marxian outlook. In fact, his amazing insights are due to his
     mastery of the "Marxian key." Like Marx, he saw a basic tension
     between the community's industrial arts and its institutional
     framework. Institutional principles, perhaps well suited to the
     earlier epoch in which they were developed, persist beyond their
     useful span to hamper the progressive potentialities of the
     present. Veblen equated progress with the advance of the peace-
     ful industrial arts toward maximum productivity.

9   _____. "Thorstein Veblen Reconsidered." Science and Society
     21 (Winter):52-85.
         Reassesses Veblen's thought on the centennial anniversary
     of his birth. Veblen stands close to the Marxian tradition; his
     Darwinism is largely a facade. Although at points mistaken or

weak, Veblen's social evolutionary approach is to be praised. He
is viewed as being critical of social institutions and this
demonstrates a tendency toward anarchism on his part. Veblen's
categories of instinct, habit, and culture lag are examined and
found inadequate as the bases of a theory of society. Veblen's
welfare standard (maximum productivity) falls short of the total
needs of a harmonious community. Likewise his analysis of conspicuous consumption is one-sided--Veblen sees only the negative
and not positive aspects. Veblen was a pioneer in the field of
business cycles, although his theory of economic crisis suffers
as a result of his preoccupation with cultural lag. His theory
of the ruling class lacks a grounding in detailed, concrete study
of primitive societies. Though flawed, his studies on imperial
Germany are brilliant and prophetic. Veblen's last papers show
him to be a proponent of the Bolshevik Revolution and socialism.

10   DOBRIANSKY, LEV E. Review of The Values of Veblen: A
      Critical Appraisal, by Bernard Rosenberg. Annals of
      the American Academy of Political and Social Science 313
      (September):165.
         Owing to the breadth and diversity of Veblen's thought,
      systematic study of his work is necessary. Finds the book essen-
      tially correct, if limited in scope. See 1956.10.

11   _____. Veblenism: A New Critique. Washington, D.C.: Public
      Affairs Press, 409 pp.
         Attempts a comprehensive analysis and critique of Veblen's
      ideas from the point of view of the philosophia perennia. Topics
      covered include Veblen's personality and experience, his methodo-
      logical premises and approach, his conception of science, and his
      economic, cultural, and institutional analyses. Assesses Veblen's
      "managerialism" and concludes with an appraisal of his achieve-
      ments. States that while Veblen had a "brilliant and probing
      mind" his work, stripped of style, is not particularly profound.
      Argues that Veblen's ideas are rooted in British empiricism and
      bear a kinship to modern pragmatism. While Veblen's philosophi-
      cal stance is skeptical, it is not determinist. He engages in
      disguised moralism, and his critiques are often unbalanced and
      contradictory. Sees Veblen as a technocrat managerialist, not a
      democratic Socialist. Published revision of Ph.D. dissertation,
      see 1950.6.

12   GEIS, GILBERT. "Conspicuous Dissenter." New York Times
      Magazine, 11 August, pp. 66-67.
         Celebrates the centennial anniversary of Veblen's birth and
      surveys his major contributions. Emphasizes Veblen's peculiar
      traits.

13   HACKER, LOUIS M. Introduction to The Higher Learning in
      America. New York: Hill and Wang, pp. v-ix.
         Provides biographical information and highlights the major
      points of The Higher Learning in America. Relates Veblen's ideas

to the conditions of America in his time. Argues that while
Veblen at times carries his polemic too far, many of the criticisms he leveled at American universities remain valid. Claims
that the book shows a "high order of art . . ." and is "intelligent, clear and sharp. . . ."

14   HALL, STUART A. "Veblen: A Centenary Memorial." Current
Economic Comment 19 (November):39-48.
      Assesses Veblen's contributions to the study of economics,
particularly his critique of orthodoxy. Describes his theories
of income distribution and depression and finds the latter to
have been the most satisfactory for his time. Stresses Veblen's
realism and rejects the notion that Veblen was a "prophet" who
was an enemy of the upper class.

15   HILL, FOREST G. "Discussion." American Economic Review:
Papers and Proceedings 47 (May):15-18.
      Responds to Boulding's remarks on institutionism and Veblen
in the same journal issue. Defends Veblen by pointing to his
influence on the theory of the firm, consumer economics, and
industrial organization. Stresses his use of the "instinct of
workmanship" and denies that he had a "racist anthropology" or
"instinct psychology" and that his greatest influence was on the
study of law. See 1957.4.

16   HUTCHINSON, T.W. "An Economist Outsider." Listener 58
(28 November):877-78.
      Notes the relative lack of knowledge of Veblen in England.
Surveys his life and major works. Credits his critique of orthodox economics, compares Veblen to Marx, and praises his satiric
ability and power of prophecy--especially his views regarding
Germany and Japan. "Much may be lost if Veblen's kind of writing
entirely disappears, as indeed seems the case."

17   JOHNSON, ALVIN. "Cycles in Climate of Opinion." Social
Research 24 (June):330.
      In claiming that intellectual history appears to move in
cycles, now finds Veblen less relevant than he once thought.
States that "Veblen's engineers" have not scuttled the price
system but have actually helped to sustain it.

18   LANDSMAN, RANDOLPH H. "The Philosophy of Veblen's Economics."
Science and Society 21 (Fall):333-45.
      Describes Veblen's attack on classical economics and Marxian
socialism. Veblen's reconstruction of economics via Darwinism
and pragmatism "stands out as the bulwark of current philosophical attacks on Marxian socialism." Veblen never abandoned his
behaviorist psychology and logics of induction and experiment in
favor of materialist dialectics. Essentially he belongs to the
nineteenth century and "arrived at an arrested stage of development." Veblen's philosophy is neither feudal nor Socialist; it
stands for liberalism and a "modified capitalism."

19   McDOUGALL, A. KENT. "Conspicuous Consumption: 1957." Nation
      184 (2 March):185-87.
         Updates Veblen's concepts to the present. Refers to Veblen
      as "a rumpled-suited professor . . . coiner of the phrase 'con-
      spicuous consumption,' a phrase that has become as integral a
      part of the compleat intellectuals verbal baggage as, say,
      Freud's 'Oedipus complex.'"

20   MATSUO, HIROSHI. "Veblen no keizaigaku hōhōron" [The method-
      ology of Veblen's economics.] Hikone ronsō [Hikone review] 39
      (September):17-33.
         Assesses Veblen's critique of classical economic theory.
      Agrees with the general thrust of Veblen's argument but suggests
      that he goes too far in the direction of empiricism. Veblen can
      be faulted for not reconciling the deductive and inductive methods.

21   MORRISON, PHILIP. "The Place of Science in Modern Civiliza-
      tion." Monthly Review 9 (July-August):99-105.
         Outlines Veblen's ideas concerning the growth of science
      and its role in contemporary civilization. Although "idle curi-
      osity" might have once been based on social institutions, it is
      probably less the case in the present.

22   NOBLE, DAVID W. "Dreiser and Veblen: The Literature of
      Cultural Change." Social Research 24 (June):311-30.
         Compares Veblen and Dreiser with respect to human progress.
      Suggests that Veblen's faith in the emancipatory effect of tech-
      nology is countered by Dreiser's view of industrialism as "a
      truly autonomous and unpredictable force. . . ." Claims that
      most of the academic social thinkers of Veblen's time hailed from
      small towns or rural backgrounds and did not experience directly
      the destructive impact of industrialism that Dreiser did in his
      own life. Abridged and reprinted: 1960.5; 1968.15.

23   ROGOW, ARNOLD A. "Veblen and the Society of Consent." Nation
      185 (31 August):94-96.
         Calls Veblen a "pessimist throughout his life and a fatal-
      ist at the end." Notes that among recent commentators on Veblen,
      Riesman was the most critical while Mills, Rosenberg, and Davis
      are more favorably impressed by his depth and vision. Feels that
      Riesman "tends to minimize the substantive application of
      Veblen's work to the present. . . ." Defends Veblen's analysis
      of the price system, explaining that so far it has paid off
      through mass consumption and gimmicks. While much in Veblen is
      oversimplified (e.g., the instinct of workmanship), he leaves
      behind a rich legacy. Those to the left of center politically
      will be more likely to respond favorably to Veblen.

24   SCHLESINGER, ARTHUR M., Jr. The Age of Roosevelt. Vol. 1,
      The Crisis of the Old Order, 1919-1933. Boston: Houghton
      Mifflin Co., pp. 130, 136-39, 144, 205, 211, 461.

Discusses the intellectual influence Veblen's ideas exerted
on New Deal thought. Veblen's criticisms of classical economics,
business, and his emphasis on an ordered economy are emphasized.

25 SCHULTZE, ROBERT O. Review of The Values of Veblen: A
    Critical Appraisal, by Bernard Rosenberg. American Journal
    of Sociology 63 (November):335-36.
        Questions Rosenberg's elevation of Veblen to the level of
    Max Weber and Karl Marx. Much of what Rosenberg writes about
    Veblen is common knowledge. See 1956.10.

26 STEENBERGEN, TH. J. "Thorstein Veblen, 1857-30 juli-1957"
    [Thorstein Veblen, 1857-30 July 1957]. Economist [Economist]
    105 (July-August):481-93.
        Begins with a biographical account of Veblen's life.
    States that his theories were mostly brilliant intuitions rather
    than careful inductions from the facts of American life. Veblen
    had a stimulating effect on the study of economics and inspired a
    generation of progressive American intellectuals. His theory of
    overcapitalization is considered, and the falling of his star,
    with the ascendancy of Keynesian economics, noted.

27 SWEEZY, PAUL M. "The Theory of Business Enterprise and Absen-
    tee Ownership." Monthly Review 9 (July-August):105-12.
        Veblen's diagnosis of the American economy in the early part
    of this century is extremely accurate and relevant even today.
    He was probably correct in stating that monopolies would evolve
    as a cure for chronic depressions, but he appears to be somewhat
    uncertain on this matter. The fundamental weakness in Veblen is
    his failure to solve the problem of the relation between the
    process of monopoly and the tendency to chronic depression. In
    spite of certain weaknesses in his analysis of economic proces-
    ses, Veblen is unsurpassed since Marx as a critical analyst of
    capitalism.

28 [SWEEZY, PAUL, and LEO HUBERMAN]. "Thorstein Bunde Veblen,
    1857-1957." Monthly Review 9 (July-August):65-75.
        Describes Veblen's life and work. Although he was not a
    Marxist, he was a Socialist and great critic of capitalism. The
    evils brought about by capitalism, according to Veblen, could be
    traced to absentee ownership. Veblen was convinced, as was Marx,
    that capitalism contained the seeds of its own destruction.
    Veblen was also an internationalist--critical of the "national
    politics" practiced by capitalist countries in their desire to
    expand their markets.

29 WHITE, MORTON G. Social Thought in America: The Revolt
    against Formalism. Boston: Beacon Press, 301 pp. passim.
    Reprint. 1964.
        Incorporates material from 1947.10. Reprint of 1949.20
    with a new preface and epilogue.

30   WILLIAMS, WILLIAM APPLEMAN. "The Nature of Peace." <u>Monthly</u>
    <u>Review</u> 9 (July-August):112-17.
        Discusses Veblen's study of foreign relations. Veblen
understood that foreign policy is integrally tied to domestic
policy. Veblen likewise demonstrates a keen understanding of
international events. He recognized that mid-Victorian imperialism was essentially noncolonial in nature, and he also noted the
significance of the Bolshevik Revolution for international relations. Moreover, Veblen's "emphasis on the supremacy of the
military offensive due to advances in technology has proven valid
in terms of the present nuclear stalemate."

31   WILSON, H.H. "<u>The Higher Learning in America</u>." <u>Monthly</u>
    <u>Review</u> 9 (July-August):117-22.
        Describes the main features of Veblen's volume. He criti-
cized the modern university using a standard derived from his
concepts of the instinct of workmanship and idle curiosity.
Veblen felt that the modern university had come under the domination of business practices and methods. Since Veblen's time,
however, universities have turned to the government for funding
and research support. Veblen's prescription for freeing the
university from external pressures by abolishing the academic
executive and the governing board is inadequate.

32   WOLFE, DON M. <u>The Image of Man in America</u>. Dallas: Southern
    Methodist University Press, pp. 146, 295-306, 434, 455.
    Reprint. New York: Thomas Y. Crowell Co., 1970.
        Provides some biographical information and stresses
Veblen's preoccupation with human nature and the peaceful
traits of primitive man. Argues that Veblen does not answer the
question of whether the instinct of workmanship is a product of
heredity or environment. Sees Veblen as indebted to Rousseau.

<u>1958</u>

1   AYRES, CLARENCE E. "Veblen's Theory of Instincts Recon-
    sidered." In <u>Thorstein Veblen: A Critical Reappraisal</u>.
    Edited by Douglas F. Dowd. Ithaca: Cornell University Press,
    pp. 25-37.
        Considers Veblen to be a first-rank social theorist whose
most important contribution was his theory of instincts. Veblen
revolutionized the field of economics by understanding the anthropological view that human behavior is cultural. His major criticism of classical economic theory is that it assumed human nature
to be a given. Veblen was among the first in economics to real-
ize the distinction between making "things" and making "money"
and recognize its significance. Critics have suggested that
Veblen never understood the complexities of American business;
the author disagrees, arguing that Veblen appreciated even the
simplest skill and this appreciation aided his investigations into
the American business structure. Veblen attributed the polariza-
tion of human behavior to instinct. He is criticized for his

vagueness, and his theory of instincts is discredited because "no such complex behavior patterns are in any literal sense inborn." Emphasizes the symbolism in Veblen's work and his awareness of "cultural operational efficiency," which contributed to his conception of the "savage state." Suggests that Veblen was correct in representing workmanship and ceremonialism as constants that hark back to the origins of man and have persisted through all cultures. The study of this conflict was Veblen's lifework as seen throughout his writings. Veblen identified workmanship, technology, science, the arts, and crafts as "the life process of mankind."

2   BARNES, HARRY ELMER. "A New Assessment of Veblenian Economics." Southern Economic Journal 25 (July):88–96.
        Reviews Veblenism: A New Critique by Lev E. Dobriansky (1957.11). Claims that the book correctly describes Veblen "as being more of an encyclopedic social scientist . . . than an orthodox economist. . . ." Notes the Catholic author's underlying sympathy with Veblen's antibusiness attitude. Argues that there is no point to criticizing Veblen for not doing systematic economic theory à la J.B. Clark, Marshall, or Taussig; he had other aims.

3   BROCKIE, MELVIN D. "The Cycle Theories of Veblen and Keynes Today." In Thorstein Veblen: A Critical Reappraisal. Edited by Douglas F. Dowd. Cornell University Press, pp. 113–28.
        Compares Veblen's theory of "overcapitalization with Keynes's "trade cycle analysis." Defines Veblen's theory in terms of conditions that relate crisis, depressions, and brisk times to business, prices, and capitalization. Defines Keynes's cycle analysis as "cyclical change in the marginal efficiency of capital. . . ." Considers Keynes's concern with underinvestment and underconsumption and Veblen's emphasis on overcapitalization as instructive for understanding the modern economy. Compares and contrasts the two theories and concludes that they are overlapping and the areas of divergence between the two are largely terminological. The Keynesian framework is broadly theoretical and comprehensive, and the more specific Veblenian model serves to supplement Keynes.

4   COPELAND, MORRIS A. "On the Scope and Method of Economics." In Thorstein Veblen: A Critical Reappraisal. Edited by Douglas F. Dowd. Ithaca: Cornell University Press, pp. 57–76.
        Assesses Veblen's contributions to the scope and method of economic study. Veblen's incorporation of physical and historical scientific method is cited as his most significant contribution. Considers Veblen's proposal that economics should be an evolutionary science in six contexts: (1) his conception of evolution; (2) the historical relativity of economic truths; (3) the need for a cultural perspective; (4) explanation, causation,

and genetic process; (5) public policy; and (6) the scope of
economics. Perhaps the most significant of Veblen's contributions is the proposition that economics should be understood in
an evolutionary context.

5   CORDERO, FREDERICO A. "La teoria institutionalista de
    Thorstein Veblen" [Thorstein Veblen's institutionalist
    theory]. Torre [Tower] 6 (January-March):131-44.
        Summarizes the institutionalist theory of Veblen. Contends
    that Veblen, in spite of his alleged detachment, was not in fact
    an impersonal observer of the economic system. "His analytic
    concepts are full of judgmental prejudices." Finds Veblen's
    distinction between industry and finance too simple and denies
    that mechanized industry is gaining influence among broader seg-
    ments of the population. Praises, however, Veblen's analysis of
    consumer behavior, his ideas concerning the modern industrial
    system, and his penetrating analysis of the world of finance.
    "We must admit that the theoretical system that he constructed has
    been a rich source of ideas for social scientists."

6   DILLARD, DUDLEY. Review of Veblenism: A New Critique by
    Lev E. Dobriansky. American Economic Review 48 (June):456-57.
        Notes Dobriansky's Catholic postulates in assessing Veblen's
    ideas. Economists not trained in philosophy may find the book
    difficult. Others may disagree with his philosophical assump-
    tions. Feels that some of Dobriansky's interpretations of Veblen
    are open to question. See 1957.11.

7   DIRLAM, JOEL B. "The Place of Corporation Finance in Veblen's
    Economics." In Thorstein Veblen: A Critical Reappraisal.
    Edited by Douglas F. Dowd. Ithaca: Cornell University Press,
    pp. 199-220.
        The most important feature of Veblen's general theory of
    the economic process is the significance he gives to financing
    the modern corporation. He is careful to differentiate between
    the era of the petty capitalist and that of the speculator and
    financier who are free of the earlier restraints imposed by both
    owning and managing the enterprise.

8   DORFMAN, JOSEPH. "The Place of a Titan." New York Times Book
    Review, 26 January, p. 6.
        Reviews The Values of Veblen: A Critical Reappraisal by
    Bernard Rosenberg (1956.10) and Veblenism: A New Critique by
    Lev E. Dobriansky (1957.11). "Both volumes testify to the fact
    that Veblen promises to continue to be the subject of a vast
    variety of viewpoints for many years to come." Notes that
    Rosenberg is more favorably disposed toward Veblen than is
    Dobriansky.

9   _____. "Source and Impact of Veblen." American Economic
    Review: Papers and Proceedings 48 (May):1-10.

Veblen is both artist and economist. As an artist, he
"merely picked up his Don Quixotes from the realm of economics."
Veblen was both a "theorist and catalyst of reform." Being less
doctrinaire than many of the greats who preceeded him, he was
able to construct an open system which explained the relationship
of man to technology. Mentions several of Veblen's prominent
students including Hoxie, Davenport, and Mitchell, who went on to
establish solid reputations for their work in various fields of
economics. Veblen's influence on his contemporaries is also
surveyed. Figures such as Commons, Clark, Berle, Means, and
others are cited. "Ultimately, his value lies in his role as an
emancipator of the human mind." Revised: 1958.10.

10   . "The Source and Impact of Veblen's Thought." In
    Thorstein Veblen: A Critical Reappraisal. Edited by
    Douglas F. Dowd. Ithaca: Cornell University Press, pp. 1-12.
        Discusses Veblen's development, his educational experi-
    ences, the climate of the times when he taught and wrote, and his
    influence on other thinkers. Veblen is described as artist as
    well as economist. He incorporated knowledge of linguistics,
    anthrolopology, philosophy, psychology, history, and biological
    sciences into his economic theory. Revision of 1958.9.

11 DOWD, DOUGLAS F., ed. Preface to Thorstein Veblen: A
    Critical Reappraisal. Ithaca: Cornell University Press,
    pp. vii-ix.
        Claims that Veblen "was and remains the most eminent and
    seminal thinker in the area of social analysis yet to emerge in
    America." The unorthodox and uncompromising Veblen was in
    "greatest vogue in the twenties and thirties, especially the
    latter." Contemporary social science would benefit if it were to
    adopt some of his perspectives and attitudes.

12   . "Technology ad Social Change: Japan and the Soviet
    Union." In Thorstein Veblen: A Critical Reappraisal.
    Ithaca: Cornell University Press, pp. 283-301.
        Assesses Veblen's study of Japan's industrialization and
    utilizes his analytical insights in order to understand the case
    of the Soviet Union. Praises Veblen as a great generalizer, but
    one who did not develop a "system of thought." Veblen saw "cumu-
    lative causation and blind drift--not reason"--as the force be-
    hind social change. The outlook for world peace is then rather
    gloomy.

13 FISHMAN, LESLIE. "Veblen, Hoxie, and American Labor." In
    Thorstein Veblen: A Critical Reappraisal. Edited by
    Douglas F. Dowd. Ithaca: Cornell University Press, pp. 221-34.
        Contends the major problem of Veblen's time and the present
    is that of adjusting pecuniary institutions to a changing and
    modernizing industrial world. Veblen's concern is with a growing
    disparity between scientific progress and social institutions.
    Both Veblen and Hoxie incorporate an evolutionary theory of

change into their evaluations of American labor. Criticizes
Veblen for not adequately describing the operative forces of
change and assimilation that allow institutions to be consistent
with industrial technology and science. Expands on the foundations provided by Veblen. Veblen's insights into the problems of
American labor are often neglected because he is misinterpreted.
His conception of human interaction with the environment on all
levels of consciousness is the key to understanding the operative
forces at work. Veblen fails to explain what force will be
responsible for disestablishing the dominant institutions. Both
Hoxie and Veblen conclude that the impetus to change American
institutions will not come from organized labor.

14   GALBRAITH, JOHN KENNETH. The Affluent Society. Boston:
      Houghton Mifflin Co., pp. 50, 52-55.
         Portrays Veblen's unique position in economics and de-
scribes his iconoclasm. Contends that there will always be a
debate regarding his influence. Notes also Veblen's pessimism
concerning reform and progress.

15   GOODRICH, CARTER. "The Case of the New Countries." In
      Thorstein Veblen: A Critical Reappraisal. Edited by
      Douglas F. Dowd. Ithaca: Cornell University Press, pp. 265-81.
         Reviews Veblen's contributions to the field of comparative
economic history. Veblen compares nations that developed techno-
logically over a longer period of time with those that borrowed
technology and institutionalized rapidly. Cites Imperial Germany
and the Industrial Revolution and "The Opportunity of Japan" as
Veblen's most significant works in this field. Veblen describes
the penalties for taking the technological lead and emphasizes
the resistance to change of habits of thought in industrializing
countries. He contrasts the degree to which economic individualism is checked and modified by collective and state actions in
"new countries." In Australia and New Zealand, labor unions had
as much political power as pecuniary interests while in the
United States only a minority supported labor. This is attributed to the American habit of concern with economic individualism
and helps to explain why the United States was less inclined to
develop Socialist institutions. Latin-origin and British-origin
"new countries" are compared for differences in their economic
levels and standards of living. Veblen theorizes that Latin-
origin countries have a lower standard of living because of their
medieval, military Spanish and Portuguese heritage whereas British-
origin countries enjoy a higher standard of living because of
their more industrial-business heritage. Veblen's insights need
to be supplemented and qualified by analysis based on geographic
location.

16   GRUCHY, ALLAN G. "The Influence of Veblen on Mid-Century
      Institutionalism." American Economic Review: Papers and
      Proceedings 48 (May):11-20.

Surveys the major similarities and differences between
Veblen's economics and that of present-day institutionalists.
Points to Veblen's critique of Marshallian economics for largely
ignoring oligopoly and aggregate product. Modern institutionalists continue to theorize within a micro-/macroframework outlined
by Veblen. Also, Veblen's interest in the administered price
problem has been extended by later institutionalists. There are
differences, however, between Veblen and modern institutionalists
concerning the future course of capitalism. Veblen thought that
capitalism would evolve into either socialism or fascism, while
the modern institutionalists feel that there exist other possibilities such as democratic socialism or welfare statism. The
institutionalists tend to see the state in a more favorable light
than did Veblen, viewing it as a protector of less powerful
interests and a positive economic agent. Although many of
Veblen's ideas are "outmoded," it is "also apparent that the
broad contours of his economic thought have stood the test of
time successfully." See 1958.32, 34.

17   . "Veblen's Theory of Economic Growth." In Thorstein
        Veblen: A Critical Reappraisal. Edited by Douglas F. Dowd.
        Ithaca: Cornell University Press, pp. 151-76.
        The problem of how to achieve and sustain adequate economic
growth is one that commands much attention. Suggests that Veblen
does not urge a jettisoning of neoclassical economic theory;
rather he stresses that it be revised and modernized. Two types
of economic growth theories are presented: one is concerned with
consistency and congruency, the other with evolution. Veblen's
evolutional theory of economic growth focuses attention upon
institutions and attitudes and includes changes in the nature of
the system as well as increased output. Interprets Veblen's
early efforts as elementary but rates his generalizations about
the growth process as significant. Veblen devotes much time to
the qualitative aspects of the problem of economic growth. His
theory relies on his concept of a national economic account, and
he claims that economic growth is facilitated by the use of
labor, natural resources, and capital equipment. Economic growth
is a strenuous process, and for Veblen the capitalist economy of
his time was in transition. Changes were occurring in the character of capital and there was an increase in the size and scale
of operations. There was also progress in science and technology
and in the attitudes of those who participated in the nation's
economic activity. Veblen recognized that there are obstacles in
the path of obtaining the goal of economic surplus. He argues
that though the breakdown of the capitalist system may be delayed
by expansion and by wasteful expenditures, it will occur. He
does not make any attempt, as does Marx, to predict what economic
system will follow the demise of capitalism.

18   HAMILTON, WALTON. "Veblen--Then and Now." In Thorstein
     Veblen: A Critical Reappraisal. Edited by Douglas F. Dowd.
     Ithaca: Cornell University Press, pp. 13-23.

Veblen's contributions to social science are still relevant today. His theories are catalysts for further inquiry. Veblen is described as both "a recluse and a man of the world." He incorporated humor and a confusing style of English language into his writing. Three contemporary problem areas worthy of Veblen-ian analysis are: "the case of the sulfa drug" (patents); the "so-called squeeze play" or the power of a major firm to favor its own affiliates and discriminate against competing independents; and the "corporate imperium." Veblen was the least dogmatic of scholars. His inquiries were expanded on by his students and contemporaries. His greatest contribution: "he made the generation of scholars following him sensitive to the question of 'Why do you want to know?'"

19   HARRIS, ABRAM L. "Thorstein Veblen: Toward a Soviet of Technicians." In Economics and Social Reform. New York: Harper and Brothers, pp. 156-213. Expanded revision of 1953.6.

20   HILL, FOREST G. "Veblen and Marx." In Thorstein Veblen: A Critical Reappraisal. Edited by Douglas F. Dowd. Ithaca: Cornell University Press, pp. 129-49.
      Veblen regarded Marx as an important and original thinker but questioned his theory of value and Hegelian concept of social change. Veblen also claimed that Marx's theory of increasing misery lacked empirical verification and considered his theory of the reserve army as vulnerable. Contends that Veblen revised Marxism for his own purposes and asserts that "Marxism became Veblenism." Veblen suggested that Marxism needed to be subjected to post-Darwinian insights to gain credibility. Compares the strengths and weaknesses of Marx and Veblen in terms of strong emphasis on economic development, processes, and causation. Marx was less willing and able to study psychological processes involved in economic development. Marx was also constrained by his Hegelian preconceptions and oversimplified theory of class structure whereas Veblen demonstrated a recognition of class complexities. Argues that Veblen's framework of occupational discipline is more flexible than Marx's doctrine of class struggle. On the other hand, Veblen's reluctance to make explicit value judgments like Marx is a weakness in his theory. Veblen produced confusion with his theory of instincts; Marx is easier to interpret. Marx made predictions and policy prescriptions whereas Veblen, for the most part, did not. Both Veblen and Marx have a tendency to engage in sweeping generalizations; both believe in determinism; both demonstrate an inadequate treatment of the state, reform, immediate policy, and labor unions. The normative theoretical orientation of both is their greatest weakness.

21   KAPLAN, NORMAN. "Idle Curiosity." In Thorstein Veblen: A Critical Reappraisal. Edited by Douglas F. Dowd. Ithaca: Cornell University Press, pp. 39-55.

States that the notion of idle curiosity was central to
Veblen's work and is one of his most important contributions.
Defines idle curiosity as the disinterested pursuit of both
scientific and scholarly knowledge in the absence of an ulterior
end. Idle curiosity is the quest for knowledge for its own sake.
Veblen theorized that science and research flourished in societies that provided opportunities for idle curiosity. He argued
that idle curiosity and the instinct of workmanship are basic
traits of human nature. Also examines Veblen's educational theories in light of this motif. The function of the university is
to encourage scientific inquiry and the instruction of students;
as such, the university environment should ideally provide for
idle curiosity. Contends that the no-strings-attached pursuit of
knowledge is now a concern in modern society.

22   KRETSCHMANN, JENNY GRIZZIOTTI. "La dottrina
      instituzionalista americana" [The American institutionalist
      doctrine]. In Il pensiero americano contemporaneo
      [Contemporary American thought]. Edited by Ferrucio Rossi-
      Landi. Vol. 2. Milan: Edizioni di Comunità, pp. 187-221.
       Discusses American economic thought and contrasts the deduc-
tive and inductive schools. Veblen is considered to be of the
inductive school that emphasizes the dynamic process and empirical studies.

23   MACCHIORO, AURELIO. "Il problema del benessere nell'economia
      politica fra 19 e 20 secolo" [The problem of well-being in
      political economy in the nineteenth and twentieth centuries].
      Società [Society] 14 (January):52-72.
       Traces the controversy between individualism and collective
well-being, referring to the works of Marshall, Pigou, Pareto,
and others. Veblen is mentioned in regard to his discussion of
trusts and fair play in his Theory of Business Enterprise.

24   MATSUO, HIROSHI. "Veblen shihon-shugi-ron ni kansuru ichi
      kōsatsu" [A study of Veblen's theory of capitalism]. Hikone
      ronsō [Hikone review] 42 (March):19-41.
       A descriptive account of Veblen's theory of capitalism.
Finds his theory too superficial and lacking in scientific rigor.
Veblen also underestimated the exploitative nature of capitalism
and fails to comprehend the theory of surplus value. Although
Veblen's theory tends toward idealism, it is nonetheless an
important stepping stone to a fuller critique of contemporary
capitalism.

25   MORRISON, PHILIP. "The Ideology of the Engineers." In
      Thorstein Veblen: A Critical Reappraisal. Edited by
      Douglas F. Dowd. Ithaca: Cornell University Press, pp. 237-48.
       Veblen was acutely aware of the importance of the engineer
in the American economy. Veblen's theory of workmanship and idle
curiosity equate the nature of scientific theories with the
processes of machine production. The Darwinian perspective of

continuous building is incorporated in Veblen's analysis. Veblen
is faulted for arguing that the machine is impersonal and functions only to serve human needs. Claims that there exists no
such guarantee to human value in science or technology. Engineers are limited to rational and scientific designs that serve
to limit the output of their production.

26   NABERS, LAWRENCE. "Veblen's Critique of the Orthodox Economic
      Tradition." In Thorstein Veblen: A Critical Reappraisal.
      Edited by Douglas F. Dowd. Ithaca: Cornell University Press,
      pp. 77-111.
          Analyzes Veblen's critique of the economic theory of his
      times, which he found to be irrelevant to extant conditions.
      Orthodox economics was described by Veblen as "not serviceable
      for an explanation of the operation of the economic mechanism or
      as a guide for policies conducive to the welfare of the popula-
      tion." Veblen also attacked the neoclassical conception of the
      rational businessman and its natural law underpinning. Contends
      that "Veblen nowhere spells out an explicit alternative value
      theory to serve as a point of departure for his analysis of
      distribution and allocation." It can be stated, however, that
      for Veblen serviceability for the community as a whole, and not
      merely profits for the individual businessman, constitute an
      implicit value criterion. Economic theory must be cognizant of
      the inherent conflict between industry and the pecuniary behavior
      of businessmen.

27   NOBLE, DAVID. "Thorstein Veblen: The Economist as Scientist
      and Prophet." In The Paradox of Progressive Thought.
      Minneapolis: University of Minnesota Press, pp. 138, 199-227.
          Explains Veblen's personal misfortunes by presenting the
      fact that he had a personality "both withdrawn and belligerent."
      Interprets Veblen as believing that although civilization was a
      return to savagery, it was not a simple imitation of the primi-
      tive past. Attempts to demonstrate that there was no paradox in
      Veblen's blending of the environment of industrial complexity
      with the spiritual qualities of prehistoric man. Veblen is also
      portrayed as evolving toward a reformist position during the
      First World War and after, a period in which he began to sound
      much like the Christian economist Richard Ely and the quasi-
      Christian thinker Simon Patten. Veblen had come to believe that
      Western civilization was based at the moment on two major tradi-
      tions, those of competitive business and Christianity, and asks
      whether or not it is possible for Western civilization to survive
      if one or the other of these traditions disappears. See also
      1955.6.

28   OHARA, KEISHI. "Veblen to Marx" [Veblen and Marx]. Keizai
      kenkyū [Economic research] 9 (April):97-103.
          Compares Veblen with Marx. Agrees with those who classify
      Veblen as a non-Marxian Socialist. Although not a Marxist,

Veblen is not a mere petit-bourgeois reformer either. Veblen was an iconoclast, an opponent of nationalism and a critic of capitalism who displayed impressive insights into the nature of the economy.

29 SCHNEIDER, LOUIS. Review of Veblenism: A New Critique, by Lev E. Dobriansky. American Sociological Review 23 (June):345.
    Credits the author with discerning what is valuable in Veblen (his sociologically based economic theory, for example) from "that measure of outright foolishness which no conscientious reader of Veblen can miss." See 1957.11.

30 SWEEZY, PAUL M. "Veblen on American Capitalism." In Thorstein Veblen: A Critical Reappraisal. Edited by Douglas F. Dowd. Ithaca: Cornell University Press, pp. 177-97.
    The general features of Veblen's theory of capitalism are derived from Marx. Unlike Marx, however, Veblen attributes to the industrial process a logic of its own, quite independent of the capitalist economy. The main weaknesses in Veblen's economic analysis stem from his assuming the "operation of Say's Law in the extreme form in which total income is automatically spent and remains constant over time." Had Veblen lived longer he might have extended "the theory of unproductive public consumption as a remedy for depression." Revision of 1958.31.

31 _____. "Veblen's Critique of the American Economy." American Economic Review: Papers and Proceedings 48 (May):21-29.
    Assembles Veblen's theory into a coherent whole: the machine process is seen as the force behind capitalist development and operates independent of the will of the businessman. The machine process causes certain institutional changes that lead to chronic depression and then to monopoly. Profits are protected but resources remain underutilized. Class struggle intensifies and the principles upon which capitalism rest are undermined. Vested interests mount an aggressive counterpolicy leading to the policy state. The main weaknesses in Veblen's economic analysis stem from his assuming the "operation of Say's Law in the extreme form in which total income is automatically spent and remains constant over time." Had Veblen lived longer he might have extended "the theory of unproductive public consumption as a remedy for depression." Revised: 1958.30. See 1958.32, 34.

32 VUKASIN, PETER N. "Discussion." American Economic Review: Papers and Proceedings 48 (May):30-32.
    A brief discussion of the presentations of Gruchy and Sweezy in the same journal issue (1958.16, 31). Calls attention to the role of the state in economic analysis.

33 WATKINS, MYRON W. "Veblen's View of Cultural Evolution." In Thorstein Veblen: A Critical Reappraisal. Edited by Douglas F. Dowd. Ithaca: Cornell University Press, pp. 249-64.

Veblen is considered to be a cultural geneticist basing his theories on Darwinian notions. He did not accept the prevailing views of his time and his theories were not widely accepted. Veblen's theory of reality, like Kant's, was a theory of becoming rather than being. Proposes that Veblen, Marx, and Schmoller are basically in agreement. Although Marx is a Hegelian and Veblen is considered a Darwinian, their views of cultural patterns are largely consistent. Veblen argues that human behavior is not fixed though much of it is instinctive. Veblen's view of human nature is illustrated in his theories of workmanship and idle curiosity. Argues that Veblen saw no evidence for the assured class conflict that Marx did. Veblenian theory emphasizes two aspects of the process of social change: institutional borrowing in a positive sense and contamination of human positive instincts. Points out that Veblen's equation between technological advancement and progress cannot be overlooked. Veblen's tendency to present scientific innovation and technological advancement as progressive may raise doubts as to whether Veblen presents his ideas in a Darwinian context. His theories remain valid. He is best described as a humanist.

34   ZINKE, GEORGE W. "Discussion." American Economic Review:
     Papers and Proceedings 48 (May):32-34.
        A brief discussion of the presentations of Gruchy and Sweezy
     in the same journal issue (1958.16, 31). Calls attention to
     Veblen's desire for peace and the "quality of cultural living."

35   ZINKE, G[EORGE] W. "Veblen's Macroinstitutionalism." In
     Thorstein Veblen: A Critical Reappraisal. Edited by Douglas F.
     Dowd. Ithaca: Cornell University Press, pp. 303-17.
        Veblen's interpretation of technological change is the
     least explored aspect of his work. His theory of change is
     related to his concept of the quality of human behavior in the
     institutional environment. What Veblen perceives as workmanship
     is contaminated by waste. The manner in which the common good is
     damaged by political institutions is qualitative. His uniqueness
     is demonstrated in his approach to the topic of the economic
     conditions of cultural decline. Veblen views social change as
     all-inclusive and inevitable. He emphasizes the quality of work-
     manship and employs quantitative methods only to test the quality
     of production or furnish a comparison between the rate of con-
     sumption and waste. Both Veblen and Marx devote attention to the
     entire scenario of institutionalism and the interaction of vari-
     ous economic institutions. Veblen's theory, unlike Marx's, does
     not lay the foundation for a value theory. Veblen was critical
     of classical and neoclassical theory although he drew upon
     aspects of both. Suggests that Veblen's theory provides for a
     qualitative standard to be utilized for scientific inquiries into
     "community needs" and a macroinstitutional approach to both com-
     munity and foreign policy concerns.

1959

1   BANKS, J.A. "Veblen and Industrial Sociology." British
      Journal of Sociology 10 (September):231-43.
        Veblen is a technological "fundamentalist" (determinist).
Technological change and cultural change in Veblen's view may
conflict with each other. This conflict is the result of an
occupational differentiation between pecuniary and industrial
interests. Veblen's work on absentee ownership and the vast
changes in corporate structure are duly noted. His ideas continue to provide opportunities for further research into contemporary industrial conflict.

2   BAZELON, DAVID T. The Paper Economy. New York: Random
      House, pp. 12-377 passim.
        Praises Veblen's contributions to a theory of credit and
capitalization. Refers to his ideas on property and other related subjects. Claims that "Veblen made an original, non-
Marxist and uniquely American contribution" to economic theory.

3   BLAUG, MARK. Review of Thorstein Veblen: A Critical
      Reappraisal, edited by Douglas F. Dowd. American Economic
      Review 49 (September):726-27.
        Finds the various essays rather "informal" and unoriginal.
Claims that Veblen was guilty of overtheorizing at the expense of
facts and his criticism of economics has an air of "irrelevancy"
about it; for what else might economists do? It is not acci-
dental that Veblen's influence has come to be felt more in sociology than economics. Suggests that Veblen can "still provoke
and inspire." Wants fewer works on Veblen and bids the reader to
read Veblen for himself.

4   BROWN, NORMAN O. Life against Death: The Psychoanalytic
      Meaning of History. Middletown, Conn.: Wesleyan University
      Press, pp. 37-38, 245, 254-57, 279, 288, 318.
        Praises Veblen for exposing the irrational motives behind
pecuniary emulation and recognizing the problem of waste. While
his psychological theory is an improvisation, his masterpiece
must be deemed his concentration on the main problem of the next
generation--that of consumption. Along with Plato and Thoreau,
Veblen saw that human neurosis is tied to economic surplus.

5   CHANDLER, CHARLES CLARENCE. "Institutionalism and Education:
      An Inquiry into the Implications of the Philosophy of
      Thorstein Veblen." Ph.D. dissertation, Michigan State
      University.
        Deals with the educational implications of Veblen's theo-
ries. Argues that his influence has spread beyond economics into
psychology, sociology, anthropology, history, and legal theory
but has been neglected in the sphere of education. Although he
did not actually develop a general theory of education, there is
in Veblen's writings an implicit theory. Argues that his work

does not provide an adequate basis for a theory of education and
finds totalitarian implications in it that do not fit with a
democratic philosophy. In spite of his rejection of individual
sovereignty, Veblen is praised for having made brilliant critiques of American culture.

6   CLARK, JOHN MAURICE. Review of Thorstein Veblen: A Critical
     Reappraisal, edited by Douglas F. Dowd. Political Science
     Quarterly 59 (September):426-29.
          Claims that while Veblen used "basically Marxian themes,"
     he added other concepts, notably biological ones. Notes that it
     is a "severe test" to evaluate Veblen's work by present-day
     conditions. While Keynesianism and the welfare state have become
     popular, finds it interesting that Veblen remains "currently
     relevant." Veblen "was one of the great formative influences in
     the transformation of economic thought in the past half-century."

7   DEWEY, ERNEST W. "Thorstein Veblen: Radical Apologist for
     Conservatism." American Journal of Economics and Sociology 18
     (January):171-80.
          Attempts to show that Veblen was "philosophically an opti-
     mist" and sound apologist for the extrinsic value of the conser-
     vative's role in society. Contends that Veblen saw man as an
     efficient organism characterized by an instinct of workmanship.
     "Immanent but impermanent absolutes" may be used to describe
     Veblen's concept of principles and truth. Truth is limited to
     the case or situation-at-hand. Veblen "saw the institution as a
     functional social instrument which, though retardative in many
     instances, represents the means by which society preserves what
     it believes to be the best principles of individual and social
     adoptation."

8   DORFMAN, JOSEPH. The Economic Mind in American Civilization,
     1918-1933. Vols. 4 and 5. New York: Viking Press, pp. 62-
     770 passim.
          Discusses Veblen's later writings and concludes that his
     place in the American intellectual scene had been secured. Notes
     Veblen's recognition that the prosperity of the era in which he
     wrote "masked a number of grave problems." Veblen, the dissident
     and heterodox thinker, was attacked by conservatives and Marxists
     alike, and in spite of his dour analysis, many of his ideas came
     to exert a powerful influence on subsequent thinkers.

9   FREDERICKSON, GEORGE M. "Thorstein Veblen: The Last Viking."
     American Quarterly 11 (Fall):403-15.
          Veblen's writings, very popular in radical circles during
     the thirties, are to be read differently in the fifties. Refers
     to Riesman's interpretation of Veblen as alienated and marginal
     and states that this does not fully explain Veblen and his theo-
     ries. Then goes on to explain that Veblen's Norwegian and farm
     background was influential in his theorizing--the "anarchistic-
     morality" of the Scandinavian farmer is said to loom large in

Veblen's thinking. Likens Veblen to the "wandering Viking" and stresses his rural background.

10   HARRIS, ABRAM L. Review of The Values of Veblen: A Critical Reappraisal, by Bernard Rosenberg. Journal of Political Economy 67 (August):422-24.
     Discusses some of Veblen's major ideas and comments on his experience at the University of Chicago. See 1956.10.

11   KNIGHT, FRANK H. Review of Veblenism: A New Critique, by Lev E. Dobriansky. Annals of the American Academy of Political and Social Science 321 (January):196-97.
     Finds the book to be sheer nonsense for chastizing Veblen for not explaining the origin of the universe; "such an aim was contrary to Veblen's intention. . . ." See 1957.11.

12   LEKACHMAN, ROBERT. A History of Economic Ideas. New York: Harper and Brothers, pp. 263, 283, 287, 296, 298, 314-25, 328-78, 356, 365.
     Surveys Veblen's major ideas and provides biographical material. Sees Veblen's theory as resting on the distinction between business enterprise and the machine process. Treats his critique of business society and makes a brief comparison with Marx. Notes Veblen's intellectual relationship to John R. Commons and Wesley C. Mitchell.

13   LEVI, ALBERT W. Philosophy and the Modern World. Bloomington: Indiana University Press, pp. 198-243.
     Contrasts Veblen's views with those of Lenin. Sees Veblen's originality in having taken the Marxian standpoint, developed in an age which had not yet solved the problem of production and distribution, and utilized it in an age where the problem was related to consumption. Notes Veblen's critique of Marxism for the latter's metaphysical and romantic qualities. Veblen demonstrates a clear understanding of class relationships.

14   MARCHAL, ANDRÉ. Method scientifique et science economique [Scientific method and economic science]. Vol. 1. Paris: Éditeurs M. Th. Genin, pp. 139-45, 167-70, 240, 249.
     Writes that Veblen was unquestionably the originator of sociological economics or institutionalism as it is known in the United States. This school of thought was a reaction against abstract, deductive economics. Notes Veblen's influence on W.C. Mitchell and others.

15   MAY, HENRY F. The End of American Innocence. New York: Alfred A. Knopf, pp. 29, 103, 135, 180-81, 290, 303, 309, 374-75, 377.
     Describes Veblen as an innovative and skeptical social scientist. In spite of his scoffing indictment of capitalist society and his pessimism Veblen, like Marx, partook of that nineteenth-century brand of optimism. Veblen's influence on

young radicals is mentioned, as well as his troubled support of
World War I.

16   MURPREE, IDUS. "Darwinism in Thorstein Veblen's
Economics." Social Research 26 (June):311-24.
      Veblen used Darwinism as a "convenient label" and added to
it "a whole series of implications." In contrast to Spencer and
other cultural evolutionists, Veblen viewed history "soberly and
warily," and he remained somewhat skeptical of progress. Veblen
turned his evolutionary method on the study of economics, laying
bare the basic conflict between pecuniary and industrial interests. In criticizing Marx, Veblen contended that he was "a
disciple of Bentham as well as of Hegel," and he rejected Marx's
optimism. Veblen represents a transition from an older intellectual period to a newer one. He can be charged with failing to
provide an alternative for the economic system he attacked.

17   SPENGLER, JOSEPH J. "Veblen and Mandeville Contrasted."
Weltwirtschaftliches Archiv [International economic relations
archive] 82, no. 1:35-67.
      Contrasts the ideas of Veblen with those of Bernard de
Mandeville (1670-1733). While some writers have suggested that
Veblen was heavily in Mandeville's debt, Spengler argues that
"Veblen was influenced little if at all by Mandeville." Goes on
to interpret both writers in terms of structural-functional analysis. Finds that Mandeville emphasized the progressive effects
of such things as pride and emulation while Veblen saw them as
wasteful and detrimental to progress. Veblen, unlike Mandeville,
underestimates the importance of political order. Feels also
that Veblen did not see that vice would continue to exist even in
the ideal industrial society he envisaged. Veblen also attached
more importance to thrift, efficiency, and capital formation than
did Mandeville.

18   VIANELLO, MINO. "Per il centenario vebliano" [For Veblen's
centenary]. Nuova rivista storica [New historical review] 43
(May-August):267-88.
      Discusses the publication in 1958 of Thorstein Veblen: A
Critical Reappraisal, edited by Douglas F. Dowd. Also provides a
general discussion of Veblen's main ideas and his impact. Notes
Benedetto Croce's negative review of Veblen (1949.6) but defends
Veblen, referring to his work as "precious," and concurs with the
judgment that he is the best critic of America produced by that
country.

19   VINE, MARGARET WILSON. "Thorstein Veblen: Conspicuous Consumption." In An Introduction to Sociological Theory. New
York: David McKay Co., pp. 190-212.
      Treats in summary fashion the broad outlines of Veblen's
contributions to sociology. His position in social theory can be
attributed more to his description of the leisure class and its
emulation by other classes than to his theory of technological

evolution. Veblen's analysis of upper class behavior is unequaled.

1960

1   HALL, ROBERT A., Jr. "Thorstein Veblen and Linguistic Theory." American Speech 35 (May):124-30.
Contends that Veblen's The Theory of the Leisure Class deserves to be recognized for its contributions to linguistic theory. Veblenian concepts such as conspicuous waste and invidious distinctions provide insights in helping us to understand speech and spelling patterns and the use of obsolescent forms.

2   MARTINDALE, DON. The Nature and Types of Sociological Theory. Boston: Houghton Mifflin Co., pp. 326, 393-99, 411.
Claims Veblen held a type of social-action theory that embodies human purposes, intentions, and aims. Compares Veblen's instinct of workmanship with Weber's rational-purposeful type of social action. Attention is given to Veblen's "instincts" theory, his predatory-constructive dichotomy, and his intellectual influences. Believes that economists ignore Veblen because they think him to be a sociologist, and many sociologists do not think that he has a sociological theory. "His proper field, it appears, is sociology; it is high time sociologists claimed him for their own."

3   MENCKEN, HENRY L. "'The Great Thinker' in America." In The Intellectuals. Edited by George B. de Huszar. Glencoe, Ill.: Free Press, pp. 139-49.
Excerpted revision of 1919.14. Excerpted from 1919.15. See also 1949.13; 1965.8.

4   NAKAYAMA, MASARU. "Thorstein Veblen no shihon-shugi-ron ni kansuru ichi kenkyū" [A study of Thorstein Veblen's theory of capitalism]. Keizai ronsō [Economic review], 85 (May), 66-83.
Describes Veblen's theory of capitalism, arguing that only a few commentators on Veblen have devoted attention to his analysis of the industrial, as opposed to the monopoly, stage of capitalism. Goes on to describe Veblen's emphasis upon the decisive role played by technology in the transition to monopoly capitalism and the subsequent growth of parasitic and pecuniary values.

5   NOBLE, DAVID W. "Dreiser and Veblen and the Literature of Cultural Change." In Studies in American Culture. Edited by Joseph J. Kwiat and Mary C. Turpin. Minneapolis: University of Minnesota Press, pp. 139-52.
Abridged from 1957.22. Reprinted: 1968.15.

6   RIESMAN, DAVID. Thorstein Veblen: A Critical Interpretation. New York: Seabury Press, 221 pp.

Reprint of 1953.17. Contains a new preface in which
Riesman relates Veblen's thought to the populist movement and
also attempts to demonstrate the contradictions and ambiguities
in his writings on the nature of peace. See also 1960.7-8.

7   RIESMAN, DAVID, and STAUGHTON LYND. "The Relevance of
    Thorstein Veblen." American Scholar 29 (Autumn):543-51.
        Generally unsympathetic reconsideration of Veblen's con-
    tributions. Finds "contradictions in his work as a whole and
    evinces bewilderment over his praise of technology and the
    alleged virtues of small-scale neighborly life." Belittles
    Veblen's "populist" background and his comparisons of late
    nineteenth-century stock manipulators with medieval landlords.
    Finds it "remarkable that Veblen has found no place in the main-
    stream of Socialist thought in America, or abroad." Moreover,
    Veblen could not bridge the gap between the industrial/
    technological and the "literary" worlds. See also 1960.6, 8.
    Reprinted: 1964.15.

8   _____. "The Relevance of Thorstein Veblen." New Statesman 59
    (9 April):526-28.
        Analyzes the evidence of Veblen's The Theory of the Leisure
    Class and the impact of Veblen's comparison of the members of the
    progressive movement and the feudal lords of the Middle Ages.
    Discusses his animus toward conventional theories of social eco-
    nomics and the Jeffersonian influence on his work. Argues that
    Veblen has yet to find a place in American social thought and
    attributes his lack of widespread popularity to his ironic liter-
    ary style. Points to the influence of Charles Darwin, John
    Dewey, and William James on Veblen. Argues that there are "seri-
    ous flaws" in The Theory of the Leisure Class and Veblen himself
    was aware of many of them. See also 1960.6-7; 1964.15.

9   SCHNEIDER, LOUIS. Review of Thorstein Veblen: A Critical
    Reappraisal, edited by Douglas F. Dowd. American Sociological
    Review 25 (February):119-20.
        Provides brief synopses of the contributed articles.
    Notes that Veblen was not a systematic writer but had a "good
    deal to say that is still worthy of reflection and investigation
    in the fields of social stratification and institutional
    interrelations. . . ."

                                1961

1   ANDERSON, THORNTON. Jacobson's Development of American
    Political Thought. 2d ed. New York: Appleton-Century-
    Crofts, pp. ix, 515-19, 564, 566, 589, 592.
        Treats Veblen's major ideas in summary fashion. Topics
    include Veblen on property, waste, exploit, technology, capital-
    ism, and revolution.

2   AYRES, CLARENCE E. Toward a Reasonable Society. Austin:
University of Texas Press, pp. 28-31, 198-99, 201-2, 216, 235,
239, 241, 265-66, 277.
Contains various references to Veblen's ideas and how
the author follows his leads, especially the notion of "life
process."

3   BERGER, MORROE. "Thorstein Veblen's Literary Style." Cairo
Studies in English 4:17-25.
Analyzes Veblen's literary style. Shows how Veblen used
loaded expressions, "studied exaggeration," circumlocution, and
other devices to satirize and criticize business culture. Claims
that Veblen's indirect style misled many readers who did not
grasp his "innocent" yet "devastating irony."

4   DOWNS, ROBERT B. Molders of the Modern Mind. New York:
Barnes and Noble, pp. 339-42.
Summarizes the major ideas of The Theory of the Leisure
Class. Notes Veblen's eccentricities and discusses his far-
reaching influence on economists and other social thinkers. Sub-
sequent reprints are entitled Famous Books since 1492.

5   ELLIS, JOHN M. "Cannan and Veblen as Institutionalists."
American Journal of Economics and Sociology 20 (April):305-12.
Compares Veblen with Edwin Cannan. Both were aware of the
deficiencies of classical economic theory and the point of closest similarity between them "lies in their treatment of technology." Both men emphasized the group nature of economics and
later criticized orthodox economics for its individualistic bias.
Neither could abide waste. Cannan and Veblen differ in that the
former had less to say about institutional arrangements; in fact,
he had nothing to say about corporations. Veblen had more to say
about monopoly and business restriction of production.

6   VIANELLO, MINO. Thorstein Veblen. Milan: Edizioni di
comunità, 405 pp.
In Italian. Presents a comprehensive treatment of Veblen's
ideas. Topics include his biography, methodological premises,
critique of orthodox economics, social theories, and analysis of
democracy and imperialism. Veblen is compared to other significant writers including Marx, Sombart, Weber, and Freud. Suggests
that the only unarguable point about "Veblen is the devilish
difficulty of his strange prose—that Veblen must think in
Swahili or ancient Bulgarian then translate his thoughts into
rococo English." Finds Veblen valuable and attempts a critical
reconstruction of his writings.

1962

1   ADORNO, THEODOR W. Foreword to Functionalismus und
Irrationalität: Studien über Thorstein Veblen's "Theory of

the Leisure Class" [Functionalism and irrationality: studies
of Thorstein Veblen's Theory of the Leisure Class], by Peter
von Haselberg. Frankfurt a.M.: Europäische Verlagsanstalt,
pp. 5-7.
Credits Veblen with helping to transform a narrow economic
analysis into an institutional-sociological one. Sees Veblen's
approach as highly technocratic and suggests that he did not
really provide sufficient evidence for his questionable ethnological thesis.

2   HAMILTON, DAVID. "Why Is Institutional Economics Not Institutional?" American Journal of Economics and Sociology 21
(July):309-17.
Argues that orthodox economists hold a mistaken conception
about what actually constitutes institutionalism. Many think
that the institutionalists have abandoned theory in favor of
description. A close look at Veblen, however, will dispel this
notion. Goes on to demonstrate Veblen's theoretical concerns and
make a case for a Veblenian theory of value.

3   HARTER, LAFAYETTE G., Jr. John R. Commons. Corvallis:
Oregon State University Press, pp. 211-12, 219, 241-48, 250-
51, 254-55.
Describes the intellectual relationship between Commons and
Veblen, the similarities and differences in their thought.

4   LAYTON, EDWIN, Jr. "Veblen and the Engineers." American
Quarterly 14 (Spring):64-72.
Assesses Veblen's ideas regarding a soviet of technicians
that would presumably lead a revolution in the United States.
Contends that Veblen misunderstood the self-serving nature of the
engineering profession and its dominance by big business. While
Veblen understood that engineers tended to be conservative, he
was nonetheless overly impressed with the ideas and actions of
such men as Morris Cooke, Henry Gantt, and Guido Marx. "Veblen's
attempt to influence the engineers was not successful." His
misunderstanding of the engineers can be explained by his position as a transitional figure in the growth of social science.
He eschewed the more empirical approach he helped bring about,
and traces of the "animism" he detected in the thinking of others
were ironically present in his fervent desire to see the engineers assume control of production. See also 1956.6; 1971.11.

5   LEKACHMAN, ROBERT. The Varieties of Economics. Vol. 2.
Cleveland: Meridian Books, World Publishing Co., pp. 116-18.
Holds that today Veblen is probably more respected by
economists than read by them. Many see him as a sociologist
rather than as an economist. The key to Veblen is in the
Darwinian doctrine of evolution. Sees Veblen as a "savage"
critic of capitalism and its apologists.

6   MacIVER, ROBERT M., and CHARLES H. PAGE. "The Strict Technological Explanation of Social Change." In Society: An Introductory Analysis. New York: Holt, Rinehart, and Winston,
pp. 565-71.
    Emphasizes the role of habituation to the environment in
Veblen's theory of technological determinism. In contrast to the
optimism of Marx, Veblen offers no "goal" or "revelation." Questions whether the theory of habituation is too all-inclusive an
explanation of social change.

7   OHARA, KEISHI. "Thorstein Veblen ni okeru shihon no gainen"
[Thorstein Veblen's concept of capital]. Keizai kenkyū
[Economic research] 13 (January):1-8.
    Emphasizes Veblen's dualistic view of life and society--the
instinct of workmanship versus pecuniary emulation, peaceable
savagery versus predatory barbarism, industry versus finance, and
others. Notes how Veblen's approach differs from Marx's and
Weber's and takes account of some critiques of Veblen's ideas
concerning corporation finance and business enterprise.

8   SCHULMAN, ROSALIND. "Absentee Ownership Reread." American
Journal of Economics and Sociology 21 (July):319-30.
    Laments the fact that Absentee Ownership and Business
Enterprise in Recent Times remains largely unread even though it
is a work "which today has greater meaning for our society" than
any other book by Veblen. Credits Veblen with pinpointing the
problems arising out of credit loans and the Federal Reserve
Board.

9   Von HASELBERG, PETER. Functionalismus und Irrationalität:
Studien über Thorstein Veblen's "Theory of the Leisure Class"
[Functionalism and irrationality: studies of Thorstein
Veblen's Theory of the Leisure Class]. Frankfurt a.M.:
Europäische Verlagsanstalt, 111 pp.
    Veblen's analysis in The Theory of the Leisure Class is
criticized for failing to take into account the irrational main-
springs of human behavior. Veblen did not understand that wasteful and ostentations consumption by the leisure class can be just
as necessary and compelling as the urge to destroy surplus goods
that cannot be sold or the irrational urge to wage war when there
exists an abundance of weaponry and armaments. Disagrees with
Veblen's assumption that waste can be eliminated by a rationally
ordered economic arrangement. Veblen fails to explain the psychological factors which compel ostentatious display and waste.
Contrary to Veblen, aggression is not eliminated by machine
discipline--technology itself produces violence as a necessary
mechanism to overcome impediments to its own functioning.
Charges that Veblen was more concerned with waste than economic
exploitation, his aesthetic theory is faulty in that it does not
take into account the aesthetic norms of consumer behavior, and
in general Veblen's analysis is one-sided and does not sufficiently stress the element of aggression in conspicuous display.

10   ZINGLER, ERVIN K. "Thorstein Veblen: An Economic Iconoclast."
     Mimeographed. San Antonio, Tex.: Saint Mary's University
     Graduate School.
         Provides a biograpical sketch of Veblen along with remarks
     on several of his major ideas. Finds Veblen rewarding and worth
     rereading but points to his dogmatism and sometimes unjustified
     criticisms of other economic doctrines.

                                1963

1   BELL, DANIEL. Introduction to The Engineers and the Price
     System. New York: Harcourt, Brace, and World, pp. 2-35.
         Reprint of 1963.2; reprinted with additional footnotes:
     1980.2.

2   _____. "Veblen and the New Class." American Scholar 32
     (Autumn):616-38.
         Summarizes Veblen's efforts to promote the idea of a ruling
     class constituted by engineers. Veblen overemphasized the polit-
     ical possibility of rule by engineers; nevertheless his book, The
     Engineers and the Price System, "is surprisingly accurate and
     relevant to the present day American economy." Recent findings
     of administered prices "read like a gloss of the opening chapter"
     of the book. Contends that he betrays an elitist stance and his
     suggestions for revolution and the abolition of the price system
     are utopian. Asserts that what Veblen disliked about capitalism
     was its waste rather than its exploitation. Claims that there is
     a spiritual link between his ideas and the earlier stages of the
     technocracy movement. Reprinted: 1963.1; with additional foot-
     notes: 1980.2.

3   DIGGINS, JOHN P. "Dos Passos and Veblen's Villains." Antioch
     Review 23 (Winter):485-500.
         Emphasizes the Veblenian themes present in several Dos
     Passos novels. Like Veblen, Dos Passos admired craftsmanship and
     distinguished between pecuniary and industrial occupations. Un-
     like Veblen, Dos Passos longed for a return to agrarian society.
     "The modern scientist and the engineer, Veblen's heroic emancipa-
     tors, have now alienated the worker and deprived him of his sole
     source of salvation--his workmanship. Veblen's hero has become
     Dos Passos' new villain."

4   KAPP, KARL WILLIAM, and LORE L. KAPP, eds. History of
     Economic Thought: A Book of Readings. 2d ed. New York:
     Barnes and Noble, pp. 383-84.
         Claims that Veblen did more than simply critique neoclass-
     ical economics; he laid down all the distinguishing elements of
     social economy. He pointed to the pecuniary habits of economic
     actors, the cumulative nature of economic change, and the nature
     of business fluctuations.

5   KOLKO, GABRIEL. The Triumph of Conservatism: A Reinterpreta-
     tion of American History, 1900-1916. New York: Free Press,
     pp. 214, 288, 300-301.
        Claims that while Veblen had his shortcomings, he alone
     among the progressive era intellectuals understood the dynamics
     of that time. Veblen attributed more power to finance than it
     actually had, and he did not understand the conditions of eco-
     nomic insecurity that government intervention was designed to
     remedy. "For all Veblen's deficiencies, his contribution toward
     a theoretical comprehension of American history in this century
     has never been equalled."

6   OSER, JACOB. The Evolution of Economic Thought. New York:
     Harcourt, Brace, and World, pp. 245-60.
        Summarizes Veblen's major ideas, noting his criticisms of
     standard economic theory and ideas concerning work and capital-
     ism. Argues that Veblen was not a reformer; he was fundamentally
     opposed to the system he thought so wasteful. Although Veblen
     flirted with the idea of rule by engineers, he was basically a
     pessimist who held a rather dim view of future prospects owing to
     the pervasive influence of those institutions he so disliked.

7   ROSENBERG, BERNARD, ed. Introduction to Thorstein Veblen.
     New York: Thomas Y. Crowell Co., pp. 1-14.
        The revival of interest in Veblen has to do with the wide-
     spread pessimism of the second half of the twentieth century.
     Veblen was successful in broadening the field of economics and
     enriching it through the application of insights gleaned from
     anthropology, psychology, and sociology. Veblen's insistence
     upon the study of change or process is a felicitous result of his
     exposure to the Darwinian evolutionary approach. It can be said
     that his anthropological sources are dated and his excesses can
     be readily identified in those passages that smack of technolog-
     ical determinism. Yet Veblen was surely aware of the fact that
     technology, in the wrong hands, could "lay waste to any given
     country of the habitable globe." He clearly grasped the fact
     that latecomers to industrialization might eventually outstrip
     those nations which preceded them. Hence, his analyses of
     Germany and Japan demonstrate the potential that lesser-developed
     nations have for future growth. The tremendous development of
     bureaucracy in advanced nations also bothered Veblen. The bureau-
     crat and the specialist would come to constitute the major power
     centers in the future. The forces and institutions which haunted
     him have arrived: war, nationalism, stifling bureaucracy, and
     wasteful consumption are in great abundance. Chronic complainer
     that he was Veblen, were he living today, would be profoundly
     depressed. Perhaps we should, however, emulate his "perpetual
     discontent" with things as they are, and by doing so "we might
     help mankind to survive."

8   ROTH, GUENTHER. Review of Functionalismus und Irrationalität:
     Studien über Thorstein Veblen's "Theory of the Leisure Class"

[Functionalism and irrationality: studies of Thorstein
Veblen's Theory of the Leisure Class], by Peter von Haselberg.
American Sociological Review 28 (April):300-301.
    Notes that social critics from Veblen to Adorno have argued
that many of the "most crucial problems in the study of society
tend to vanish in the interstices of the various social sciences,
especially economics and sociology." Feels that Veblen's satirical treatment of conspicuous waste as regards property has been
weakened by von Haselberg's argument. The latter stresses more
the aggressive tendencies embedded in the display. See 1962.9.

9   SCHLESINGER, ARTHUR M., Jr. "Sources of the New Deal." In
    Paths of American Thought. Edited by Arthur M. Schlesinger
    and Morton White. Boston: Houghton Mifflin Co., pp. 379-80.
        Veblen's call for organizing the American economy into a
    "systematic whole" and his general critique of business practices
    are assessed in an attempt to survey sources of the New Deal.

                            1964

1   AYRES, CLARENCE E. "The Legacy of Thorstein Veblen." In
    Instutional Economics: Veblen, Commons, and Mitchell
    Reconsidered. Berkeley and Los Angeles: University of
    California Press, pp. 45-62.
        Assesses the significance of Veblen's legacy. Argues that
    Veblen rejected marginal utility theory in order to postulate an
    altogether different conception of the economy--one based on
    anthropology. History has confirmed his insight. The role of
    technology is pervasive, and the study of economic institutions has
    become less deductive and in many cases quite empirical. While
    recognizing the importance of Keynes for the study of macro-
    economics, it can be said that the central concept of macro-
    economics is Veblenian.

2   BOSKOFF, ALVIN. Review of Thorstein Veblen: Selections from
    his Work, edited by Bernard Rosenberg. American Sociological
    Review 29 (April):311-12.
        Suggests that this selection of readings might benefit by
    inclusion of parts of The Engineers and the Price System in order
    to provide a richer introduction to "the brilliant satirical
    Veblen . . . a unique figure."

3   DORFMAN, JOSEPH. "The Background of Institutional Economics."
    In Institutional Economics: Veblen, Commons, and Mitchell
    Reconsidered. Berkeley and Los Angeles: University of
    California Press, pp. 1-44.
        Discusses the intellectual background of the institutional
    school of economics, including Veblen's contributions.

                            117

4 _____. Introductory Note to The Instinct of Workmanship and
   the State of the Industrial Arts. New York: Augustus M.
   Kelley, pp. vii-x.
       Provides information regarding Veblen's preparations prior
   to publishing The Instinct of Workmanship. Contains parts of
   letters by Veblen and Frank Taussig, who praised the book.

5 DOWD, DOUGLAS F. "On Veblen, Mills . . . and the Decline of
   Criticism." Dissent 11 (Winter):29-38.
       Compares Veblen with C. Wright Mills. Both were radicals
   in the analytical sense; they explored the dark side of modern
   society. Veblen and Mills were concerned with exploring the
   phenomenon of power, and while their theories fall short of
   adequacy, they are the two American social scientists of this
   century "who most persistently kept such questions in view." As
   academic practitioners of social criticism, both Veblen and Mills
   often suffered the disdain of their colleagues. Both stand in
   sharp contrast to the prevailing uncritical social science of
   today. Reprinted: 1964.7.

6 _____. Thorstein Veblen. New York: Washington Square Press,
   205 pp.
       A general introduction to the ideas of Thorstein Veblen.
   Covers Veblen's social theory, his views on American capitalism,
   economics, and his observations of the great events of his time.
   Contains a chapter analyzing his strengths and weaknesses. Concludes with a selection of Veblen quotes.

7 _____. "Thorstein Veblen and C. Wright Mills: Social Science
   and Social Criticism." In The New Sociology. Edited by
   Irving L. Horowitz. New York: Oxford University Press, pp.
   54-65.
       Reprint of 1964.5.

8 GORDON, R.A. "Institutional Elements in Contemporary Economics." In Institutional Economics: Veblen, Commons, and
   Mitchell Reconsidered. Berkeley and Los Angeles: University
   of California Press, pp. 123-47.
       Discusses the continuing role played by institutional con-
   cepts in contemporary economics. Refers to Veblen's attack on
   static orthodoxy and claims that today's orthodoxy is subject to
   many of the same criticisms leveled by Veblen years ago.

9 GRAÑA, CESAR. Bohemian versus Bourgeois. New York: Basic
   Books, pp. 75, 162-67, 172, 187.
       Argues that The Theory of the Leisure Class "is a treatise
   on the concept of aristocratic behavior and its relation to work,
   productivity, and spiritual excellence." Those who charge Veblen
   with bogus or opportunistic scholarship have missed the point of
   the book. "Veblen's accounts are really theoretical evocations
   aimed above all at uncovering the symbolic content of our social
   heritage." Assesses Veblen's theory and relates it to specific

historical periods. Suggests that his notion of polite society finds its best expressions in the Renaissance and classical periods of European cultural history, in particular, French classicism. Reprinted with a new title: 1967.9.

10   HANSEN, NILES M. "Weber and Veblen on Economic Development." Kyklos 17, fasc. 3:447-69.
       Compares Veblen with Weber and Marx. Finds that the Veblenian institutional approach has much to offer in attempting to understand economic development. Shortcomings of this approach include an inadequate treatment of economic motivation; a tendency to substitute a study of institutions for price theory; and an inadequate treatment of alternative institutions as they relate to economic development. By adding the insights of Weber, improvements can be made both methodologically and theoretically.

11   JAHER, FREDERIC COPLE. Doubters and Dissenters: Cataclysmic Thought in America, 1885-1918. Glencoe, Ill.: Free Press, pp. 28-29.
       Portrays Veblen as an alienated dissenter who adopted "a guise similar to Crane and Dreiser, posing as the tough-minded, objective observer with little patience for spiritual reformers and sentimental theorists. . . ." Veblen was too abrasive to express his views in the style of Christian brotherhood. Like Donnelly and London he attacked the predatory behavior of the economic elite. "Seldom has a man turned more bitterly on his age than did Veblen."

12   LOVEJOY, ARTHUR O. Reflections on Human Nature. Baltimore: Johns Hopkins Press, pp. 208-15, 220.
       A set of lectures delivered at Swarthmore College in 1941. Argues that many of the ideas set forth in Veblen's The Theory of the Leisure Class were anticipated by earlier writers such as Mandeville, Rousseau, and Adam Smith. Veblen revived and elaborated the themes put forth earlier by others.

13   MEYNAUD, JEAN. La technocratie: mythe ou realite? [Technocracy: myth or reality?]. Paris: Payot, pp. 202-3.
       Sees Veblen as a forerunner of technocratic ideology. Cites Veblen's distinction between the businessman and engineer and his call for the latter to replace the former in organizing economic affairs. Claims that the technocrat Howard Scott drew inspiration from Veblen's works. Translated and reprinted: 1968.14.

14   RIESMAN, DAVID. "The Social and Psychological Setting of Veblen's Economic Theory." In Abundance For What? Garden City, New York: Doubleday & Co., pp. 374-87.
       Reprint of 1953.16; a section of 1954.14.

15   RIESMAN, DAVID, and STAUGHTON LYND. "The Relevance of
     Thorstein Veblen." In Abundance For What?, by David Riesman.
     Garden City, New York: Doubleday & Co., pp. 388-401.
        Draws on 1953.17 and 1960.8. Reprint of 1960.7.

16   SILVER, CHERRY BUSHMAN. "William James, Oliver Wendell Holmes
     Jr., Thorstein Veblen: American Intellectual Prose, 1870-
     1910." Ph.D. dissertation, Harvard University.
        Treats the prose of James, Holmes, and Veblen. Analyzes
     and evaluates Veblen's word patterns, syntactical structure, verb
     roots, and use of imagery. Defends Veblen against criticisms of
     his prose style, finding that his writings are subtle and refined
     rather than bland or bombastic.

17   VATTER, BARBARA. "Veblen: The Analyst and His Critics."
     American Journal of Economics and Sociology 23 (April):155-64.
        Laments the fact that Veblen has been ignored, slighted,
     unjustly criticized, and misunderstood. Points to Veblen's acute
     insights and contemporary relevance. "Should we not reward his
     faith in us with monuments to him for his critical, probing
     method of social analysis resulting in findings which are useful
     still years after his death? He was interested in what was good."

                                1965

1   ANON. "Institutional Economics." In The McGraw-Hill
     Dictionary of Modern Economics. New York: McGraw-Hill
     Book Co., p. 266.
        Considers Veblen to be the leader of the institutional
     school of economic thought. Economic activities are shaped by
     institutions which are psychological and customary.

2   ANON. Review of The Instinct of Workmanship and the State of
     the Industrial Arts. Choice 2 (April):132.
        "Athough Veblen is often unnecessarily obtuse for the gen-
     eral reader he is also often so clear and correct in his observa-
     tions that this book might have been written today." Finds
     Veblen quite "in tune" with the integrated approach of con-
     temporary social science.

3   ARMYTAGE, W.H.G. The Rise of the Technocrats. London:
     Routledge and Kegan Paul, pp. 238-39, 248, 401.
        Refers to Veblen's meeting with Charles P. Steinmetz; his
     relationship to Howard Scott; and the fact that he was aware that
     his ideas in The Engineers and the Price System were indeed
     utopian. While Veblen was "wise" and "shrewd," Scott was not.

4   DORFMAN, JOSEPH. Prefatory Note to The Theory of Business
     Enterprise. Clifton, N.J.: Augustus M. Kelley, unpaginated.

Provides information regarding the publishing of the book, how the title was changed, and Veblen's hopes to have it published in England.

5   FREDERICK, WILLIAM O. "Was Veblen Right about the Future of Business Enterprise?" American Journal of Economics and Sociology 24 (July):225-40.
Argues that while Veblen has been proven to be "essentially correct" about the course of business enterprise since his day, "he faltered on the more fundamental and actual matter of the future course to be taken by cultural development in general. On this question we might hope Professor Ayres has been the better prophet."

6   GINGER, RAY. Age of Excess: The United States from 1877-1914. New York: Macmillan Co., pp. 290, 308, 317-19.
Refers to Veblen's notion of "trained incapacity," his theory of how the leisure class is emulated by the lower classes, and his analysis of business practices put forth in The Theory of Business Enterprise.

7   LIEBEL, HELEN. "Thorstein Veblen's Positive Synthesis." American Journal of Economics and Sociology 24 (April):201-16.
Argues that although most of Veblen's major works stress his Darwinian and positivist postulates, it should not be forgotten that he utilized a Kantian ontology as well. It was probably his preoccupation with Kant that prevented Veblen from formulating his philosophical system entirely along Darwinian lines. Contends that, in spite of his pessimism, Veblen entertained a belief that in the remote future, a better age might come about.

8   MENCKEN, HENRY L. "Professor Veblen." In The American Scene. Edited by Huntington Cairns. New York: Alfred A. Knopf, pp. 200-210.
Excerpted revision of 1919.14. Excerpted from 1919.15. Reprint of 1949.13. See also 1960.3.

9   SRIVASTAVA, S.K. "Thorstein Bunde Veblen." In History of Economic Thought. 2d ed. Dehli: Atma Ram and Sons, pp. 470-76.
Surveys Veblen's life, his criticism of orthodox economics, his theory of institutions, views on corporations, trade cycles, class conflict, and economic versus pecuniary values.

1966

1   ANON. Review of Imperial Germany and the Industrial Revolution. Science and Society 30 (Fall):510.
Claims that this book "exhibits all the salient characteristics of Veblen's style--irony, complexity, reticence, and a massive apparatus of indirection and concealment."

2   CAMENSON, HERBERT S.   Review of Thorstein Veblen, by Douglas F.
     Dowd.   Library Journal 91 (August):3706.
         "If economists are mistakenly forgetting one of the great-
     est of American thinkers, political scientists, sociologists,
     anthropologists and historians are not. . . ." Veblen "forced
     economists to think in social science terms." See 1964.6.

3   CARAHER, CATHERINE ANN.   "Thorstein Veblen and the American
     Novel." Ph.D. dissertation, University of Michigan, Ann
     Arbor.
         Claims that Veblen's influence can be seen in the writings
     of such early twentieth-century novelists as Robert Herrick,
     Sinclair Lewis, and John Dos Passos. These writers were either
     directly influenced by Veblen or came to share his critical
     perspective as a result of the pervasive spread of his ideas in
     society in general. Demonstrates that Veblen's views regarding
     the instincts of workmanship, idle curiosity, the parental bent,
     his attack on the country town, and his distinction between
     industry and exploit have close parallels in the authors exam-
     ined. Emphasizes Veblen's influence on writers of the early
     twentieth century.

4   DORFMAN, JOSEPH.   Thorstein Veblen and His America. New York:
     Augustus M. Kelley, 572 pp.
         Reprint of 1934.9. This reprint edition contains some
     corrections, new items in Veblen's bibliography, and new appendices.

5   FUSFELD, DANIEL R.   The Age of the Economist. Glenview, Ill.:
     Scott, Foresman, & Co., pp. 90-94.
         Highlights Veblen's major ideas and provides some biograph-
     ical information. Emphasizes Veblen's theory of technological
     change and his influence on Wesley C. Mitchell, Gardiner Means,
     Adolf Berle, Clarence Ayres, and others.

6   GOULD, JAY M.   The Technical Elite. New York: Augustus M.
     Kelley, 118 pp. passim.
         Argues that Veblen's indictment of business rests on
     grounds of relative inefficiency. Among the business practices
     that tend to negate the productive efforts of the engineer Veblen
     included salesmanship, advertising, monopoly control, absentee
     ownership, financial speculation, and, in general, any failure of
     a market-oriented economy to achieve full capacity levels of
     output. It is easy to understand the reasons for Veblen's popu-
     larity during the Great Depression. The hearings of the famous
     Temporary National Economic Committee in the late thirties, in
     which attention was focused on the precise quantitative measure-
     ment of unused capacity, could be regarded as official recogni-
     tion of the validity of Veblen's analysis as applied to the
     inadequate functioning of the American economy of those years.
     Further argues that business today, although it frequently uses
     science inadequately, probably needs the scientist more than the
     scientist needs business, and this is why the balance between

them is being shifted in favor of the scientist, as was foreseen
by Veblen. Concludes that much of what Veblen saw in the relationship between business and the creators of new technology is
valid today. His analysis helps us understand the nature of the
conflict between them and the direction in which resolution of
that conflict must move.

7   SILK, LEONARD S. Veblen: A Play in Three Acts. New York:
     Augustus M. Kelley, 138 pp.
        A semifictional play depicting the life and times of
     Veblen. Concerned mainly with his family relationships.

8   SVIGOVA, MILADA. "Hlavni smery sociologie volnebo casu"
     [Principal trends in the sociology of leisure]. Sociologicky
     casopis [Sociological magazine] (Czechoslovakia) 2, no. 5:
     664-72.
        Summarizes the main points of The Theory of the Leisure
     Class.

9   VISSER, DERK. "Thorstein Veblen's Imperial Germany and the
     Industrial Revolution." Ph.D. dissertation, Bryn Mawr
     College.
        Argues that Veblen's "essay on Germany was a compilation of
     generalizations that do not pass the test of factual examina-
     tion." Adds that Veblen's economic history is faulty and based
     upon an "almost Manichaean" set of preconceptions. Veblen
     greatly overemphasizes the Prussian element in German economic
     history and fails to show the similarity between German business-
     men and their English-speaking counterparts. If Imperial Germany
     and the Industrial Revolution is an example of Veblen's case
     study approach, then his theories are open to serious question.
     See also 1969.16.

1967

1   ADORNO, THEODOR W., ed. "Veblen's Attack on Culture." In
     Prisms. Translated by Samuel and Shierry Weber. London:
     Neville Spearman, pp. 73-94.
        Reprint of 1941.1. Translation and reprint of 1955.1.

2   BELL, JOHN FRED. "Thorstein Veblen." In A History of Economic
     Thought. 2d ed. New York: Ronald Press, pp. 539-53.
        Describes Veblen as the most critical of all economists
     with respect to accepted doctrines. Surveys his life, attack on
     traditional assumptions in economics, notion of the pecuniary
     element in society, business cycles, and contribution to institu-
     tional economics. Veblen was instrumental in creating a new
     intellectual climate.

3   COMMAGER, HENRY STEELE, ed. Introduction to Lester Ward and
     the Welfare State. Indianapolis: Bobbs-Merrill Co., pp. xxi-
     xxii, xxvii-xxviii, 279.

Notes that Ward anticipated and influenced Veblen in some important respects. The two shared much in common—both were outsiders and rebels.

4   DOWD, DOUGLAS F. "Veblen, Thorstein Bunde." In The Encyclopedia of Philosophy. Edited by Paul Edwards. Vol. 8. New York: Macmillan Co. and Free Press, pp. 237-38.
    Provides a biographical sketch of Veblen and highlights his major ideas. Sees Hume, Darwin, and Marx as the greatest influences on Veblen. "Darwinian concepts aside, the starting point of Veblen's analysis of society and of social change was fundamentally Marxian." Nonetheless there are significant differences between Veblen and Marx.

5   ELSNER, HENRY, Jr. The Technocrats: Prophets of Automation. Syracuse: Syracuse University Press, pp. 17-35 passim, 94, 154, 215, 222.
    Describes Veblen's involvement with those who were later to become known as "technocrats" and discusses Veblen's ideas concerning a society administered by technicians and how his ideas influenced the technocracy movement. Considers The Engineers and the Price System to be a basic document of the movement. Partisans of both Veblen and Howard Scott argue over who influenced whom with regard to the engineers. Scott himself stated that he disagreed with the conclusions in The Engineers and the Price System.

6   FERRAROTTI, FRANCO. "Thorstein B. Veblen: l'agiatezza vistosa" [Thorstein B. Veblen: conspicuous leisure]. In Saper tutto: enciclopedia del XX secolo [To know everything: encyclopedia of the twentieth century]. Vol. 406. Italy: Garzanti Editore, pp. 169-91.
    Describes and analyzes the major ideas of Veblen that are labeled technological determinist. Notes the integral relationships between society, economy, and culture in his writing.

7   GIACALONE, JOSEPH A. "Thorstein Veblen: uno schema di sviluppo istituzionalistico" [Thorstein Veblen: a scheme of institutional development]. Rivista internazionale di economiche e commerciale [International review of economics and commerce] 14 (August):806-15.
    A general account of Veblen's evolutionary theory of economics. Points to Veblen's biological orientation and his emphasis on cumulative change. Covers Veblen's pecuniary-technological distinction, the cultural incidence of the machine process, and the leisure class.

8   GILL, RICHARD T. "Institutions: The Sweeping Critique of Thorstein Veblen." In Evolution of Modern Economics. Englewood Cliffs, N.J.: Prentice-Hall, pp. 66-70.
    Details Veblen's criticisms of the theories of utility, consumer, and business behavior. Veblen proposed an evolutionary

economics stressing the conflict between the predatory (business)
habit of mind and the workmanlike or machine-disciplined habit of
mind. Veblen's contribution lies in his skeptical attitude
toward an easy acceptance of theories and doctrines.

9   GRAÑA, CESAR. Modernity and Its Discontents: French Society
     and the French Man of Letters in the Nineteenth Century. New
     York: Harper Torchbooks, pp. 75, 162-67, 172, 187.
          Reprint of 1964.9 with a new title.

10   HILL, FOREST G. "Veblen, Berle, and the Modern Corporation."
     American Journal of Economics and Sociology 26 (July):279-95.
          Describes the views of two leading theorists of corporate
     growth in America. Veblen was "a grand theorist of finance
     capitalism, perhaps with too oversimplified a version of it."
     Veblen displayed a dislike for financiers and "gave entire credit
     to the industrial engineers and technicians" rather than the
     financiers and business types. States also that many have misun-
     derstood Veblen's call for a soviet of technicians and claims he
     uses the concept to throw light on the existence of absentee
     ownership.

11   LEAKACHMAN, ROBERT. Introduction to Absentee Ownership and
     Business Enterprise in Recent Times. Boston: Beacon Press,
     pp. v-xviii.
          Claims that this is not Veblen's most popular book. Finds
     the notion of "absentee ownership" vague but "full of suggestive
     overtone" when read in light of subsequent works on corporations.
     States that his "major theories are shown to rest on foundations
     of sand." That is the fate he shares with Marx. Nonetheless,
     people still read him. "Veblen appeals to the deep vein of
     subversion buried in the souls of even the most respectable."

12   _____. Introduction to The Theory of the Leisure Class. New
     York: Viking Press, pp. v-xi.
          After highlighting The Theory of the Leisure Class, con-
     cludes that Veblen's evolutionary faith and instinct psychology
     are not at this time very convincing. What endures, however, is
     the distinction he drew between pecuniary and mechanical values.
     Moreover, Veblen is certainly more subversive of business values
     than some earlier commentators had realized.

13   MARSHALL, HOWARD D. "Thorstein Bunde Veblen. In The Great
     Economists: A History of Economic Thought. New York: Pitman
     Publishing Corp., pp. 286-97.
          Provides a biographical sketch and discusses Veblen's cri-
     tiques of classical economics, the marginal utility school, and
     capitalism. His views on business cycles are also described.
     Emphasizes his fascination with the machine process. "It would
     be impossible to award Veblen anything but the highest honors for
     originality and brilliance." Veblen's theory of instincts is
     questionable and his critique of orthodox theory has not had a

significant impact upon later economists. What influence he did
exert was eclipsed by the rise of popularity of Keynesian theory
beginning in the thirties.

14   MAYER, ARNO J. "Historical Thought and American Foreign
     Policy in the Era of the First World War." In The Historian
     and the Diplomat. Edited by Francis L. Loewenheim. New York:
     Harper and Row, pp. 73-90.
         Describes Veblen's penetrating analysis of President
     Wilson's peace program after World War I.

15   MERTON, ROBERT K. On Theoretical Sociology: Five Essays, Old
     and New. New York: Free Press, pp. 19-20, 29, 112, 123-24,
     151.
         Reprint of 1949.14.

16   ROUCEK, JOSEPH S. Review of Thorstein Veblen, by Douglas F.
     Dowd. American Political Science Review 61 (June):503-4.
         Refers to Veblen as a "great theoretician." Feels that the
     book stresses Veblen's influence on economics rather than sociol-
     ogy "although Veblen's conspicuous influence has persisted and
     continues today not only in economics but also in sociology and
     history." Notes that Veblen contributed to social-action theory,
     particularly in political sociology, and that his theory in this
     latter regard bears comparison with that of Max Weber. See
     1964.6.

17   SOWELL, THOMAS. "The 'Evolutionary' Economics of Thorstein
     Veblen." Oxford Economic Papers 19 (July):177-98.
         Suggests that more is understood about Veblen the social
     satirist and literary critic than is understood about Veblen the
     economist. Analyzes Veblen's critique of orthodox economics and
     notes that his harshest critique was directed at preclassical
     economics while at the same time he had kind words for contempo-
     raries such as Alfred Marshall and Edwin Cannan. Argues that
     Veblen's distinction between "taxonomic" and "evolutionary"
     approaches to economic theory "is operationally identical" with
     Marx's distinction between "metaphysical" and "dialectical"
     thought. Claims that Veblen has an original theory pertaining to
     the business cycle, but much of what he has to say about econom-
     ics and business practices are unfalsifiable ad hoc predictions.
     Scattered throughout his work are adumbrations of concepts that
     would receive fuller treatment by later thinkers. For a dissent-
     ing opinion see 1969.3.

18   WARD, LESTER F. Review of The Theory of the Leisure Class.
     In Lester Ward and the Welfare State. Edited by Henry Steele
     Commager. Indianapolis: Bobbs-Merrill Co., pp. 279-90.
         Reprint of 1900.3. Reprinted: 1973.23.

19   WEINSTEIN, JAMES. "Notes on the Need for a Socialist Party."
     Studies on the Left 7 (January-February):336-37.

Refers to Veblen's analysis of the possibility of abolishing the price system. States that his emphasis on efficiency
distorts his vision "somewhat," but he was correct in his charge
that business was wasteful and ran at cross-purposes with the
good of the community.

20 WEST, THOMAS REED. "Thorstein Veblen and Carl Sandburg." In
    Flesh of Steel. Nashville: Vanderbilt University Press,
    pp. 71-84.
        Analyzes Veblen's attitude toward the machine. Emphasizes
    Veblen's concern with the instinct of workmanship, the discipline
    of the machine, and his animus toward business. Contends that
    Veblen had a very flexible approach to social problems and dis-
    played great subtlety in his analysis of economic psychology.
    Regarding the impact of the machine discipline on men's thinking
    in general, writes that "Veblen's thesis cannot look to extensive
    psychological documentation and can be considered only a bold
    guess." While Sandburg "represents the Whitmanesque tradition,"
    Veblen speaks for scientific rationality.

1968

1 ANON. Review of Absentee Ownership and Business Enterprise in
   Recent Times. Science and Society 32 (Winter):122.
       "The note appended to Chapter XI comparing business sales-
   manship to the commercialization of religion surely is the most
   irreverent and excruciatingly funny exposure extant of the role
   of organized religion in American life."

2 APOSTLE, CHRIS N. "Veblen's Contribution to a Societal Theory
   of Boredom." Indian Journal of Social Research 9, no. 1:1-13.
       Argues that Veblen's ideas in The Theory of the Leisure
   Class have a broad application to the "overwhelming majority of
   the American people today." Attempts to relate Veblen's ideas to
   the problem of boredom.

3 COCHRAN, THOMAS C. "Business in Veblen's America." In
   Thorstein Veblen: The Carleton College Veblen Seminar Essays.
   Edited by Carlton C. Qualey. New York: Columbia University
   Press, pp. 47-71.
       Veblen's analysis of American capitalism was formed during
   a troubled period and some of his principles of capitalist dynamics have become outdated. Veblen's expectations that free enterprise capitalism would be ended by chronic depression were based
   on his hypothesis that the influence of the investment banker was
   on the rise. His solution for reorganizing production and distribution was never clearly defined. Nationwide competition,
   falling prices, and continuous depression characterized Veblen's
   time. Local monopolies and industrial trusts furthered the business of marketing securities carried on by investment bankers.
   In the 1890s life insurance companies became financial giants and

advertising expenditures grew rapidly. The nonagricultural population greatly increased. Veblen miscalculated the growth and
impact of the professional manager and his influence on the
change of corporate ethics. A new availability of capital and
fresh emphasis on increasing mass consumption brought about basic
alterations in the managerial capitalist ethic difficult to foresee in Veblen's time.

4   CONROY, STEPHEN S. "Thorstein Veblen's Prose." American
Quarterly 20 (Fall):605-15.
     Argues that many commentators on Veblen have been wide of
the mark. Mencken failed to grasp Veblen's meaning; Howells missed
the serious social and economic criticism contained in The Theory
of the Leisure Class; Riesman appears in doubt as to Veblen; and
Dorfman "does not demonstrate" that The Theory of the Leisure
Class "is not satirical." In spite of the "explanations" of
Veblen's style, it has to be said that he simply chose to write
in the manner he did. When Veblen wanted to make a point
clearly, he did. Contends that Veblen's prose is overwhelmingly
Latinate and that he "was a self-conscious stylist" who used
alliteration and incongruous word sets to suit his taste. While
Veblen's prose is a parody of the leisure class, it is probably
also a conscious self-parody—a form of satire itself.

5   DAVIS, ARTHUR K. "Veblen, Thorstein." In International
Encyclopedia of the Social Sciences. Edited by David L.
Sills. Vol. 16. New York: Macmillan Co. and Free Press,
pp. 303-8.
     Argues that there is a strand of utopian anarchism in
Veblen's thought. Relates Veblen to Marx, finding that the two
share much in common. Unlike the Marxists, however, Veblen
tended to rely upon broad sociological and psychological mechan-
isms rather than tightly reasoned economic analysis to explain
social change.

6   DORFMAN, JOSEPH. "Background of Veblen's Thought." In
Thorstein Veblen: The Carleton College Veblen Seminar Essays.
Edited by Carlton C. Qualey. New York: Columbia University
Press, pp. 106-30.
     Discusses Veblen's development, his educational experi-
ences, the climate of the times when Veblen taught and wrote, and
his influence on other thinkers. Veblen is described as artist
and economist. He incorporated knowledge of linguistics, anthropology, philosophy, psychology, history, and biological sciences
into his economic theory.

7   FRIDAY, CHARLES B. "Veblen on the Future of American Capi-
talism." In Thorstein Veblen: The Carleton College Veblen
Seminar Essays. Edited by Carlton C. Qualey. New York:
Columbia University Press, pp. 14-46.

Veblen's controversial theories of economic development in
modern society are critical of classical and neoclassical economic
thought. He argued that traditional theories were irrelevant to
modern economic issues. The ultimate extinction of capitalism
was crucial for him. Veblen differs from Marx in that he does
not prescribe action nor does he predict what is to follow the
demise of capitalist society. Two dominant themes in his analysis are the goal of maximum production and his animus toward
institutionally supported inequality. An important distinction
for Veblen is the one between business and industry. Industry is
the factor in modern civilization that brings about growth
whereas business is concerned with profit and property rights.
Veblen points out that the invisible hand is no longer effective
in dealing with modern monopoly, allowing great profits for
business at the expense of the community. His theory of crisis
or depression was generally considered to be inadequate, and
critics argue that he lacked a theory of aggregate demand.
Veblen presented the idea that monopoly and depression supplement
each other, but he fails to adequately tie them together. The
tendency of business toward wasteful production inhibits economic
growth. Veblen did not distinguish between economics and politics. For Veblen, business interests dominate both industry and
politics and that domination results in a stagnant economy.
Notes that Veblen has been criticized for not considering that
social legislation and government control of business might serve
as an indefinite perpetration of capitalism. Veblen's emphasis
on the conflict in modern society may have been exclusive of the
virtues of welfare reform, but it is in this emphasis that the
basics for his analyses lie.

8   GRUCHY, ALLAN G. "Economic Thought: The Institutional
     School." In International Encyclopedia of the Social
     Sciences. Edited by David L. Sills. Vol. 4. New York:
     Macmillan Co. and Free Press, pp. 462-67.
        Cites Veblen as the intellectual forefather of the institu-
tional school of economics. Summarizes several of his major
contributions.

9   JUNKER, LOUIS J. "Theoretical Foundations of Neo-
     Institutionalism." American Journal of Economics
     and Sociology 27 (April):197-213.
        States that for Veblen the concept of culture is the master
principle of social analysis. Sees Veblen's analytical framework
as resting upon the fundamental distinction between technology
and institutions. Technology is a cumulative process of workmanship and tools. Opposed to this pattern of behavior are the
"forces of ceremonialism." Demonstrates the linkage between the
ideas of Veblen and Clarence Ayres, an important figure in the
history of institutionalism. Sees Veblen's major failure as "his
relative incapacity to move from analysis to policy." A fruitful
step forward would involve the integration of Veblen and his

followers' general theory "with some of the insights" of
Keynesianism.

10   KAPP, K. WILLIAM. "In Defense of Institutional Economics."
      Swedish Journal of Economics 70, no. 1:1-18.
            Holds that institutional economists have always been con-
      cerned with issues that appear unorthodox to other economists--
      such as conflict, coercion, and power. Credits Veblen for his
      work on those topics and also for his originality in criticizing
      orthodox economics and his contributions to the theories of
      culture lag and circular causation.

11   LeCLAIR, EDWARD E., Jr., and HAROLD K. SCHNEIDER, eds.
      Economic Anthropology: Readings in Theory and Analysis. New
      York: Henry Holt & Co., pp. 486-87.
            Credits Veblen with leading a "substantive revolution" in
      economics that paved the way for empirical analysis of economic
      institutions. His impact has been significant and helpful in the
      construction of an economic anthropology.

12   LEIBENSTEIN, HARVEY. "Bandwagon, Snob, and Veblen Effects in
      the Theory of Consumer's Demand." In Readings in
      Microeconomics. Edited by W. Breit and H.M. Hochman.
      New York: Holt, Rinehart, and Winston, pp. 123-29.
            Reprint of 1950.10. Reprinted: 1969.7; 1975.8. Incor-
      porated into a chapter of a book: 1976.13. See also 1978.1.

13   LUBIN, ISADOR. "Recolletions of Veblen." In Thorstein
      Veblen: The Carleton College Veblen Seminar Essays. Edited
      by Carlton C. Qualey. New York: Columbia University Press,
      pp. 131-47.
            Former student and colleague recounts impressions of
      Veblen. Indicates Veblen did not consider reformism as func-
      tional but rather as purely analytical. Argues that Veblen had
      no animus toward the economic system or the people who ran it.
      Points to Veblen's distinction between the individual as a human
      being and the individual as part of the mechanism and to Veblen's
      appreciation and respect for the small businessman as support.
      Describes Veblen's recommendations to the Food Administration in
      Washington to reconcile with the I.W.W. (Industrial Workers of
      the World) and take over certain phases of retail distribution in
      order to end food problems and win the war. Says Veblen's dissec-
      tion of the economic system led to preconceived conclusions.
      Claims Veblen's false notion that "vested interests" could not
      adapt to and gain from social reform was based on early conclu-
      sions. Veblen would be "pleasantly disappointed" with the devel-
      opment of our economic system over the past three-and-one-half
      decades.

14   MEYNAUD, JEAN. Technocracy. Translated by Paul Barnes. New
      York: Free Press, pp. 202-3.
            Translation and reprint of 1964.13.

15   NOBLE, DAVID W. "Dreiser and Veblen: The Literature of
      Cultural Change." In Intellectual History in America. Edited
      by Cushing Strout. Vol. 2. New York: Harper and Row,
      pp. 60-72.
      Abridged from 1957.22. Reprint of 1960.5.

16   _____. "The Sacred and the Profane: The Theology of
      Thorstein Veblen." In Thorstein Veblen: The Carleton College
      Veblen Seminar Essays. Edited by Carlton C. Qualey. New
      York: Columbia University Press, pp. 72-105.
      A major paradox rested on the foundation of theories put
      forth by liberal social philosophers in early twentieth-century
      America. Equates twentieth-century liberals with seventeenth-
      century Puritans. Veblen sought a return to a natural and sim-
      plified order; his attack was directed at those who argued that
      the status quo was the natural order. Veblen attempted to show
      that capitalism and capitalist economics were unnatural. He also
      argued that industrialism would eventually destroy the leisure
      class and in doing so, liberate the masses to return to "the time
      of origin." Veblen's third book, The Instinct of Workmanship,
      was written to show that man had fallen from the "sacred time of
      origin" into the "profane time of barbarism" and that he would
      triumphantly return to the "time of origin." Veblen taught that
      there was no private property in nature and that for the primi-
      tive man the rights to productive property were held in common.
      Veblen also argued that capitalism and Christianity supported
      each other. He thought World War I would mark the time when
      reversion to the "sacred time" would occur. If finance capital-
      ism was to survive, there would be no future opportunities to
      return to the "sacred time of origin."

17   QUALEY, CARLTON C., ed. Introduction to Thorstein Veblen:
      The Carleton College Veblen Seminar Essays. New York:
      Columbia University Press, pp. 1-15.
      Sketches Veblen's life, research interests, and reactions
      to his work. Maintains that Veblen "defies labelling." Few
      would dispute that "Veblen was America's greatest social critic
      of the first half of the twentieth century."

18   SMITH, OLIVER WENDELL. "Thorstein Veblen's Evaluation of
      American Capitalism." Ph.D. dissertation, University of
      Alabama.
      Considers Veblen's analysis of American capitalism.
      Although Veblen's style makes him difficult to understand,
      he has made significant contributions to economic theory. Notes
      Veblen's "dichotomous" approach to economics and his concern with
      exploit, waste, and sabotage. Claims that while Veblen disliked
      both big government and business enterprise, he nonetheless sug-
      gested a far-ranging program of economic reconstruction. Exam-
      ines Veblen's predictions and policy prescriptions, noting his
      half-hearted endorsement of a soviet of engineers. More impor-
      tant are his practical proposals to ensure peace, eliminate

waste, and his early use of statistics and data gathering as aids
to the study of economics.

1969

1 BANKS, J.A. "Thorstein Veblen." In The Founding Fathers of
   Social Science. Edited by Timothy Raison. Baltimore:
   Penguin Books, pp. 119-27.
   Provides biographical information and assesses Veblen's
   major books and ideas. Argues that many of his ideas have been
   absorbed into the language of sociology and we have forgotten
   that it was Veblen who first originated them. "The empirical
   content of his writings, as we should understand it today, was
   slender to the point of emaciation. But as an interpretive
   sociologist he has had few equals."

2 BOLLER, PAUL F., Jr. American Thought in Transition: The
   Impact of Evolutionary Naturalism, 1865-1900. Chicago: Rand
   McNally & Co., pp. 88, 175-98.
   Provides biographical information and describes Veblen's
   major ideas and, in some cases, critical reaction to his writings.
   Notes Veblen's hostility to business and his fondness for the
   long-forgotten peaceful state of man. In some of his work Veblen
   gave the impression that he regarded the United States "as a kind
   of vast theater of the absurd." Writes that Veblen cherished the
   values of liberty, equality, and democracy but felt that these
   ideals would never be achieved through war and predation.

3 CORNEHLS, J.V. "On the Use and Misuse of Veblen's 'Evolutionary Economics.'" Oxford Economic Report 21
   (November):433-37.
   Challenges Professor Sowell's interpretation of Veblen's
   economics. Argues that Veblen was critical of classical economics because the system was closed and limited. Argues that
   Sowell has misinterpreted Veblen's critique. Responds to
   Sowell's position that Veblen approved of classical economic
   practices with only some reservations. See 1967.17.

4 FURNAS, J.C. The Americans: A Social History of the United
   States, 1587-1914. New York: G.P. Putnam's Sons, pp. 882-84,
   923, 925-26.
   Claims that Veblen "produced a psychology of the culture of
   private property." Only by restoring free will to economic
   behavior could Veblen denounce the plutocratic values so con-
   spicuously displayed at the turn of the century. Calls Veblen
   pessimistic, even nihilistic. "Veblen's implicit gospel of hate
   and black destructiveness became eventual preparation for the New
   Left of the 1960s. For our purposes it is a striking token of
   America's growing cultural independence—it was a homegrown radicalism that, like the industrial union, proved more important to
   following generations than to its own."

5   GRESSLEY, GENE M.   Review of <u>Thorstein</u> <u>Veblen:</u>   <u>The</u> <u>Carleton</u>
    <u>College</u> <u>Veblen</u> <u>Seminar</u> <u>Essays</u>, edited by Carlton C. Qualey.
    <u>Library</u> <u>Journal</u> 94 (January):68.
        "Veblen reached high eminence in American intellectual
    thought with his trenchant social criticism and his iconoclastic
    economics."

6   HERMAN, SONDRA R.   <u>Eleven</u> <u>against</u> <u>the</u> <u>War:</u>   <u>Studies</u> <u>in</u> <u>Amer-</u>
    <u>ican</u> <u>Internationalist</u> <u>Thought</u>.   Stanford, Calif.:   Hoover
    Institution Press, pp. 150-78, 217, 221-26, 228-29.
        Portrays Veblen as a catalyst for radical discontent.
    Basing his instincts theory on the new psychology and anthro-
    pology, Veblen tried to determine why men fight. Veblen's ideas
    concerning the relationship between war and business are explained.
    His dislike of nationalism is noted, as well as his proposals for
    peace, a possibility about which he was nonetheless skeptical.
    Credits Veblen for pointing out rather early that capital invest-
    ment in the underdeveloped areas would not benefit the native
    population.   Veblen eventually came to despair over the common
    man's patriotism and turned his attention to the engineers and
    the possibility of revolution.

7   LEIBENSTEIN, HARVEY.   "Bandwagon, Snob, and Veblen Effects in
    the Theory of Consumer's Demand."   In <u>Readings</u> <u>in</u> <u>Micro-</u>
    <u>economics</u>.   Edited by D.R. Kamerschen.   New York: John Wiley
    and Sons, pp. 95-119.
        Reprint of 1950.10; 1968.12.   Reprinted: 1975.8.   Incor-
    porated into a chapter of a book: 1976.13.   See also 1978.1.

8   MAYBERRY, THOMAS C.   "Thorstein Veblen on Human Nature."
    <u>American</u> <u>Journal</u> <u>of</u> <u>Economics</u> <u>and</u> <u>Sociology</u> 28 (July):315-24.
        Argues that Veblen "operates with a normative theory of
    human nature" where that theory functions as a guiding principle
    rather than an empirical theory.   Explains Veblen's theory of
    instincts and concludes that his "description of human nature is
    not a neutral scientific description."   His theory of human
    nature is a device "used to interpret, explain and evaluate any
    facts concerning 'schemes of life' or social institutions."   It
    is clear that Veblen utilizes a moral vocabulary in order to
    approve or disapprove--he is not, correctly speaking, a detached
    social scientist.

9   MICHELMAN, IRVING S.   <u>Business</u> <u>at</u> <u>Bay:</u>   <u>Critics</u> <u>and</u> <u>Heretics</u>
    <u>of</u> <u>American</u> <u>Business</u>.   New York: Augustus M. Kelley,
    pp. 1-63, pp. 65-291 passim.
        Provides considerable biographical information and treats
    Veblen as a major critic of business.   Notes his puritanical
    streak and his careful avoidance of the label "revolutionary."
    For all his grousing about business, Veblen is squarely in the
    American tradition.   Muses about what he might have thought of
    Henry Ford, who actually shared many of Veblen's misgivings about
    capitalism and his affection for efficiency.   Also relates

Veblen's ideas to those of Herbert Marcuse, John Kenneth
Galbraith, and others. Claims that Veblen's theory of industrial
sabotage by businessmen is tendentious and unproved and most of
his claims turn out to rest on "foundations of sand." Nonetheless, the "morose" Veblen, always the nonconformist outsider, had
a gift for prophecy.

10   MORGAN, H. WAYNE. Review of Thorstein Veblen: The Carleton
      College Veblen Seminar Essays, edited by Carlton C. Qualey.
      American Historical Review 74 (April):1371-72.
           Comments briefly on the collected articles. States that
      Veblen overestimated the role of business in politics.

11   RADER, BENJAMIN G. Review of Thorstein Veblen: The Carleton
      College Veblen Seminar Essays, edited by Carlton C. Qualey.
      Journal of American History 55 (March):874-75.
           Writes that the collection of essays is of mixed value.

12   RUCKER, DARNELL. The Chicago Pragmatists. Minneapolis:
      University of Minnesota Press, pp. 13, 18, 142-48, 153-56.
           Discusses Veblen's role and influence during his stay at
      the University of Chicago. The parallels and differences between
      Veblen and the Chicago Pragmatists are treated.

13   SMITH, BENJAMIN. "Political Theory of Institutional Eco-
      nomics." Ph.D. dissertation, University of Texas, Austin.
           Argues that Veblen exerted an important influence on
      Wesley C. Mitchell, C. Wright Mills, and John Kenneth Galbraith.
      There are also important parallels between his work and that of
      John R. Commons although Commons was more conservative. Veblen's
      critics have mistakenly claimed that he was an advocate of the
      gospel of efficiency, constant economic quantities, and technol-
      ogy. A close reading of Veblen shows that these claims are not
      true.

14   SOWELL, THOMAS. "Veblen's Higher Learning After Fifty Years."
      Journal of Economic Issues 3 (December):66-78.
           Discusses Veblen's work on universities and colleges, The
      Higher Learning in America. Veblen was critical of business in-
      fluence on the conduct of the university. Although much of what
      he wrote has contemporary significance, he failed to note that
      pressures other than those stemming from the business community
      influence the behavior of the university--the faculty themselves,
      government, and in special cases, military and ecclesiastical
      groups.

15   VINOKUR, ANNIE. Thorstein Veblen et la tradition dissidente
      dans la pensée économique americaine [Thorstein Veblen and the
      dissident tradition in American economic thought]. Paris:
      R. Pichon et R. Durand-Auzias, pp. 1-156.
           Covers Veblen's critiques of orthodox theory and capital-
      ism, his cultural analysis, and soviet of technicians. Holds

that he was the leading figure in American institutional economics and his role as a dissenting economist can be explained in
part by the fact that he hailed from a socially marginal background. Veblen's work is noteworthy for its penetrating and
original critique of neoclassical economics. His theory is also
significant for its introduction of Darwinian evolutionism into
economic analysis. Veblen's theory of business cycles and his
prophecy of fascist barbarism make him an important figure in the
history of American social thought.

16   VISSER, DERK. "The German Captain of Enterprise: Veblen's
      Imperial Germany Revisited." Explorations in Entrepreneurial
      History 6 (Spring-Summer):309-28.
          Claims that the study of German captains of industry "shows
      that Germany's economic development was a continuous and cumula-
      tive process, refuting Veblen's thesis of the sudden phenomenal
      industrial expansion that was an incidental result of the politi-
      cally inspired unification of 1870." Veblen's study has also
      added "to the myth of German technical proficiency" by depicting
      Germans as "non-wasteful." See also 1966.9.

1970

*1   ARON, RAYMOND. Introduction to Theorie de la classe de loisir
      [The Theory of the Leisure Class]. Paris: Gallimard, pages
      unknown.
      Source: 1971.9, p. 977.

2   AYRES, CLARENCE I. "Institutionalism and Economic Develop-
      ment." Social Science Quarterly 50 (March):1034-54.
          Writes that many scholars have found it impossible to
      dissociate Veblen's conception of technology from the rubrics in
      which he couched it. In so doing, they have overlooked an impor-
      tant notion. As is often the case, Veblen's language and "in-
      stinct" psychology have made it difficult to get at his sound
      points.

3   HAMILTON, DAVID. Evolutionary Economics: A Study of Change
      in Economic Thought. Albuquerque: University of New Mexico
      Press, 132 pp. passim.
      Reprint of 1953.4 with a new title.

4   KEARNEY, EDWARD N. "Thurman Arnold, Social Critic: The
      Satirical Challenge to Orthodoxy. Albuquerque: University of
      New Mexico Press, pp. 11-14, 16, 18, 25, 28, 33, 35, 55-56.
          Assesses Veblen's role in the tradition of dissent which
      influenced Thurman Arnold. Stresses Veblen's distinction between
      business and industry and finds his ethical norm in the "instinct
      of workmanship." Veblen is viewed as a critic of orthodox theo-
      ries with no stated pretentions to reform.

5   LAUMANN, EDWARD O., and JAMES S. HOUSE. "Living Room Styles and Social Attributes: The Patterning of Material Artifacts in a Modern Urban Community." Sociology and Social Research 54 (April):321-42.
Refers to Veblen and other social theorists to test theories and ascertain patterns of material consumption in households. Veblen's "notion of the standard-setting function of the leisure in establishing matters of taste and style in consumption" is utilized and found to be correct in some, but not all, cases.

6   MAIER, CHARLES S. "Between Taylorism and Technocracy." Journal of Contemporary History 5, no. 2:27-61.
Discusses Veblen's prescriptions for rule by technicians. Argues that Veblen probably misunderstood the temper of the engineers.

7   ROMANO, RICHARD, and MELVIN LEIMAN. Views on Capitalism. Beverly Hills, Calif.: Glencoe Press, pp. 318-19, 352-54.
Summarizes some major ideas in Veblen's work and notes both similarities and differences between him and Marxist writers. Sees Veblen as hostile to capitalism although he was not fully committed to any alternative economic arrangement.

1971

1   ALLEN, FRANCIS R. Socio-Cultural Dynamics: An Introduction to Social Change. New York: Macmillan Co., pp. 170-80.
Assesses Veblen's contribution to a theory of social change. Finds Veblen guilty of overgeneralizing his critique of business enterprise and improperly lumping together different types of economic activities. Veblen moreover failed to demonstrate that industry is the basic factor (independent variable) in socioeconomic dynamics and business secondary (dependent variable). It does not follow that the solution to abuses in business is to entrust the operation of the economy to production-oriented engineers or technicians.

2   ARANDA, THEODORE ROOSEVELT. "Thorstein Veblen on Education." Ph.D. dissertation, University of Illinois, Urbana-Champaign.
Argues that there is a great deal of validity in Veblen's indictment of the pervasive influence of business on American education. Veblen's writings are important because they show how and why business has come to infiltrate education to such a large degree. Describes Veblen's theory of instincts and his critique of American culture and relates them to all levels of the American system of education. Veblen's analytical framework lends itself to a study of current educational problems and demonstrates the overwhelming power of business in contrast to the relative low status and power of education. It should not be surprising then

that some educators will emulate business practices in the hope
of enhancing their prestige.

3   ARONOWITZ, STANLEY. "Does the United States Have a New
     Working Class?" In The Revival of American Socialism.
     Edited by George Fischer. New York: Oxford University
     Press, pp. 188-216.
          Credits Veblen with anticipating recent debates over the
     conservative nature of organized trade unions and the role that
     technical experts would play in industrial society. Stresses
     that Veblen was neither technocrat nor elitist; he simply wished
     to comprehend the situation as it existed. Although he acutely
     recognized the important function of corporate managers, he
     (through no fault of his own) did not yet see the distinctions
     between technocrats and technicians.

4   BREIT, WILLIAM, and ROGER L. RANSOM. "Thorstein Veblen--The
     Abrogation of Consumer Sovereignty." In The Academic Scrib-
     blers: American Economists in Collision. New York: Holt,
     Rinehart, and Winston, pp. 33-44.
          Asserts that Veblen's work on consumer behavior abrogates
     the claim that the consumer is sovereign. Veblen has largely
     succeeded in establishing the view that consumer preferences are
     molded by exogenous factors, especially the existence of status
     emulation. Veblen's influence on later public policy provides a
     rationale for government intervention in the market to alter
     consumer choice in the direction of satisfaction of organic needs
     rather than emulatory consumption. Although Veblen died without
     succeeding in setting economics on what he considered to be the
     right track, his influence on succeeding generations of econo-
     mists was to become continually more pronounced. It culminated
     in the writings of Galbraith, where Veblen's efficiency experts
     and conspicuous consumers were to "reappear in a form and at a
     time that seemed eminently ripe for them."

5   COSER, LEWIS A. "Thorstein Veblen, 1857-1929." In Masters of
     Sociological Thought. New York: Harcourt Brace Jovanovich,
     pp. 262-302.
          Provides a biographical account of Veblen and an exposition
     of his ideas. Veblen's "main thrust" comes in his "discussion of
     contemporary or near-contemporary society." "Veblen is at his
     best when he analyzes the various means by which men attempt to
     symbolize their high standing in the continuous struggle for
     competitive advantage." Praises his contribution to both the
     sociology of knowledge and functional analysis. The most endur-
     ing aspect of Veblen's sociology is his "theory of the socially
     induced motivations for competitive behavior" rather than his
     theory of instincts. States the major influences on Veblen were
     Herbert Spencer and Edward Bellamy and then Marx. His debt to
     pragmatism and the populist movement is also noted. While not a
     thinker of the first rank, Veblen's seminal thoughts are likely
     to "stimulate social theory for a long time to come." States

that Veblen "was more nearly a sociological Montaigne than a sociological Weber. His place in the ongoing history of social thought will be largely determined retroactively by future generations of scholars."

6   DAWSON, HUGH JOSEPH. "The Rhetoric of Veblen." Ph.D. dissertation, University of Illinois, Urbana.
        Analyzes Veblen's rhetoric in light of Kenneth Burke's criticism. Shows how Veblen's rhetoric is related "to his life, the behavior and values of his society, and universal human history." Examines Veblen's psychogenetic theory of social evolution, his understanding of social history, his criticism of contemporary society, and his expectations regarding the future. Emphasizes Veblen's use of irony and his unique rhetorical ability. Argues that Veblen is more than philosopher and historian-- he is also a prophetic writer; he has "translated man's essence into myth." Defends him against the charge that his writing is essentially negative.

7   DOWNS, ROBERT B. "Predatory Man: Thorstein Veblen's The Theory of the Leisure Class." In Famous American Books. New York: McGraw-Hill Book Co., pp. 198-205.
        Highlights some major points in The Theory of the Leisure Class. Claims that there is "little dissent from the view that he was one of the most remarkable intellects produced by America."

8   FERGUSON, FRANCIS PERCY. "Analysis, Interpretation, and Institutional Change: Marx and the Institutionalists, Commons and Veblen." Ph.D. dissertation, University of Wisconsin, Madison.
        Veblen and John R. Commons are compared with Karl Marx on the topics of theories of history, the capitalist crisis, and the utopian vision. Asserts that in spite of differences between the two Americans and Marx, all are in fundamental agreement. Argues that Veblen went furthest in developing a theory of culture and ideology but never did develop a psychological theory capable of explanation.

9   FRIEDMAN, GEORGES. "Veblen: un precurseur" [Veblen: a precursor]. Annales: économies, sociétés, civilisations [Annals: economies, societies, civilizations] 26 (September-October):977-81.
        A positive assessment of Veblen's impact and relevance. Feels that Veblen achieved more as a moralist and social anthropologist than as a critic of classical economics. Writes that Veblen was an original spirit and one who is not easily categorized.

10 LAWSON, R. ALAN. The Failure of Independent Liberalism (1930-1941). New York: G.P. Putnam's Sons, pp. 13-310 passim.
        Shows Veblen's influence on such prominent figures of the 1930s as John Dewey, Lewis Mumford, Paul Douglas, Stuart Chase,

Alfred Bingham, Thomas Amlie, George Soule, and others. Emphasis is on Veblen's critique of capitalism and higher education and his elucidation of the cultural incidence of the machine process.

11   LAYTON, EDWIN T., Jr. The Revolt of the Engineers: Social Responsibility and the American Engineering Profession. Cleveland: Press of Case Western Reserve University, pp. 1, 64, 226-27.
        Asserts that Veblen's point to the contrary, business and science may in fact benefit each other. Feels that Veblen was in a sense an optimist in thinking that the tension between business and engineering was reconcilable. Deals with Veblen's attempts to recruit engineers to his programs and ideas. See also 1956.6; 1962.4.

12   NAMASAKA, BOAZ NALIKA. "William B. Dubois and Thorstein B. Veblen: Intellectual Activists of Progressivism, A Comparative Study, 1900-1930." Ph.D. dissertation, Claremont Graduate School.
        Compares the economic, social, educational, and political ideas of Dubois and Veblen. Argues that both thinkers believed in evolutionary progress and the need for socialism and economic planning to end the injustices and waste caused by capitalism. While both men began as writers, they eventually "moved from theoretical activism to practical planning." Provides biographical information on the two thinkers and their ideas concerning both domestic and international affairs and assesses those ideas within the context of the progressive era.

13   SPIEGEL, HENRY W. The Growth of Economic Thought. Englewood Cliffs, N.J.: Prentice-Hall, pp. 628-34.
        Explains Veblen's major ideas on economics and subjects them to criticism. Veblen is faulted for denigrating the higher law tradition as well as for his false dichotomy between captains of industry and productive technicians.

1972

1   BEITZINGER, A.J. A History of American Political Thought. New York: Dodd, Mead, & Co., pp. 444-47, 455, 524.
        Provides a general summary of Veblen's major ideas. Focuses on Veblen's instinct theory, the relationship between technology and social change, the stages of history, and his critique of business and politics.

2   CHAMBERLAIN, J.E. "Oscar Wilde and the Importance of Doing Nothing." Hudson Review 25 (Summer):194-218.
        Argues that Veblen missed the point concerning the psychological function of art. It is both used and useless--it satisfies the urge to "abstraction" as well as the urge to "empathy."

Veblen's analysis is one-sided in that he sees only the need for conspicuous display.

3   CHARNEY, GEORGE. "Thorstein Veblen." New Republic 166 (22 January):30-32.
    Recounts Veblen's life and reconsiders the impact of The Theory of the Leisure Class. Compares Veblen with Marx, stating that "Veblen's emphasis was on the mythology of business rather than on its exploitative character." Veblen is important for recognizing the role that science was to play in shaping social forces and "because of his brilliant and courageous demonstration of the role of the critic at an important juncture in history." Veblen, however, tended to underestimate the force of democratic institutions in this country.

4   CYWAR, ALAN SIGMUND. "An Inquiry into American Thought and the Determinate Influence of Political, Economic, and Social Factors in the Early Twentieth Century: Bourne, Dewey, Dubois, Nearing, Veblen, and Weyl." Ph.D. dissertation, University of Rochester.
    Describes Veblen's theories and points to his major influences. Argues that Veblen's value structure was permeated by ambivalence; he endorsed rule by the engineers but was fond of democracy. Veblen was a materialist, yet he could not commit himself to thoroughgoing prediction. Asserts that Veblen elaborated a sociology of knowledge through which he tried to show how modes of thought in contemporary capitalist society were but slight modifications of earlier barbarian modes. Veblen's work in social science made him the preeminent figure in American political economy.

5   GRUCHY, ALLAN G. Contemporary Economic Thought. Clifton, N.J.: Augustus M. Kelley, pp. 1, 16-36, 40-130 passim.
    Sees Veblen as the major figure in the founding of institutional economics. He wrote in a time, however, when there was less governmental intervention in the economic sphere than there is today. Surveys Veblen's major economic ideas, including his critique of orthodox economics, his famous dichotomy between industry and business, and his critique of the latter. Argues that Veblen failed to look at industrialization in as critical a fashion as he did business. He also failed to do much with value theory and might have been much more systematic in his writings in both micro- and macroeconomic theory. In general, Veblen is vague concerning the future course of the economy under industrialization.

6   McILVAINE, ROBERT M. "Dos Passos's Reading of Thorstein Veblen." American Literature 44 (November):471-74.
    Claims that Veblen's influence on Dos Passos was so persuasive that Dos Passos must have read Veblen at a young and impressionable age. States also that the young Dos Passos more than likely read Veblen's The Theory of Business Enterprise where, in

a footnote, Veblen referred to the testimony before the U.S.
Industrial Commission of Dos Passos's father.

7   . "Thorstein Veblen and American Naturalism." Ph.D.
dissertation, Temple University.
   Discusses Veblen's relationship to literary naturalism.
Claims that Veblen influenced such writers as Robert Herrick,
John Dos Passos, Sinclair Lewis, F. Scott Fitzgerald, and
Nathanael West and Veblenian themes can be found in the novels of
Harold Frederic, Kate Chopin, and Frank Norris. Compares Veblen
with Theodore Dreiser, noting the similarity of their views
regarding life in capitalist society. Argues that the naturalist
authors all agree with Veblen's charge that modern society is too
barbarian. Maintains that The Theory of the Leisure Class does a
better job of describing what actually happens in American naturalist novels than does purely literary theory and that "Veblen
is the key figure in the second great American literary movement,
the naturalistic."

8   MILLER, EDYTHE S. "Veblen and Womens' Lib: A Parallel."
Journal of Economic Issues 6 (September):75-86.
   Argues that Veblen's analysis of the role of women in
society is valid and instructive. Veblen is correct in stating
that society views women as objects, property, and symbols of
status.

9   SPENGLER, JOSEPH J. "Veblen on Population and Resources."
Social Science Quarterly 52 (March):361-78.
   Claims that population plays a secondary role in Veblen's
evolutionary approach. For Veblen population growth is under
"the dominance of two sets of forces, one making for growth of
net product and the other making for curtailment of output and
unproductive use of that which was produced. . . . Perhaps
Veblen oversaw an Age of Overkill in which man's capacity for
waste would keep pace with whatever increase he might achieve in
his capacity to produce."

10   STANFIELD, J.R. "Veblen's 'Revolutionary Overturn' and The
New Industrial State." Review of Social Theory 1
(September):12-18.
   Compares Veblen with Galbraith and shows the similarities
and differences between them. The two are probably closest in
their views of the technostructure. They differ, however, in
that Veblen stresses pecuniary profit (maximation of earnings)
while Galbraith sees "a level of earnings sufficient to sustain
or enhance the autonomy and prestige of the technostructure" as
primary. Differences can also be seen in their respective attitudes toward labor and advertising.

11   TILMAN, RICK. "Veblen's Ideal Political Economy and Its
Critics." American Journal of Economics and Sociology 31
(July):307-17.

Argues against those who charge that Veblen was a technocratic elitist. Critics of Veblen such as Bell and Riesman
distort Veblen's work by overemphasizing aspects of The Engineers
and the Price System. In actuality, Veblen's values of egalitar-
ianism and his anarchist tendencies clearly overshadow any commit-
ment to elitism. There can be found in Veblen a "dialectical
tension between anarchism and centralism"; any recognition on
Veblen's behalf of the need for planning does not entail a preference for elitism.

12   WEED, FRANK. "Thorstein Veblen's Sociology of Knowledge."
      Review of Social Theory 1 (September):1-11.
      Claims that Veblen has made a significant contribution to
the sociology of knowledge. Veblen started with Kant and detailed the effect of machine technology on habits of thought.
His work is, however, often marred by a clumsy set of instincts
and vague concepts. For Veblen, knowledge within a society is to
a great extent influenced by dominant social institutions.

13   WILLIAMS, WILLIAM DEAN. "The Mathematics of Veblenian Eco-
      nomics." Ph.D. dissertation, Union Graduate School.
      Subjects various elements of Veblen's economic theory to
mathematical analysis; cites, for example, his income, employ-
ment, productivity, investment, and consumption theories. Claims
that Veblen has been unduly neglected as an economic theorist and
hopes to help rectify this through a systematic presentation of
his work. Veblenian economics offers a genuine alternative to
orthodox economics by emphasizing dynamics and growth. Sees
Veblen as a heterodox economist.

1973

1   ANON. Review of The Higher Learning in America. In Thorstein
      Veblen: Essays, Reviews, and Reports, Previously Uncollected
      Writings. Edited by Joseph Dorfman. Clifton, N.J.:
      Augustus M. Kelley, pp. 659-64.
      Reprint of 1919.4.

2   BARKIN, KENNETH D. "Germany's Path to Industrial Develop-
      ment." Laurentian University Review 5 (June):11-33.
      Refers to Veblen's explanation of Germany's rapid indus-
trial growth near the turn of the century. Agrees with his
theory in its essentials but demurs on his contention that rapid
growth would do nothing to materially benefit the "common man."

3   BENCHLY, ROBERT C. "The Dullest Book of the Month; The Theory
      of the Leisure Class: Dr. Thorstein Veblen Gets the Crown of
      Deadly Nightshade." In Thorstein Veblen: Essays, Reviews,
      and Reports, Previously Uncollected Writings. Edited by

Joseph Dorfman. Clifton, N.J.: Augustus M. Kelley,
pp. 637-42.
Reprint of 1919.7.

4   BERGEN, TIMOTHY J., Jr. "The Sociological Mind of Thorstein
     Veblen." Journal of Thought 8 (July):224-33.
     Considers Veblen's views on sociology, politics, and educa-
tion. Emphasizes his critique of pecuniary culture. Draws heavily on secondary sources.

5   BROYARD, ANATOLE. "Lumps for the Leisure Class." New York
     Times, 23 April, p. 31.
     Reviews The Theory of the Leisure Class. Describes the
book as "the most original, ironical and revealing analysis ever
to be made of American society." Suggests that Veblen's sociology has worn better than his economics and his "instinct of
workmanship" is "now a matter of wistful memory." "His prose had
a deadpan humor that was the intellectual equivalent of Buster
Keaton and W.C. Fields."

6   CLARK, JOHN MAURICE. "Thorstein Bunde Veblen, 1857-1929." In
     Thorstein Veblen: Essays, Reviews, and Reports, Previously
     Uncollected Writings. Edited by Joseph Dorfman. Clifton,
     N.J.: Augustus M. Kelley, pp. 595-600.
     Reprint of 1929.3.

7   CORBO, CLAUDE. "Les théories épistémologiques et sociales de
     T.B. Veblen (1857-1929)" [The epistemological and social theo-
     ries of T.B. Veblen (1857-1929)]. Ph.D. dissertation, Univer-
     sity of Montreal.
     Analyzes the epistomological basis of Veblen's theories.
Argues that the quasi-Kantian aspects of Veblen's preconceptions
must be distinguished from the pragmatic and positivistic assumptions normally associated with science. Also analyzes his social
theories and pinpoints certain problems. Praises Veblen's ideas
concerning fascism, technocratic socialism, and capitalist
evolution.

8   DORFMAN, JOSEPH, ed. "New Light on Veblen." In Thorstein
     Veblen: Essays, Reviews, and Reports, Previously Uncollected
     Writings. Clifton, N.J.: Augustus M. Kelley, pp. 5-326.
     Presents material on Veblen discovered since the author
published Thorstein Veblen and His America in 1934. This work
contains additional information concerning Veblen's life, work,
contributions to learning, and general influence. Also contains
anecdotes, references to correspondence, and scholarly opinions
of Veblen's writings. Considers Veblen to be "the most creative
of American economists of our age."

9   GALBRAITH, JOHN KENNETH. Introduction to The Theory of the
     Leisure Class. Boston: Houghton Mifflin Co., pp. v-xxv.
     Reprint of 1973.10 with minor stylistic changes.
Reprinted: 1979.7.

10 _____ . "A New Theory of Thorstein Veblen." American Heritage .
    24 (April):32-40.
       Provides a biographical sketch and highlights Veblen's
    major ideas. Attempts to separate Veblen the man from Veblen the
    legend. Veblen is the nearest thing to an academic legend we
    have in the United States. He is to academia what Scott
    Fitzgerald is to fiction and the Barrymores are to the theatre.
    Reprinted with minor stylistic changes: 1973.9; 1979.7.

11 GUARALDO, ALBERTO. "Diffusione e critica dell'opera di
    Thorstein Veblen in Italia: alcuni testi chiave" [Diffusion
    and critique of the work of Thorstein Veblen in Italy: some
    key writings]. Quaderni di sociologia [Notebooks of
    sociology] 22 (January-March):62-68.
       Discusses the critical reception by Italians of Veblen's
    work. Reference is made to the critical comments by Benedetto
    Croce (1949.6), the "hasty" comments of Antonio Gramsci (1948.9),
    and the balanced observations of Franco Ferrarotti (1950.7).
    Writes that the issue of the relationship between Veblen and Marx
    has not been resolved.

12 HACKETT, FRANCIS. "An Inquiry into the Nature of Peace." In
    Thorstein Veblen: Essays, Reviews, and Reports, Previously
    Uncollected Writings. Edited by Joseph Dorfman. Clifton,
    N.J.: Augustus M. Kelley, pp. 651-57.
       Reprint of 1917.7; 1918.2.

13 HOWELLS, WILLIAM DEAN. "An Opportunity for American Fiction
    [First Paper]." In Thorstein Veblen: Essays, Reviews, and
    Reports, Previously Uncollected Writings. Edited by Joseph
    Dorfman. Clifton, N.J.: Augustus M. Kelley, pp. 630-33.
       Reprint of 1899.3.

14 _____ . "An Opportunity for American Fiction [Second Paper]."
    In Thorstein Veblen: Essays, Reviews, and Reports, Previously
    Uncollected Writings. Edited by Joseph Dorfman. Clifton,
    N.J.: Augustus M. Kelley, pp. 633-37.
       Reprint of 1899.4.

15 LEATHERS, CHARLES G., and JOHN S. EVANS. "Thorstein Veblen and
    the New Industrial State." History of Political Economy 5
    (Fall):420-37.
       Maintains that much of the institutional structure of the
    American economy described by Galbraith is a mature version of
    Veblen's "New Order of the early 1900's." Compares the kinship of
    ideas of Veblen and Galbraith in the areas of technology and
    institutional change. Similarities of viewpoint are noted re-
    specting the technostructure, organized labor, consumer manipula-
    tion, and interfirm competition. "The works of Galbraith and
    Veblen tend to lead the reader to the conclusion that the eco-
    nomic system is badly in need of reform." For comments, see

1980.14. For a reply to the comments, see 1980.6; for the rejoinder, 1981.9.

16   MacKENNA, STEPHEN. "The Luxury of Lazihead." In Thorstein
      Veblen: Essays, Reviews, and Reports, Previously Uncollected
      Writings. Edited by Joseph Dorfman. Clifton, N.J.:
      Augustus M. Kelley, pp. 615-19.
      Reprint of 1899.5.

17   McNULTY, PAUL J. "Hoxie's Economics in Retrospect: The
      Making and Unmaking of a Veblenian." History of Political
      Economy 5 (Fall):449-84.
          Demonstrates the influence of Veblen on Hoxie and explains
      why the latter eventually abandoned much of the Veblenian frame-
      work. Hoxie could not abide Veblen's pessimistic conclusions nor
      did he agree with the latter's views on "labor mentality" and
      economic determinism.

18   MITCHELL, WESLEY C. "Thorstein Veblen, 1857-1929." In
      Thorstein Veblen: Essays, Reviews, and Reports, Previously
      Uncollected Writings. Edited by Joseph Dorfman. Clifton,
      N.J.: Augustus M. Kelley, pp. 601-6.
      Reprint of 1929.7.

19   _____. "Thorstein Veblen, 1857-1929." In Thorstein Veblen:
      Essays, Reviews, and Reports, Previously Uncollected Writings.
      Edited by Joseph Dorfman. Clifton, N.J.: Augustus M. Kelley,
      pp. 606-14.
      Reprint of 1929.8.

20   O'DONNELL, L.A. "Rationalism, Capitalism, and the Entre-
      preneur: The Views of Veblen and Schumpeter." History of
      Political Economy 5 (Spring):199-214.
          Provides a biographical sketch of Veblen and notes the
      influences on his outlook. Veblen's ideas regarding business
      sabotage are discussed, as are the evolving stages of capitalism.
      Veblen held a negative view of entrepreneurs while Schumpeter's
      attitude was generally favorable.

21   TILMAN, RICK. "Thorstein Veblen: Incrementalist and Uto-
      pian." American Journal of Economics and Sociology 32
      (April):155-69.
          Argues that while critics have charged that Veblen fails to
      provide policy prescriptions, analysis of his work will reveal
      policy proposals of an incremental nature mixed in with those of
      a clearly utopian nature. Refers to various proposals and re-
      search articles that reveal Veblen's policy prescriptions. "A
      key to an understanding of the relationship between Veblen's role
      as a social critic and theorist, and his role as a policy-
      prescriber, is his use of ideal types as polar opposites; and his
      intermittent realization that society contains mixed types upon

whose growth and development depends the inexorable drift of history."

22   TUFTS, JAMES HAYDEN. Review of The Theory of Business Enterprise. In Thorstein Veblen: Essays, Reviews, and Reports, Previously Uncollected Writings. Edited by Joseph Dorfman. Clifton, N.J.: Augustus M. Kelley, pp. 643-50. Reprint of 1904.4.

23   WARD, LESTER F. Review of The Theory of the Leisure Class. In Thorstein Veblen: Essays, Reviews, and Reports, Previously Uncollected Writings. Edited by Joseph Dorfman. Clifton, N.J.: Augustus M. Kelley, pp. 619-30. Reprint of 1900.3; 1967.18.

1974

1   ANDERSON, CHARLES. The Political Economy of Class. Englewood Cliffs, N.J.: Prentice-Hall, pp. 2, 80-173 passim, 205, 222, 241-85 passim, 324, 331-32.
   Believes that he has written a Marxist sociological critique of class-stratified capitalist society in which Veblen's work on social class is presented as a part of the Marxist tradition. Veblen is seen as sharing with Marx a belief that capitalism tends toward overproducing exchange values and responding by cutting back on production. He also shares with Marx a similar view of the relationships between property, class, and power. Feels that critics of Marx and Veblen fail to visualize a truly socially efficient productive system planned and controlled by the workers themselves, a system where pride and satisfaction in the quality and social contribution of labor overrides wage labor, private appropriation, and emulation of unearned wealth and consumption. In the realm of status, critics fail to grasp that achievement and workmanship may produce differential prestige without correlating class and economic inequalities and that the money economy can itself be eliminated. However, somewhat contrary to Marx, Veblen held that the working class is exploited but nonrevolutionary and nonradical; this is a deficient view because it fails to identify any real, serious oppositional efforts and tendencies within the working class.

2   ANON. Review of Thorstein Veblen: Essays, Reviews, and Reports, Previously Uncollected Writings, edited and with an introduction, "New Light on Veblen," by Joseph Dorfman. Choice 10 (February):1908.
   Claims that "Veblen is a seminal figure in modern social philosophy, and his writings, once recognized only in the circle of American progressive intellectuals, are now acknowledged by European social scientists as profound and prescient, comparable to the scholarship of Weber and Mannheim."

3   Den HOLLANDER, A.N.J. "Thorstein Veblen." In Hoofdfiguren
     uit de sociologie [Major figures in sociology]. Edited by L.
     Rademaker and E. Petersma. Utrecht: Spectrum; Antwerp:
     Intermediair, pp. 138-55.
        Provides biographical information and surveys some of
     Veblen's major contributions to sociology. Considers Veblen to
     be a very creative and original theorist who influenced such
     thinkers as A.A. Berle, Gardiner Means, Robert Brady, and others.

4   DOBRONRAVOV, I.S., ed. "Veblen, Thorstein." In Great Soviet
     Encyclopedia. Vol. 4. New York: Macmillan Co., p. 554. [No
     translator given].
        Claims that Veblen's ideas are contradictory and his theory
     combines petit-bourgeois utopianism with a critique of certain
     aspects of capitalism. He undervalued the importance of property
     and did not grasp the connection between substructure and super-
     structure. Credits Veblen with having exerted influence on Amer-
     ican non-Marxist sociology.

5   DOWD, DOUGLAS F. The Twisted Dream: Capitalist Development
     in the United States since 1776. Cambridge: Winthrop
     Publishers, pp. 4-293 passim.
        Writes that although Marx and Veblen have much in common,
     they differ in the following ways. Marx had a more coherent and
     more powerful economic theory of capitalist development than
     Veblen. On the other hand, the looseness and breadth of Veblen's
     analysis and the later period in which he wrote allowed him to
     examine the behavior and meaning of modern monopolistic business
     organization and the state in ways going beyond Marx. Thus, what
     is essential is to combine the strengths of Marx, Veblen, and
     Keynes with contemporary data and social analysis. Secondly,
     Veblen's "instinct of workmanship" virtually equates with Marx's
     notion of work as the life activity of human beings, in the sense
     that workmanship and what Veblen calls "the parental bent" refer
     to the production and reproduction of life. If Veblen is gloom-
     ier than Marx, part of the reason is that he sees workmanship and
     sportsmanship as running a sort of race between life- and death-
     giving activities, with little reason to believe that a society
     controlled by force and fraud would allow the race to be won by
     life. Neither Veblen nor Marx evince a "truly systematic under-
     standing of the state"; both, however, study society through a
     proper historical method. Revised: 1977.9.

6   FERRAROTTI, FRANCO. Il pensiero sociologico da August Comte a
     Max Horkheimer [Sociological thought from August Comte to Max
     Horkheimer]. Milan: Arnoldo Mondadori Editore, pp. 135-91.
        Provides a biographical treatment of Veblen's work. Argues
     that in order to understand Veblen one must look at his life.
     His experiences account for the sarcasm and bitterness of this
     American sociologist. Contains a bibliography of Veblen's
     writings and critical assessments by others.

7 _____. "Variazoni su Veblen" [Variations on Veblen]. Critica
   sociologica [Sociological critique] 29 (Spring):199.
      Argues that John Kenneth Galbraith's reduction of Veblen's
   social critique in The Theory of the Leisure Class to mere "deri-
   sion" is simplistic.

8 FORMAN, JAMES D. Capitalism: Economic Individualism to
   Today's Welfare State. New York: New Viewpoints, pp. 46-47.
      Describes Veblen's role in turn of the century attacks on
   capitalism and the foibles of the well-to-do.

9 GLYNN, KATHLEEN. "Thorstein Veblen: A New Critique." Case
   Western Reserve Journal of Sociology 6 (May):44-62.
      Explores Veblen's contribution to the history of ideas,
   especially his sociological insights and criticism. Treats
   Veblen's philosophical lineage, distinction between industrial
   and pecuniary employments, theories of social stratification, and
   sociology of knowledge. Compares his radicalism with that of
   C. Wright Mills. Contends that Veblen has contemporary relevance
   for sociology.

10 KAHN, JONATHAN. The Political Economy of Thorstein Veblen and
   John Kenneth Galbraith. Stanford Honors Essays in Humanities,
   no. 17. Stanford: N.p., 80 pp.
      Describes Veblen's ideas in the context of the modern
   liberal tradition. Veblen is compared with figures such as
   Sumner, Croly, Thurman Arnold, and Galbraith. Differences between Veblen and Galbraith, notably on unemployment, depression,
   and the pecuniary motives of businessmen, are stressed.

11 LEATHERS, CHARLES G., and JOHN S. EVANS. "Veblen's Ideal and
   the Contemporary U.S. Economy: A Contrast." American Journal
   of Economics and Sociology 33 (October):409-15.
      Rejects the contentions of writers such as Scott Gordon and
   Jay Gould that the modern corporate structure represents fulfill-
   ment of Veblen's prediction of rule by a soviet of technicians.
   If anything, the technostructure as described by Galbraith is an
   extension of what Veblen called the "business enterprise," and
   the latter would be wryly amused by the allegation that his
   prediction of rule by engineers had culminated in the modern
   business structure.

12 RIGAL, LOUIS. "Veblen et Marx" [Veblen and Marx]. Homme et
   la Societe [Man and Society] 31-32 (January-June):135-48.
      There are points of convergence and divergence between Marx
   and Veblen. Marx was a dialectical thinker whereas Veblen preferred the method of Darwinian evolutionism in his critique of
   Marx. Both emphasize the impact of technology on social struc-
   tures to explain social change. They largely agree that the
   leisure class is parasitical in nature and misuses the social
   surplus that it appropriates for its own use. However, Marx had

a more evolved and explicit theory of profits than Veblen, who
remained an aloof and isolated intellectual.

13   VERNON, RAYMOND. "The Theory of the Leisure Class." Daedalus
     103 (Winter):53-57.
         Submits that Veblen's books were on the whole remarkable
     but not very durable. Many find Veblen too old fashioned to fit
     their needs. Even if contemporary social activists agreed with
     Veblen's ideas they would be put off by his method of expression.
     Questions Veblen's distinction between business and industry,
     arguing that it does not seem to apply to the running of the
     modern corporate complex. Nonetheless, Veblen has had his in-
     fluence. "The clue to Veblen's genius lays in his alienation, in
     his resistance to the conventional wisdom of his time. . . ."

14   ZINGLER, ERVIN K. "Veblen vs. Commons: A Comparative Evalua-
     tion." Kyklos 27, fasc. 2:322-44.
         Compares the economic theories of Veblen and John R.
     Commons. Argues that Veblen was more the theorist and it was he
     who made the greater contribution to pure economic theory. The
     "moral absolute" in Veblen's theory stemmed from the instincts of
     workmanship and idle curiosity that also acted as forces of
     change in the economic system. Veblen's theory of economic
     development is designated as determinist, but he seeks to provide
     a psychological explanation of the actors involved.

                                   1975

1   ARROW, KENNETH J. "Thorstein Veblen as an Economic Theorist."
     American Economist 19 (Spring):5-9.
         Recounts the pervasive influence of Veblen's ideas at
     Columbia University's Economics Department in the early 1940s.
     Shows his links to neoclassical economics and his contributions
     as an economic theorist. Acknowledging that Veblen's ideas were
     at times inconsistent and incomplete by modern standards, claims
     nevertheless that he understood neoclassical thought very well
     and anticipated some very important notions. Veblen introduced
     the theme that "the requirements for optimization impose vastly
     greater demands on the calculating power of individuals than can
     be met, and too little attention is paid to the role of habit in
     individual decision making." Claims that Veblen, in opposition
     to the neoclassical theorists, distinguished sharply between
     vendibility and serviceability (private and social product). He
     recognized clearly the idea of monopolistic competition. The way
     in which Veblen anticipated the managerial theories of the firm
     of Berle and Means is also noted. His contribution to the theory
     of business cycles is treated, as well as his writings concerning
     the advantages of latecomers to industrialization or moderniza-
     tion. This latter proposition is subjected to a simple formal
     model to suggest modifications. "I think therefore that Veblen's
     intuition has not yet been formally modeled in modern growth

theory; it is clearly going to be a hard, though I would hope, rewarding task."

2　CRUISE, H.F.　"The Economic Historian and the Growth Debate." *Australian Economic History Review* 15 (September):83-106.
　　　"Thorstein Veblen ought to be coming back into vogue today." Attempts to show the relevance of Veblen's ideas to the debate over economic growth and conservation of resources. Emphasizes his dark prophecies concerning the "doom of contemporary institutions" and man's "incapacity to control his own future." A good reason to read Veblen is that he talked about the long-term trends of the total economy and sought to "evaluate one path of that economy in terms of another." Veblen's satirical style and use of put-ons are duly noted.

3　DENTE, LEONARD A.　"Veblen's Theory of Social Change." Ph.D. dissertation, New York University.
　　　Subsequently published in book form, see 1977.6.

4　EDGELL, STEPHEN.　"Thorstein Veblen's Theory of Evolutionary Change." *American Journal of Economics and Sociology* 34 (July):267-80.
　　　Suggests that most of Veblen's critics have "failed to comprehend the totality of his contribution. . . ." The core of Veblen's contribution lies in his "macro-economic sociology." Contends that the major influences on Veblen were Kant, Bellamy, and the evolutionist aproach of Darwin and Spencer. Provides examples of what he thinks are mistaken interpretations of Veblen's theory of social change and offers counterarguments. Places Veblen in the company of Marx and Weber as social theorists of industrial capitalism. Concludes by arguing that isolated elements of Veblen's thought must be understood in terms of his general theory and insufficient attention has been given to his theory of the processes that either encourage or discourage predatory or workmanlike behavior.

5　ELLIOT, JOHN, and JOHN COWNIE.　*Competing Philosophies in American Political Economics.* Pacific Palisades, Calif.: Goodyear Publishing Co., pp. 106-14.
　　　Writes that Veblen was the most iconoclastic economist of the era in which he lived. His theory was an alternative to both neoclassical economics and Marxism. Veblen's insights helped to undermine orthodox patterns of thought as well as the main power system.

6　HICKMAN, CHARLES A.　*J.M. Clark.* New York: Columbia University Press, pp. 71-73.
　　　Notes that Clark believed that Veblen's style and satire often bewildered critics but his broader contribution to the field obliged economists to reexamine their premises in order to gain greater objectivity.

7   KRAETZER, MARY C. "The Sociology of Knowledge of Thorstein
     Veblen and C. Wright Mills: A Study of the 'Radical' Tradi-
     tion in American Sociology." Ph.D. dissertation, Fordham
     University.
         Argues that an injustice was done to Veblen and C. Wright
     Mills by the "covert or overt excommunication of their work from
     their proper place in American intellectual history. Both men
     were not less, but, in some ways, more authentically emergent out
     of the Anglo-American Protestant tradition than the celebrated
     and 'established' thinkers such as Charles Peirce, William James
     and John Dewey." Both Veblen and Mills expressed the ethical
     individualism that originated in Puritan thought and continued in
     the pragmatic tradition. In this sense the "radical" tradition
     in America has been conservative. Working from the Puritan-
     Pragmatist viewpoint, both attacked the contamination of society
     and the warping of thought by its nonproductive and nonefficient
     elements--the leisure class and the power elite.

8   LEIBENSTEIN, HARVEY. "Bandwagon, Snob, and Veblen Effects in
     the Theory of Consumer's Demand." In Microeconomics:
     Selected Readings. Edited by E. Mansfield. New York:
     W.W. Norton & Co., pp. 12-30.
         Reprint of 1950.10; 1968.12; 1969.7. Incorporated into a
     chapter of a book: 1976.13. See also 1978.1.

9   MacRAE, DONALD. "The Sociologist of Money." Times Literary
     Supplement (London), 25 July, p. 824.
         Sees Veblen as part of an "underground" tradition in
     economics--unorthodox and grounded in social reality. This
     tradition goes back at least to Adam Smith and includes sub-
     sequent figures such as John Hobson. Shows how Veblen con-
     tributed to sociology through his originality and his elaboration
     of the thought of his predecessors. "Veblen's prose is arguably
     the most extraordinary in the history of the social sciences in
     the English language. It is not barbarous or incompetent, but it
     involves a vocabulary more than Latinate, with every sentence
     supplying a commentary on its own content, a sneer, an apology, a
     concealment, a joke, an evasion, perhaps ultimately a confession
     of weakness." Feels that Veblen both admired and deplored the
     world he saw. Considers Imperial Germany and the Industrial
     Revolution to be his "masterpiece." He saw more clearly than any
     previous writer that the "economic life is part of culture and
     that culture is in perpetual change."

10   MAI, LUDWIG H. "Thorstein Bunde Veblen." In Men and Ideas in
     Economics. Totowa, N.J.: Littlefield, Adams, & Co.,
     pp. 230-31.
         Provides a brief biographical sketch and sees Veblen as the
     founder of institutional economics. Notes his emphasis on evolu-
     tionary change and conflict and describes his criticisms of
     existing institutions and approaches to economics.

11   MUMFORD, LEWIS. "Thorstein Veblen." In Findings and
     Keepings. New York: Harcourt Brace Jovanovich, pp. 209-10.
     Excerpt of 1931.4.

12   NOE, FRANCIS, and KIRK W. ELIFSON. "An 'Invidious Compari-
     son,' Class and Status, 1920-60: Effects of Employment, Cost,
     and Time on Veblen's Theory of Class." American Journal of
     Economics and Sociology 34 (October):381-96.
           Focuses on time, employment, personal debt, and cost series
     as central in leisure class "outcome." Research findings tend to
     support Veblen's theory of the leisure class. Authors find many
     flaws in Veblen's theory but appear to agree with his "belief
     that the upper class possesses a superior advantage in asserting
     a right to leisure. . . ."

13   ROBBINS, LIONEL. Foreword to Thorstein Veblen and the Insti-
     tutionalists: A Study in the Social Philosophy of Economics,
     by David Seckler. Boulder: Colorado Associated University
     Press, pp. ix-xi.
           Writes that the institutionalists intensely admired Veblen,
     but as a school of economics institutionalism has failed to
     deliver the goods. Finds Veblen difficult to assess but admits
     that he was important and influential. Agrees with Seckler that
     Veblen had a "split personality"--part behaviorist, part
     humanist.

14   SECKLER, DAVID. Thorstein Veblen and the Institutionalists:
     A Study in the Social Philosophy of Economics. Boulder:
     Colorado Associated University Press, 190 pp.
           Analyzes major elements of Veblen's work. Claims that
     Veblen had a problem. "This problem was, in its most elemental
     terms, the problem of free will versus determinism. Veblen not
     only failed to solve this problem--a failure for which he can
     hardly be blamed; but he refused to 'choose up sides,' to create
     a consistent theory based on one or the other of these premises,
     and his fence-straddling over this issue was inexcusable." Sug-
     gests that there are actually two Veblens--one a behaviorist,
     the other a humanist. Adds that Veblen has not only been ruled
     out of economics but social philosophy as well; his method of
     grand theorizing is out of vogue.

15   Van ELDEREN, P.L., and A.J.M. WAGERMAKERS. "Thorstein Veblen
     over ledigheid en verspilling" [Thorstein Veblen on leisure
     and waste]. Sociale wetenschappen [Social science] 18,
     no. 3:153-69.
           Notes the relative lack of knowledge of Veblen in Holland
     and describes the major points of The Theory of the Leisure
     Class. While many think that Veblen was close to Marx, he was
     actually "a-Marxist." Veblen's approach was an intuitive-
     skeptical one more than a logical system of well-defined concepts
     or consistent hypotheses.

1976

1   BOULDING, KENNETH. Review of Thorstein Veblen and the Insti-
    tutionalists: A Study in the Social Philosophy of Economics,
    by David Seckler. Land Economics 52 (February):127-29.
        Argues that Veblen sacrificed truth and system for clever-
    ness and facile insight. Thinks that John R. Commons contributed
    more of substance than did Veblen but admits that Veblen can
    never again be accused of adopting a naive instinct theory.
    Allows further that Veblen should be credited with anticipating
    some of Boulding's ideas concerning the image as a source of
    behavior and his critique of Marx shows some sensitive insights.
    Concludes by arguing that Veblen is fundamentally a Darwinian,
    not a Marxist. See 1975.14.

2   BREIT, WILLIAM. Review of Thorstein Veblen and the Institu-
    tionalists: A Study in the Social Philosophy of Economics, by
    David Seckler. Journal of Economic Issues 10 (December):
    943-46.
        Argues that Veblen certainly understood the defects and
    dangers in behaviorism but also recognized the power that culture
    had over individual choice, and that is why he was ultimately
    unable to fully accept humanism. Contends that contemporary
    research regarding property rights, externalities, and public
    choice are indebted to the ground-breaking work of Veblen and his
    followers. See 1975.14.

3   COATS, A.W. "Clarence Ayres's Place in the History of Amer-
    ican Economics: An Interim Assessment." In Science and
    Ceremony: The Institutional Economics of C.E. Ayres. Edited
    by William Breit and William Patton Culbertson, Jr. Austin:
    University of Texas Press, pp. 23-48.
        Briefly discusses Ayres's intellectual debt to Veblen and
    Dewey.

4   DAY, RICHARD H. Review of Thorstein Veblen and the Institu-
    tionalists: A Study in the Social Philosophy of Economics, by
    David Seckler. Land Economics 52 (February):128-31.
        Thinks that Veblen was less confused over the conflict
    between behaviorism and humanism than Seckler alleges. Argues
    that Veblen's theory has a firm basis in modern ethological
    findings. See 1975.14.

5   DeGREGORI, THOMAS R. Review of Thorstein Veblen and the
    Institutionalists: A Study in the Social Philosophy of
    Economics, by David Seckler. Journal of Economic Issues
    10 (December):946-52.
        Argues that the book misinterprets Veblen. Veblen was
    neither positivist nor behaviorist; rather he was a humanist to
    the core, as were Dewey and Ayres. See 1975.14.

6   DIGGINS, JOHN P. "A Radical with Authority." <u>Chronicle of Higher Education</u> 13 (1 November):32.

While it might be said that Veblen was the leading problem child of higher education, he has nevertheless had a remarkable and enduring impact on learning. Points to both the strong and weak aspects of Veblen's <u>The Higher Learning in America</u>, calling attention especially to Veblen's recognition that commercial interests had come to predominate in our colleges and universities. Veblen understood what so many others did not—that thinking begins in wonder, not in "problem solving." "In Veblen contemporary higher education may find a unique social philosophy it sorely needs—a radical with authority."

7   _____. "Thorstein Veblen." <u>New Republic</u> 174 (13 March): 36-39.

Discusses the fluctuations of Veblen's stature. Mentions the reactions of various well-known sociologists and economists to his work. Brief analysis of <u>The Instinct of Workmanship</u>. Analyzes three issues explored by Veblen: alienation, reification, and mediation. Expresses belief in his Darwinian approach to history and attributes many of his most significant contributions to his Darwinian influence. Regards Veblen's discovery of the cultural hegemony of capitalism and the social stigma of labor as his most significant definition of the basic problems in contemporary society.

8   GRUCHY, ALLAN G. Review of <u>Thorstein Veblen and the Institutionalists: A Study in the Social Philosophy of Economics</u>, by David Seckler. <u>Journal of Economic Issues</u> 10 (December): 952-55.

Finds nothing new in the analysis of Veblen's philosophical underpinnings. All admit that Veblen did not deal definitively with the freewill versus determinism problem but adds "who has?" In spite of Veblen's philosophical and psychological limitations he was responsible for initiating a theoretical analysis of the evolving economic process that is lasting and important. See 1975.14.

9   HAMILTON, DAVID. Review of <u>Thorstein Veblen and the Institutionalists: A Study in the Social Philosophy of Economics</u>, by David Seckler. <u>Journal of Economic Issues</u> 10 (December): 955-57.

Argues that Veblen is misinterpreted. He did not espouse, a hedonistic position as Seckler contends. Also questions the reduction of humanism to extreme individualism. See 1975.14.

10   HARRINGTON, MICHAEL. <u>The Twilight of Capitalism</u>. New York: Simon and Schuster pp. 137, 145, 186, 197, 213.

Calls Veblen the "founding genius" of institutionalism and holds that this school of thought is "at least a cousin of Marxism." Veblen's faith in the engineers makes him a precursor of the technocrats.

11   KANEL, DON, and PETER DORNEN. Review of Thorstein Veblen and
     the Institutionalists: A Study in the Social Philosophy of
     Economics, by David Seckler. Land Economics 52
     (February):131-34.
        Agrees that Veblen refused to elaborate on the behaviorist
     aspect of his theory owing to his commitment to humanistic
     values. It is probably the case that Clarence Ayres extended
     this aspect of Veblen's thought. See 1975.14.

12   KAPP, K. WILLIAM. "The Nature and Significance of Institu-
     tional Economics." Kyklos 29, fasc. 2:209-32.
        Tries to demonstrate that institutional economists, includ-
     ing Veblen, have done more than just provide a criticism of
     orthodox economics--they have also pioneered the way for a cross-
     disciplinary approach to social problems. Early on, Veblen
     stressed the pivotal role of science and technology in social
     change. His theory of business enterprise laid the groundwork
     for the study of economic instability and his use of the princi-
     ple of circular interdependencies of a number of factors to
     analyze the leisure class, technology, and the business cycle is
     likewise an important contribution.

13   LEIBENSTEIN, HARVEY. Beyond Economic Man. Cambridge:
     Harvard University Press, pp. 48, 51-52, 62-67.
        Notes John Rae's and Veblen's contributions to a theory of
     conspicuous consumption. Consumer demand can be explained in
     terms of functional, nonfunctional, and speculative motivation.
     Sees the "Veblen effect" as a nonfunctional type of external
     effect on utility distinguished from the "bandwagon" and "snob"
     effects. Draws on 1950.10; 1968.12; 1969.7; 1975.8. See also
     1978.1.

14   LEVY, MARION J. "Clarence Ayres as a University Teacher." In
     Science and Ceremony: The Institutional Economics of C.E.
     Ayres. Edited by William Breit and William Patton Culbertson,
     Jr. Austin: University of Texas Press, pp. 181-86.
        Describes the intellectual relationship between Ayres and
     Veblen. Veblen was Ayres's starting point. "To this very day
     Veblen remains the one truly self-invented person of American
     Social Science."

15   RUSSETT, CYNTHIA EAGLE. "Thorstein Veblen: Darwinian, Skep-
     tic, Moralist." In Darwin in America: The Intellectual
     Response, 1865-1912. San Francisco: W.H. Freeman & Co.,
     pp. 147-71.
        Portrays Veblen as the complete Darwinian, critical of both
     Marxist teleology and the psychology of classical economic the-
     ory. Veblen's intellectual perspective was based on the notion
     of cumulative causation and pragmatic social psychology. His
     pessimism concerning the human prospect notwithstanding, Veblen
     occasionally displayed signs of a faith in mankind, even a uto-
     pian vision.

16   SCHNEIDER, LOUIS. Review of The Theory of the Leisure Class.
      Social Science Quarterly 57 (June):219-21.
          Claims that the book still has importance and vitality
      seventy-seven years after its original publication. Finds
      Veblen's treatment of the religious/economics connection weak and
      argues that he did not have much respect for evidence and his
      anthropology is "casual." Nonetheless the book has an impact
      that is hard to deny.

17   TIMASHEFF, NICHOLAS S., and GEORGE THEODORSON. Sociological
      Theory: Its Nature and Growth. 4th ed. New York: Random
      House, pp. 184-86, 188, 307.
          Summarizes Veblen's life and major ideas. Stresses his
      theory of the technological impact on thought processes and
      social change. Veblen made important contributions to the cri-
      tique of capitalism, the sociology of knowledge, the social
      nature of individual motivation, "and, in agreement with Cooley
      and Thomas the Social Source of Self-conception." Veblen's work
      also contributed to a more analytical notion of functionalism.
      He has influenced such diverse sociologists as David Riesman, C.
      Wright Mills, and Arthur K. Davis.

18   USELDING, PAUL. "Veblen as Teacher and Thinker in 1896-97."
      American Journal of Economics and Sociology 35 (October):
      391-99.
          Using the notes taken by James E. Hagerty, a graduate
      student at the University of Chicago, the author renders a depic-
      tion of Veblen's teaching in the years 1896-97. The notes indi-
      cate that by that time the Veblenian critique of classical
      economics "was reaching its definitive form." Attention is
      given to Veblen's insistence that psychological and teleological
      elements be purged from the science of economics. The Hagerty
      notes are approximately two pages in length and are reprinted in
      full in the appendix to the article.

19   WHITNEY, WILLIAM G. Review of Thorstein Veblen and the Insti-
      tutionalists: A Study in the Social Philosophy of Economics,
      by David Seckler. Annals of the American Academy of Political
      and Social Science 423 (January):209-10.
          Rejects the author's fundamental premise and suggests that
      Veblen was actually preoccupied with the tasks of providing an
      anthropological study of culture and a refutation of the subjec-
      tive utility theory in neoclassical economics. Veblen's work is
      more than satire, and we need more of his type of social philoso-
      phy. See 1975.14.

1977

1   AKIN, WILLIAM E. Technocracy and the American Dream: The
      Technocrat Movement, 1900-1941. Berkeley: University of
      California Press, pp. 2, 15-39 passim, 47, 71, 73, 119.

Describes Veblen's influence on and involvement in the
early stages of the technocratic movement and explains the basic
features of his theory. Contends that Veblen's writings provided
the intellectual groundwork for the movement, although Howard
Scott, a major figure in the movement, sought to minimize its
debt to Veblen. Scott's ideas can be seen as an attempt to
modify and elaborate on Veblen's writings.

2   BECKER, JAMES F. Introduction to Veblen's Theory of Social
     Change, by Leonard A. Dente. New York: Arno Press,
     unpaginated.
     Asserts that Veblen was successful in creating an evolu-
tionary explanation of economics, social development, and science
and its commercial utilization. Like Marx, Veblen perceived the
"drag of unserviceable activity." Notes Veblen's social-
psychological approach to the theory of unproductive labor and
his analysis of the subversion of science by pecuniary interests.
"What is at issue, after all, is not whether Marxism becomes
Veblenism or Veblenism Marxism, but whether or not both are to
function within a unified and serviceable social science."

3   _____. Marxian Political Economy. Cambridge: Cambridge
     University Press, pp. 22, 175, 233, 292-93, 296, 311, 313.
     Claims that Veblen's analysis of the relationship between
the engineers and managers is more penetrating than James
Burnham's. The problem with Veblen's analysis is methodological--
he does not extend his industrial/pecuniary dichotomy to an
analysis of class structure. He did not see the eventual
subjugation of the engineers by the managerial cadre of
nontechnicians.

4   BIGENWALD, MYLES M. "An Extension of Thorstein Veblen's The
     Theory of the Leisure Class to the Contemporary Consumption of
     Educational Services." Ph.D. dissertation, State University
     of New York, Buffalo.
     Discusses Veblen's ideas concerning conspicuous consumption
and empirically tests them as they relate to school district
spending. Generates a set of hypotheses and subhypotheses based
on Veblen's contention that the primary motive behind spending is
to enhance repute. Employing data from New York state school
districts, concludes that the hypotheses are generally correct.
Finds Veblen's ideas concerning display, leisure, and exploit to
be highly fruitful for purposes of testing in the field of educational expenditures.

5   CRAMER, DALE L., and CHARLES G. LEATHERS. "Veblen and
     Schumpeter on Imperialism." History of Political Economy 9
     (Summer):237-55.
     Explores the similarities and differences in Veblen's and
Schumpeter's theories of imperialism. Schumpeter's work laid
greater emphasis on the principle of rationalism in explaining
attitudes toward imperialism while Veblen's work placed more

emphasis upon the evolutionary process. Veblen's account is more humanistic than Schumpeter's in that it details the impact of imperialism on the common man. His theory of social change is also "more complex and more reassuring than Schumpeter's. He could argue that the very institutions that Schumpeter recognized as suppressing imperialism were already outmoded and contributed to the irrationality needed for the continuation of imperialism."

6   DENTE, LEONARD A. Veblen's Theory of Social Change. New York: Arno Press, 225 pp.
    Reconstructs Veblen's theories of social change and economic growth in order to illustrate the unity of his theoretical system and the important role of the technicians, scientists, and engineers within this system. Emphasizes Veblen's belief in the importance of political, cultural, psychological, and social elements in explaining social change and economic growth; his demonstration that economic stagnation is a chronic threat to capitalism because of the system of property relations upon which it is based; his alternative way of maximizing the rate of economic growth and level of economic welfare; the necessity for both productive and distributive efficiency in order to maximize the rate of economic growth; the resolution of the problems of proper allocation and employment of resources through avoidance of waste; and his focus on the problems of economic adjustment caused by cultural lag. Compares Veblen's theory of social change favorably with the theories of John Von Neumann, Joseph Schumpeter, and Karl Marx. Argues that in order to make Von Neumann's model more general, addition of the assumption of technological progress along with the Veblenian distinction between serviceability and disserviceable goods within a general theory of waste is needed. In contrast to Schumpeter's analysis of the process of "creative destruction" under which firms are created and destroyed, making the business cycle normal to capitalism, Veblen's analysis of the process of change under capitalism demonstrates that destruction will overshadow creativity with stagnation becoming a chronic threat. Both agree that in the long run mechanization and automation will bring a situation in which private property will cease to be functional and thus disappear. In the end, Veblen's "efficiency experts" will replace Schumpeter's "entrepreneurs." Contrasts Marx with Veblen to illuminate the Veblenian theory of economic waste and unproductive labor and demonstrate that Veblen's theoretical system differs from Marx's in that it is nonteleological. This book is based on a Ph.D. dissertation, see 1975.3.

7   DIGGINS, JOHN P. "Animism and the Origins of Alienation: The Anthropological Perspective of Thorstein Veblen." History and Theory 16 (May):113-36.
    Contrasts Marx and Veblen on alienation and the origin of private property. While Marx saw private property originating in the division of labor and surplus value, Veblen traced it to conquest and taking. Although Veblen believed that property

emerges out of conquest, he did not conclude that man is by
nature aggressive and acquisitive; rather, he claimed that man in
the savage state lost his peaceful instincts because of institutional growth and change. Veblen disagreed with Hobbes's notion
that the state of nature can be characterized as a constant war
of one against all. Veblen thought that alienation resulted from
the fact of human productivity itself. He also believed that man
has a tendency to engage in animistic thinking or anthropomor-
phism and workmanship itself is corrupted by emulation. Workmanship leads to productivity, and products made to satisfy others
lose their intrinsic value and lead to alienation and servitude.
Veblen hoped that the discipline engendered by the machine process and matter-of-fact attitude would destroy illusion, animism,
and other archaic habits of thought. Diggins feels that the
price to be paid here is too high--that man must renounce his
emotional qualities as man. Veblen's faint hope lay in the
notion of "idle curiosity" which is "a mode of cognition so
bereft of functional content that it could not be corrupted by
existing institutions. . . ." Veblen's conclusions are ultimately negative, yet his contributions to an anthropological
understanding of social institutions are important.

8   _____. "Reification and Cultural Hegemony of Capitalism: The
     Perspectives of Marx and Veblen." Social Research 44
     (Summer):354-83.
        Argues that Veblen's delvings into anthropology allowed him
to go beyond Marx in illuminating the phenomena of reification
and alienation. Marx's analysis was limited to production, while
Veblen emphasized the fact that consumption holds the key to
alienation. Unlike Marx, Veblen was not "indifferent to the
cultural significance of commodities." In effect, Veblen
"reverses the entire theoretical scheme of Marx's explanation of
reification." For Veblen, commodities are not mere disembodied
abstractions but can be seen as having a "strong personal sign-
character which enables man to impute to them human qualities
which he can recognize." Alienation results not from the "fetish-
ism in commodities but the animism in man which compels him to
impute personal and individual qualities to observed phenomena."
The dominant class in any society cements its position not only
through force but also through hegemonic display of prestige and
status. The working class, according to Veblen, emulates the
leisure class and is thus integrated "into the culture of capitalism." Veblen is credited with introducing the notion of
relative deprivation but that deprivation leads not to working
class antagonism toward the leisure class, but simply emulation.
Veblen's theory resembles both the consensus and conflict models
of society yet differs from both in marked respects. He recognized the fact of conflict but emphasized the role of the ideas
held by the dominant class and its influence in promoting consensus and integration. Veblen's work may contain the answer to the
question of why ideology has prevailed over technology and why
alienation persists in the face of the liberating potential of

machine objectivity. Veblen saw no sharp discontinuity between capitalism and feudal status sytems. What he saw was the barbarian residues of "prowess and esteem" and other aspects of predatory behavior carried over into the machine age.

9   DOWD, DOUGLAS F. The Twisted Dream: Capitalist Development in the United States Since 1776. 2d ed. Cambridge: Winthrop Publishers, pp. 4-326 passim.
     Minor revision of 1974.5.

10   GALBRAITH, JOHN KENNETH. The Age of Uncertainty. Boston: Houghton Mifflin Co., pp. 57-64, 70, 77, 192.
     Describes Veblen's life and the times in which he lived. Considers Veblen's greatest book to be The Theory of the Leisure Class and his enduring achievement to be in sociology rather than economics.

11   KOHLER, GERNOT. "Structural-Dynamic Arms Control." Journal of Peace Research 14, no. 4:315-26.
     Utilizes the "Veblen effect" in an effort to explain the arms race. Increasing militarization and arms stockpiling can be understood as a form of conspicuous display for reasons of status and invidious comparison.

12   LAPHAM, LEWIS. "Veblen Revisited." Harper's 255 (November):8, 12, 15.
     Claims that the leisure class described by Veblen has today become the leisure state. Finds no fault with Veblen's major observations and laments the fact that the passage of time has done little to blunt the force of his argument. Extends and updates many of Veblen's points to demonstrate the ever-widening spread of the behavior patterns described by Veblen. Examples include conspicuous leisure, pets, dress, devout observances, etc. Considers John F. Kennedy as "Veblen's beau ideal. He consumed the best of everything the society had to offer and employed the most exquisitely trained and therefore the most expensive servants. Who else could afford to hire the dean of Harvard College as a footman?"

13   LEATHERS, CHARLES G. Review of Thorstein Veblen: Essays, Reviews, and Reports, Previously Uncollected Writings, edited and with an introduction, "New Light on Veblen," by Joseph Dorfman. History of Political Economy 9 (Fall), 450-51.
     "While it doesn't seem likely that any radically new interpretations of Veblen will be found in these newly collected works, students of Veblen will find excellent opportunities to expand their understanding of the man and his knowledge."

14   LERNER, MAX. "Veblen, Thorstein Bunde." In Concise Dictionary of American Biography. 2d ed. New York: Charles Scribner's Sons, p. 1084.
     Revision of 1936.13; 1939.10.

15   SCOTT, WILLIAM B. In Pursuit of Happiness: American Con-
     ceptions of Property from the Seventeenth to the Twentieth
     Century. Bloomington: Indiana University Press, pp. 159-60,
     165-70, 178-79.
          Discusses Veblen along with three other "collectivists"--
     Bellamy, Croly, and Dewey. After reviewing some of Veblen's
     ideas writes that the "almost a cynic" Veblen had little to
     suggest in the way of social reform and that he did not have "a
     highly optimistic estimate of man's potential."

16   SMITH, JAMES R. "Politics from the Economic Point of View:
     An Analysis of the Political Theoretic Significance of the
     Writings of Thorstein Veblen." Ph.D. dissertation, University
     of California, Berkeley.
          Claims that while Veblen had achieved a reputation as a
     unorthodox economist, he was also a philosopher of science and
     political thinker. Veblen's political theory is based upon his
     stated economic views; both are constructed along the lines of
     his industrial-pecuniary dichotomy. Claims that Veblen's writings
     present a cogent theory of politics and a model for political
     economic organization. While Veblen no doubt owes an intellec-
     tual debt to Marx, he is not a Marxist in any sense of the word.
     Veblen's theory attempted to integrate both economics and politics
     by combining features of evolutionism and pragmatism. Signs
     of his influence can be seen in the work of such figures as
     C. Wright Mills and John K. Galbraith.

17   TOOL, MARC R. "A Social Value Theory." Journal of Economic
     Issues 11 (December):823-46.
          Discusses Veblen's theory of social value. Although Veblen
     did not formulate an explicit value theory, he nonetheless en-
     gaged in extensive evaluation that is evident in both his crit-
     ical and constructive efforts.

18   TUCKER, WILLIAM. "Environmentalism and the Leisure Class."
     Harper's 255 (December):49-56, 73-80.
          Argues that the environmental controversy surrounding the
     proposed construction of power plants at Storm King Mountain in
     New York "can only be understood in terms of Veblen's analysis of
     leisure-class behavior." In this case it is the leisure class
     that stands in the way of necessary developments in order to
     protect its social privilege.

19   WALKER, DONALD A. "Thorstein Veblen's Economic System."
     Economic Inquiry 15 (April):213-37.
          Contends that scholarship on Veblen is characterized by a
     lack of systematic studies of his contributions to economic
     theory. Finds Veblen's theory in parts contradictory and marred
     by a number of deficiencies. His theory of capitalism suffers
     from two major defects. First of all, it is weak with respect to
     technical economic problems; its theory of output, employment,
     and allocation and the pricing of resources is inadequate.

Second, Veblen's treatment of capitalism is tainted with normative elements; his bias against business in general leads him
into an ideological rather than scientific analysis of capitalism. Yet Veblen has made a useful contribution to the field of
economics. "Veblen helped to liberate the minds of his readers
from the prevailing set of values, and his writings still provide
a useful stimulus to thought and inquiry in the field of the
evaluation of business behavior."

20   WEST, PATRICK. "A Status Group Dynamic Approach to Predicting
     Participation Rates in Regional Recreation Demand Studies."
     Land Economics 53 (May):196-211.
         Argues that the concept of status-based diffusion, derived
     mainly from Veblen, is the most important one for understanding
     and predicting the growth of recreational fashions and fads.
     Explains the significance of Veblen's theory of emulation and its
     relevance.

21   WINNER, LANGDON. Autonomous Technology: Technics-out-of-
     Control as a Theme in Political Thought. Cambridge: MIT
     Press, pp. 143-46, 148, 196-98.
         Discusses Veblen's proposal for a rule by a technical elite
     and the "cultural incidence of the machine process." Veblen held
     that technology has come to exercise a pervasive and dominant
     influence over the lives of individuals.

1978

1   AFXENTIOU, PANAYIOTIS C. "Bandwagon, Snob, and Veblen Effects
     in the Theory of Consumer's Demand Revisited." Rivista
     internazionale di scienze economiche commerciale [Inter-
     national review of economic and commercial science] 25,
     no. 3:265-76.
         Notes the importance of the Veblen effect and attempts to
     correct flaws in the original article by Harvey Leibenstein. See
     1950.10.

2   ALLEN, JAMES SLOAN. Review of The Bard of Savagery:
     Thorstein Veblen and Modern Social Theory, by John P. Diggins.
     New Republic 178 (8 April):31-32.
         Sees Veblen as one of the "Great Unmaskers" along with
     Marx, Nietzsche, and Freud. Like those thinkers, Veblen saw
     mankind as self-deceived and tried to provide an analysis that
     put an end to the subjective self-deception. Charges that
     Diggins confuses Veblen's ideas concerning the impact of the
     machine process. It was not emotion that would be thwarted but
     rather the false conceptions that men entertained. See 1978.7.

3   COSER, LEWIS A. "American Trends." In A History of Socio-
     logical Analysis. Edited by Tom Bottomore and Robert Nisbet.
     New York: Basic Books, pp. 287-320.

Fixes Veblen's place in the history of American sociology
and describes him as the most original thinker of his generation.

4   _____. Review of The Bard of Savagery: Thorstein Veblen and
     Modern Social Theory, by John P. Diggins. Sociology and
     Social Research 63 (October):166-67.
     Argues that Veblen's framework of "instincts" should be
relegated to the museum of antiquities. Instead, focus should be
on his major contributions to social theory. See 1978.7.

5   CULLISON, WILLIAM E. "Examining the Effect of Interdependent
     Consumer Preferences on Economic Growth, or Rediscovering Adam
     Smith and His Eighteenth Century Contemporaries." Southern
     Economic Journal 44 (April):937-43.
     Analyzes and assesses contributions to the theory of con-
sumer choice. Sees Veblen, Adam Smith, and others as making
significant additions to the theory.

6   DIGGINS, JOHN P. "Barbarism and Capitalism: The Strange
     Perspectives of Thorstein Veblen." Marxist Perspectives 1
     (Summer):138-56.
     Assesses Veblen's contributions to several areas of social
theory and contrasts them with the views of other significant
thinkers, including Karl Marx. Questions Talcott Parsons's negative appraisal of Veblen and finds "stranger still" the view of
Veblen held by T.W. Adorno, who labeled him a positivist and
contended that he was "a typical American thinker assimilated
into the dominant values of that society." Veblen is credited
with being the first social scientist to point to the faulty
Ricardian-Benthamite-Hegelian basis of the labor theory of value.
Veblen's anthropological perspective also enabled him to shed
light on the mystery of the origin of property. For Veblen
property originated in conquest and taking--especially the taking
of women as trophies and signs of status. Veblen's explanation
of reification and hegemony is also treated. The values of the
dominant class are copied by the lower classes as signs of prestige and status, rendering coercion as a technique of social
control a less attractive alternative. Also explains the oppres-
sed conditions of women to whom fall the "unceremonious" tasks.
Veblen's distinction between business and industry is noted, as
well as his views concerning modernization. With respect to the
latter, Diggins claims that Veblen was the first social scientist
to interpret German history from the "structuralist" point of
view rather than emphasizing the actions of great statesmen.
Veblen is praised for "his unique contribution to modern social
theory" in demonstrating the brutish origins of social class
stratification, acquisitive capitalism, and male domination.

7   _____. The Bard of Savagery: Thorstein Veblen and Modern
     Social Theory. New York: Seabury Press, 257 pp.
     Focuses on topics of common interest to Veblen, Marx, and
Weber with occasional sidetracks, where appropriate, into

analysis of the related work of such luminaries as Levi-Strauss, Malinowski, Piaget, and Dewey. Deals with Veblen's view of the origins of private property, the role of status emulation, the effects of technology, and the role of religion. Diggins covers broad ground including the sociological dynamics of capitalism, cultural hegemony, value theory, modern social philosophy, alienation, mediation, and reification. Included also are discussions of Veblen's involvement with such current social issues as higher education, the woman question, and the structural causes of war and peace and his long-term impact upon American social thought and political reform. Argues that Veblen's explanation of the sociological aspects of capitalism is rooted in several basic concepts that differentiate it from Marxian analysis. The first is animism which is defined "as the tendency to attribute personal qualities to the impersonal data of nature." Diggins views animism as the original source of alienation in Veblen's work rather than attributing alienation to private property and the division of labor as does Marx. As Diggins puts it, "technological understanding is diverted and workmanship 'contaminated' when man perceives a phenomenon as animate and asks, 'What can it do on its own?'" The second and third are the concepts of status emulation and cultural hegemony that Veblen believed to have greater sociopolitical significance for the understanding of popular support for American capitalism than the Marxian ideas of class consciousness and class conflict. In much of this analysis, Veblen emerges as a more penetrating theorist than Marx and Weber. Particular emphasis is placed upon Veblen's "anthropological perspective"; he used late nineteenth-century anthropology to illuminate the problems of social and economic institutions. Argues that in order to fully appreciate Veblen we must engage in "comparative social theory," hence the analysis of Veblen's ideas in the context of the grand history of social theory. Believes that "Veblen's insights, may in the end, bring about a reorientation of modern social theory."

8   ELLIOT, JOHN E. "Institutionalism as an Approach to Political Economy." *Journal of Economic Issues* 12 (March)91-114.
     Describes Veblen's views on the nature of technological change and its impact on institutions. Considers Veblen's conjecture that "vested interests" may increasingly rely upon the political system to support their interests to be significant.

9   HAWTHORNE, GEOFFREY. Review of *The Bard of Savagery: Thorstein Veblen and Modern Social Theory*, by John P. Diggins. *New Society* 46 (19 October):837.
     Writes that whatever Veblen took seriously, it was not consistency. Veblen saw incompletely but saw very well. Sees a likeness to Rousseau, but unlike him, Veblen made no attempt to sort out his premises and offer a set of constructive inferences. See 1978.7.

10   HILL, LEWIS E. "Social and Institutional Economics: Toward
      a Creative Synthesis." Review of Social Economy 36
      (December):311-23.
           Attempts a synthesis of social and institutional economics.
      Emphasizes Veblen's contribution, followed by John R. Commons and
      Wesley C. Mitchell, to the institutional approach. Argues that
      social economics is compatible with institutionalism.

11   HUNT, E.K. "The Normative Foundations of Social Theory: An
      Essay on the Criteria Defining Social Economics." Review of
      Social Economy 36 (December):285-309.
           Argues that utilitarian economics, or contemporary neoclas-
      sical economics, cannot be described as "social economics" while
      the Veblenian and Marxian types can. Elaborates a distinction
      based on multiple criteria and analyzes the critique of utilitar-
      ian economics by both Veblen and Marx. Notes similarities be-
      tween the economic theories of the two but concludes that Veblen
      is not a disciple of Marx.

12   _____. Review of Veblen's Theory of Social Change, by
      Leonard A. Dente. Journal of Economic Issues 12
      (September):731-33.
           Asserts that Dente underestimates the degree to which
      Veblen's theory differs from neoclassical utility theory. It
      must also be emphasized that for Veblen "the interest rate was a
      pecuniary phenomenon which was historically specific to the his-
      torical conditions of modern capitalism." Veblen had no use for
      abstract, deductive models. Notes that he is difficult to inter-
      pret because of his unique style combining sarcastic humor,
      passionate feeling, and mock detachment. See 1977.6.

13   JACOBS, WILBUR. "The Great Despoliation: Environmental
      Themes in American Frontier History." Pacific Historical
      Review 47 (February):1-26.
           Argues that Veblen was far ahead of Frederick Jackson
      Turner in recognizing the social costs of environmental exploita-
      tion by vested interests. Veblen provided a penetrating analysis
      of how private interests in the fur trade, ranching, mining,
      logging, and oil drilling gained so much at public and environ-
      mental expense.

14   JAHER, FREDERIC COPLE. Review of The Bard of Savagery:
      Thorstein Veblen and Modern Social Theory, by John P. Diggins.
      Journal of American History 65 (December), 814-15.
           Argues that in the period from the late nineteenth century
      to World War I no American critics reached the level of analytic
      brilliance of Thorstein Veblen and Henry Adams. Sees Veblen as
      having probed the deepest impulses of society and economy.
      Veblen's theory would be richer yet if he had recognized the
      cultural values that gave rise to the entrepreneur as Weber did.
      See 1978.7.

15   McNEIL, KENNETH. "Understanding Organizational Power: Building
     on the Weberian Legacy." Administrative Science Quarterly 23
     (March):65-90.
        Recognizes Veblen's and John R. Commons's often-overlooked
     contributions to a theory of the dynamics of organizational
     power. Emphasizes Veblen's focus on the productive and efficient
     potential of organizational structure. Veblen understood the
     causes of tension between production and profit.

16   MACPHERSON, C.B. Property: Mainstream and Critical Posi-
     tions. Toronto: University of Toronto Press, p. 119.
        "Veblen was the first to draw attention to a significant
     change that had taken place in the nature of property by the
     early twentieth century, a change which required a new defense of
     property." Veblen pinpointed the alterations wrought by the rise
     of the modern corporation and new financial techniques and the
     corresponding changes in justifications and claims to property.

17   MUKERJI, CHANDRA. "Artwork: Collection and Contemporary
     Culture." American Journal of Sociology 84 (September):
     348-65.
        Analyzes the transformation of film from industrial commod-
     ity to art form. Sees Veblen as one of the few sociologists to
     recognize the significance, in terms of cultural meaning, of the
     design of industrial commodities.

18   PLUTA, JOSEPH E., and CHARLES G. LEATHERS. "Veblen and Modern
     Radical Economics." Journal of Economic Issues 12
     (March):125-46.
        Authors state that contemporary radical economists have
     paid little attention to the works of Veblen. Similarities
     between the modern radical and Veblen's older ideas are outlined,
     e.g., their common repudiation of the harmony of interests model
     of mainstream economics, the power held by the dominant class,
     imperialism and its causes, military spending, the use of mone-
     tary and fiscal policies to promote special interests, causes of
     unemployment, excessive advertising, and the like. On the other
     hand, it is claimed that the radicals would not agree with
     Veblen's theory of human nature with all its attendant "in-
     stincts." Other differences between the radicals and Veblen can
     be found in analysis of social change and the role of technology.
     It is also claimed that the "difference between the radicals'
     activistic stance and Veblen's detachment from policy goals seems
     of little consequence."

19   ROTHEIM, R.J. "Institutionalism and Marx: Contrasting Theo-
     ries of Value and Freedom." Social Science Journal 15
     (January):55-62.
        Compares institutionalist and Marxist approaches to certain
     questions pertaining to society and economy. Pinpoints some of

Veblen's contributions and shows how he differs from later institutionalists. Argues that recent institutionalists, unlike Marxists, wish to retain capitalism.

20   VESEY, LAURENCE. Review of The Bard of Savagery: Thorstein
     Veblen and Modern Social Theory, by John P. Diggins. Human
     Nature 1 (September):16-17, 21-22.
          Suggests that a case can indeed be made for the argument
     that "Veblen deserves his present obscurity." Feels that Diggins
     rates Veblen too highly as a thinker. Finds it strange that
     Veblen should have mistakenly pinned his hopes for a better
     society on the skills of the engineer, and that his anthropology
     was based on the writings of amateurs such as John Ferguson
     McLennon and Lewis Henry Morgan. Feels that Veblen's reliance
     upon anthropology crippled the major concerns of his works. See
     1978.7.

21   WALKER, DONALD A. "New Light on Veblen's Work and Influence."
     American Journal of Economics and Sociology 37 (January):
     87-101.
          A review of a collection of essays by Veblen edited by
     Joseph Dorfman, who also contributed a 326-page commentary on
     Veblen's influence (1973.8). The work is entitled Thorstein
     Veblen: Essays, Reviews, and Reports, Previously Uncollected
     Writings. Walker surveys the ideas of Veblen, noting his dis-
     agreement with such figures as Mallock, Sombart, and Schmoller,
     to name just a few. Claims that Veblen did indeed attach impor-
     tance to the factor of race in the analysis of culture and his
     treatment of the economics of wheat was more descriptive than
     analytical. "The principal value of the collection of repub-
     lished material is to be found in Veblen's expression of his own
     ideas, particularly in regard to business enterprise, the process
     of institutional change, and the importance of technology."

22   WHITE, RON D. "Growth versus Conservation: A Veblenian Per-
     spective." Journal of Economic Issues 12 (June):427-53.
          Attempts to apply key Veblenian concepts such as conspic-
     uous consumption and the distinction between industry and busi-
     ness to the contemporary scene. Veblen's ideas remain relevant
     and insightful and can be utilized to promote industrial effi-
     ciency, energy conservation, and more intelligent policy-making.

                                1979

1   BONJEAN, CHARLES M., and RICHARD MACHALEK. "Thorstein Veblen
     in Contemporary Perspective." Social Science Quarterly 60
     (December):418.
          Introduces a set of articles in the same journal issue
     assessing John P. Diggins's The Bard of Savagery: Thorstein
     Veblen and Modern Social Theory (1978.7). Credit is given to the
     late Veblen scholar Louis Schneider, who suggested the symposium.

The central theme of the symposium is Diggins's claim "that Weber, Marx and Veblen were the three great social theorists of industrial capitalism."

2　　BROOKS, JOHN. "A Friendly Product." New Yorker 55 (12 November):58-94.
　　　　Invokes Veblen's theories to help explain changes in fashion. Deals with the popularity of Levi's jeans. Material from this article is incorporated in 1981.3. See also 1981.2.

3　　CUFF, ROBERT D. "Veblen and Toronto." Canadian Review of American Studies 10 (Winter):347-53.
　　　　Reviews of The Bard of Savagery: Thorstein Veblen and Modern Social Theory, by John P. Diggins. Writes that Veblen unsuccessfully applied for a teaching post at the University of Toronto and speculates that he might have responded creatively in a Canadian environment. Notes his influence on such notable Canadians as Stephen Leacock, O. Skelton, Harold Innis, and MacKenzie King. Sees Veblen as having anticipated the contemporary economic critique of American national security policy. See 1978.7.

4　　DUGGER, WILLIAM M. "The Origins of Thorstein Veblen's Thought." Social Science Quarterly 60 (December):424-31.
　　　　The origins of Veblen's thought can be traced to the German historical school, Darwinian evolutionary theory, pragmatism, and Marxism. Veblen took from the German historical school the notion of holism; from Darwin he obtained an evolutionary cause and effect approach; and pragmatism led him to reject the notion of metaphysical absolutes and to view man as a "doer." His relation to Marx is complex; however, they share certain beliefs, especially regarding social change. Veblen's theory shows a varied combination of influences; it continues to be relevant and useful.

5　　_____. Review of The Bard of Savagery: Thorstein Veblen and Modern Social Theory, by John P. Diggins. Journal of Economic Issues 13 (March):219-21.
　　　　Praises the treatment of Veblen on the concept of alienation and the suppression of the instinct of workmanship. Would prefer to see more attention paid to later institutionalist thinkers such as Clarence Ayres. See 1978.7.

6　　FUHRMAN, E. R. Review of The Bard of Savagery: Thorstein Veblen and Modern Social Theory, by John P. Diggins. Contemporary Sociology 8 (July):639.
　　　　Praises the book. Agrees that the way to analyze a thinker's ideas is to compare them with appropriate competitors. See 1978.7.

7   GALBRAITH, JOHN KENNETH. "Who Was Thorstein Veblen?" In
    Annals of an Abiding Liberal. Edited by Andrea D. Williams.
    Boston: Houghton Mifflin Co., pp. 123-47.
    Reprint of 1973.9.

8   HUNT, E.K. History of Economic Thought: A Critical
    Perspective. Belmont, Calif.: Wadsworth Publishing Co.,
    pp. 299-327.
        Treats Veblen's evolutionary approach to economics, his
    critique of neoclassicism, and his theories of private property,
    class, and women. Extended analysis of Veblen's ideas concerning
    capitalism and the dominance of business over industry is pro-
    vided. Compares Veblen with Marx and finds the latter's general
    economic theory to be superior in analysis and detail; yet
    Veblen's theory of emulative consumption and all that it entails
    is decidedly superior to Marx's. "Veblen succeeded brilliantly
    in exposing the ideological elements of neoclassical economic
    theory and in promoting a clear and insightful understanding of
    both the historically transitory and the exploitive nature of
    capitalism."

9   _____. "The Importance of Thorstein Veblen for Contemporary
    Marxism." Journal of Economic Issues 13 (March):113-40.
        Argues that the ideas of Marx and Veblen concerning capi-
    talism are "quite compatible" and "significantly complement each
    other." Downplays both the "dialectical materialism" incorrectly
    attributed to Marx and the Darwinian biological theory presumably
    espoused by Veblen. Neither of the two approaches "is germane to
    a comparison of the analyses of capitalism formulated" by Marx
    and Veblen. Inconsistencies in Veblen's work "would have van-
    ished had Veblen dropped his guise as a value-free biological
    scientist and simply made explicit the human values that pervade
    all of his profound social science." Despite some differences in
    their views concerning class struggle, both the descriptions by
    Marx and Veblen are very similar. The two theorists differ most
    drastically in their analyses of prices and profits, but again,
    they supplement each other when dealing with business cycles.
    Both Marx and Veblen contributed to an understanding of false
    consciousness and the ideological hegemony of the capitalist
    class.

10 INNIS, HAROLD A. "A Bibliography of Thorstein Veblen."
    Social Science Quarterly 60 (December):420-23.
    Abridgement of 1929.6; 1956.5.

11 JUNKER, LOUIS. "Genuine or Spurious Institutionalism?"
    American Journal of Economics and Sociology 38 (April):207-23.
        A rejoinder to points made about the social philosophy of
    Thorstein Veblen and other institutionalists in David Seckler's
    Thorstein Veblen and the Institutionalists: A Study in the
    Social Philosophy of Economics (1975.14). Claims that Seckler
    does not understand Veblen's ideas and has fundamentally distorted

them. Disputes the claim that Veblen "fled into obscurantism": rather, Veblen rejected teleology, atomistic individualism, methodological dualism, orthodox economics and its metaphysical assumptions, and looked instead to cultural anthropology and the evolutionary process to explain human institutions. Suggests further that the Veblenian distinction between "ceremonial and instrumental" knowledge is ignored in Seckler's analysis. A sympathetic reading of Veblen will show that he never abandoned humanism in favor of a narrow behaviorism. Claims that Veblen, John Dewey, and Clarence Ayres "went a long way towards" showing the "directionlessness" of orthodoxy and recognized its destructive potential.

12   LORA, RONALD. Review of The Bard of Savagery: Thorstein Veblen and Modern Social Theory, by John P. Diggins. Historian 41 (August):811-13.
     Praises Veblen's multidimensional approach. Veblen held a humane vision in the midst of a rapidly changing era dominated by the machine. See 1978.7.

13   MACHALEK, RICHARD. "Thorstein Veblen, Louis Schneider, and the Ironic Imagination." Social Science Quarterly 60 (December):460-64.
     "This article explains how the work of Veblen illustrates the rich theoretical potential of the ironic imaginations." Claims that Veblen influenced the work of the late Louis Schneider, and that the latter especially found the concept of irony in the works of Veblen to be a highly productive tool for social analysis. Specific "ironic themes" to be found in Veblen's writings include: "the irony of highly adapted forms," which shows how a latecomer to industrialization can outstrip the one who originated the innovation; the irony of "contradiction, opposition, oppositeness, paradox, negation, dilemma," or the dilemmas created by adapting and rapid modernization; and third, the irony of "self-disconfirming analysis," where "analysis helps to change that which is analyzed and even turns it into its very opposite." Veblen's notion of conspicuous consumption, for example, might be understood by a conspicuous consumer, who, stung by the analysis, ceases to be a conspicuous consumer. Much of this article is devoted to the social theory of Louis Schneider and his treatment of Veblen.

14   MILLER, DONALD L. The New American Radicalism. Port Washington: Kennikat Press, pp. 5, 38, 40-42, 74-75, 80, 85, 98-99, 140, 198.
     Although the main figure in Miller's study is Alfred M. Bingham, he traces the influence of Thorstein Veblen on independent left insurgency during the 1930s. Shows that the insurgent idols of Bingham's journal Common Sense were not Marx and Lenin, but Henry George, Edward Bellamy, and Veblen. Also shows how Veblen influenced the technocratic movement led by Howard Scott,

although it is doubtful that the technocrats really understood
Veblen's message in its entirety.

15   PAGE, BARBARA S. Review of The Twisted Dream: Capitalist
      Development in the United States since 1776, 2d ed., by
      Douglas F. Dowd. Journal of Economic Issues 13
      (September):802-6.
          Commends the attention Dowd gives to Veblen but thinks that
      he has exaggerated the similarities between Veblen and Marx.
      Veblen's emphasis on pecuniary interest and his neglect of ex-
      ploitation provide only a superficial analysis of capitalist
      contradictions. See 1974.5; 1977.9.

16   ROSS, DOROTHY. Review of The Bard of Savagery: Thorstein
      Veblen and Modern Social Theory, by John P. Diggins. American
      Historical Review 84 (October):1179.
          Argues that while Veblen deserves to be ranked with Marx
      and Weber as a theorist of modern capitalist society, the author
      neglects the influence of Spencer on Veblen. Further contends
      that the issue of direct class domination in Veblen's analysis is
      likewise slighted. Also asks with whom was Veblen carrying on a
      dialogue. See 1978.7.

17   RUSSELL, S.A. "A Comment on Roger Troub and Kenneth
      Boulding." Journal of Economic Issues 13 (September):768-69.
          Takes issue with Kenneth Boulding's and Roger Troub's crit-
      ical evaluation of Veblen's theory of evolution. Quotes both
      Boulding and Veblen in order to show how the former's ideas are
      similar to the latter's. Veblen's concept of community knowledge
      looks suspiciously like Boulding's concept of "know-how." See
      response, 1979.24.

18   SAMUELS, WARREN J. "Thorstein Veblen, Heterodox Economist, in
      Retrospect." Social Science Quarterly 60 (December):454-59.
          Considers Veblen's position in the discipline of economics,
      "his conception of the economy and his role in demystification."
      Many modern economists think that Veblen's work was either not
      economics and/or misguided if not incorrect. They prefer to
      concentrate on other matters. Veblen was an astute critic of
      ideology and a master at demystifying the formal conventions of
      his time. He steered away from constructing static models of
      social theory and economics, preferring to see society in terms
      of change and evolution--but always demonstrating the continuity
      of the present with an atavistic past. Adds that Veblen's "de-
      mythicizing becomes attractive during times of dissent from and
      rebellion against established modes of thought." Veblen's eco-
      nomics should supplement rather than displace resource allocation
      economics, and his ideas should not be taken as a finished prod-
      uct but ought to be elaborated, extended, and applied. Myrdal
      and Galbraith are too alone as innovators in the Veblenian
      tradition.

19   SOBEL, IRVIN. "Adam Smith: What Kind of Institutionalist Was He?" Journal of Economic Issues 13 (June):347-68.

Compares Adam Smith with institutionalists John R. Commons and Thorstein Veblen. In spite of some basic differences, Veblen and Smith share "substantial similarities in approach, methodology, emphasis, and broad focus of concern." Both covered a wide range of intellectual inquiry, and they investigated the psychological forces behind human behavior. Both had "well articulated" theories of socioeconomic change; similarities can also be seen in the way they divided history into stages and the manner in which they described the consumption patterns of the rich and emulation of the former by other social elements.

20   SUTO, MARTIN [FRANCIS]. "Some Neglected Aspects of Veblen's Social Thought." Social Science Quarterly 60 (December): 439-53.

Discusses Veblen's place in intellectual history, his relationship to Marx and Weber, and some neglected aspects of his work. Contends that Veblen's "paradigm rests on an epistemological triad": a theory of basic human instincts; his investigations into contemporary institutions; and a theory of history. The last component is the most neglected aspect of Veblen's paradigm. Claims that Veblen was profoundly influenced by Hegel, notwithstanding the fact that his dissertation was on Kant. Contrary to the assertions of Morton White, the Hegelian philosopher George Sylvester Morris was instrumental in introducing Veblen to Hegel. Utilizes the four linguistic tropes of metaphor, metonymy, synedoche, and irony to evaluate the influence of Hegelianism on Veblen. An example can be seen in the structural similarities of both Hegel's and Veblen's theories of history. Sees Veblen's "instinct of workmanship" as an analogue to Hegel's "cunning of reason" as an operative force in the successive stages of history. Despite the fact that the current climate of opinion is not overly receptive to his ideas, Veblen's insights are of lasting quality.

21   SUTO, MARTIN FRANCIS. "Thorstein Veblen and the Crisis in Western Social Thought." Ph.D. dissertation, University of California, Los Angeles.

A detailed biographical assessment of Veblen's ideas. Argues that Veblen, along with other major thinkers of his era, created new social science paradigms in order to find an answer to the intellectual crisis around the turn of the century. This biography attempts to treat Veblen in a manner different from those utilized by Dorfman and Riesman by placing Veblen in an intellectual context that includes his European contemporaries. The author's approach differs from Diggins's in that it explicitly attempts to relate Veblen's life to his ideas. Sees Veblen as an alienated intellectual who helped establish the social sciences on a new paradigm based on anthropology. Argues that the paradigm created by Veblen can be seen in the writings of such figures as Galbraith, Brandeis, and even his detractor,

Riesman. Compares Veblen favorably with Freud, Weber, Durkheim,
and Pareto. Veblen is also compared to Nietzsche, Sumner,
Pierce, Burckhardt, and Henry and Brooks Adams. Reference is
also made to the work of Kuhn and Foucault to show how, in some
respects, Veblen anticipated their ideas with respect to preconceptions and paradigms.

22   SWANN, C.S.B. Review of The Bard of Savagery: Thorstein
      Veblen and Modern Social Theory, by John P. Diggins.
      Sociological Review 27 (August):586-89.
         Agrees that Veblen has accomplished extraordinary and wide-
ranging achievements. Also concurs in the opinion that Veblen is
a great thinker to be ranked with Marx and Weber but argues that
he is a different type of thinker--a critic of society and culture rather than a great system builder. Mentions his crucial
statements regarding language and social science. See 1978.7.

23   TILMAN, RICK. Review of The Bard of Savagery: Thorstein
      Veblen and Modern Social Theory, by John P. Diggins. Journal
      of Economic Issues 13 (March):221-24.
         Agrees that Veblen is a major social theorist to be ranked
with Marx and Weber. Contends that Veblen is the most original
and insightful radical theorist that America has produced. While
Veblen may not measure up to Marx and Weber as a general theorist, his analysis of American society is superior to theirs.
Adds that a fuller understanding of Veblen's "ceremonial-
technological" dichotomy is necessary to analyze social
institutions and processes. See 1978.7.

24   TROUB, ROGER M. "Evolutionary Visions, Frameworks, and Anal-
      yses: In Reply to S.A. Russell." Journal of Economic Issues
      13 (September):770-71.
         Claims that while there are similarities in the respective
theories of evolution formulated by Veblen and Boulding, the
differences are fundamental. Veblen's theory is more akin to
Newtonian mechanics than to Boulding's theory, which is based on
a more modern biology. Response to 1979.17.

25   WALTON, JOHN. "The Sociological Imagination of Thorstein
      Veblen." Social Science Quarterly 60 (December):432-38.
         Finds it "odd that the contemporary generation celebrates
Mills as the originator of the sociological imagination and a
radical 'new sociology' for the exemplary career and work of
Mills suggests an uncanny resemblance to Veblen's." Notes the
common experiences of both Mills and Veblen and the often observed similarities in style, outlook, and topical interests.
Veblen made important contributions to the understanding of the
relations between production organization vis-à-vis status and
the conflict between workmanship and business. He also shed
light on the notion of ideological hegemony; his work on reification predates modern semiology; and he had things to say regarding cultural liberation through science. His insights into

modernization and capitalism are exemplary. Attention is paid to
the roots of Veblen's theory, his experiences, and his place in
the history of social thought.

26   WINKELMAN, RICHARD. Review of The Bard of Savagery:
     Thorstein Veblen and Modern Social Theory, by John P. Diggins.
     Western Political Quarterly 32 (September):367.
          Emphasizes that with Veblen, as with Marx, it is difficult
     to separate the economist from the sociologist and the anthropol-
     ogist from the prophet. See 1978.7.

                              1980

1   ASHMORE, NANCY J. "Thorstein Veblen: The Last Man Who Knew
     Everything." Carleton Voice 45 (Fall):4, 6-8, 12, 16.
          Celebrates the hundredth anniversary of Veblen's graduation
     from Carleton College. Provides biographical information and
     highlights from Veblen's scholarly outputs.

2   BELL, DANIEL. "Veblen and the Technocrats." In The Winding
     Passage: Essays and Sociological Journeys, 1960-1980.
     Cambridge, Mass.: ABT Books, pp. 69-90.
          Reprint of 1963.1-2 with additional footnotes.

3   BRINKMAN, RICHARD L. "Mankind at the Starting Point."
     Journal of Economic Issues 14 (June):567-82.
          Utilizes a modified Veblen-Ayres framework in an attempt to
     demonstrate that resources are potentially unlimited. Suggests
     that Veblen and Ayres may have been correct in focusing attention
     on social structures rather than the biosphere.

4   CURTI, MERLE. Human Nature in American Thought. Madison:
     University of Wisconsin Press, pp. 247, 253-61.
          Assesses Veblen's theory of human nature and finds it vague
     and ambiguous. Even with the theory's shortcomings, Veblen's
     influence has been considerable. His critique of psychological
     hedonism was a factor in consideration by economics of the newer
     psychology.

5   DILLARD, DUDLEY. "A Monetary Theory of Production: Keynes
     and the Institutionalists." Journal of Economic Issues 14
     (June):255-73.
          Compares the economic writings of John Maynard Keynes with
     those of Veblen and demonstrates their similarities. Argues that
     both recognized the primacy of money in economic activity. Both
     explain interest in pecuniary terms and Veblen's distinction
     between industrial and pecuniary employments is compared to
     Keynes's cognate distinction between industry and finance.
     Further relationships are to be found in their writings on
     macroeconomic theory and their attitudes toward profit making
     as a way of life. Concludes by stating that Keynes's basic

theme in his monetary theory of production is the same one found in Veblen's Theory of Business Enterprise.

6 EVANS, JOHN S., and CHARLES G. LEATHERS. "Veblen on Owners, Managers, and the Control of Industry: A Reply." History of Political Economy, 12 (Fall), 441-48.
Replies to the Rutherford article in the same issue of the journal (1980.14). Authors argue that John K. Galbraith's New Industrial State is essentially a mature version of Veblen's New Order. While it is true that Veblen held a more hostile attitude toward business practices than did Galbraith, there are nonetheless "evolutionary processes at work in the New Order suggesting the emergence of the New Industrial State." Continues on to analyze Veblen's ideas concerning ownership, management and the control of credit. See also 1973.15. For the rejoinder, see 1981.9.

7 HEILBRONER, ROBERT L. "The Veblen-Commons Award." Journal of Economic Issues 14 (June):241-44.
Shows the relationships between the ideas of Veblen, Commons, and Adolph Lowe. Suggests that Lowe is more concerned with the problem of social control and the conditions of order than was Veblen or Commons. See 1980.11.

8 _____. The Worldly Philosophers. New York: Simon and Schuster, pp. 210-44.
Minor revision of 1953.8.

9 HOLSWORTH, ROBERT D. Public Interest Liberalism and the Crisis of Affluence. Boston: G.K. Hall & Co., pp. 6, 75-76, 82-93, 121, 140, 142.
Argues that Veblen's proposal for rule by an authoritarian technological elite was flawed because he did not understand the "compatibility between business mores and the requirements of technical society, nor was [he] sufficiently critical of the human problems that such a society would invariably generate." Critizes Veblen's distinction between business and technology and faults him for not adopting a critical attitude "on the transformation of the instinct of workmanship in the modern age."

10 HOROWITZ, DANIEL. "Consumption and Its Discontents: Simon N. Patten, Thorstein Veblen, and George Gunton." Journal of American History 67 (September):301-17.
Analyzes Veblen's ideas on consumption and waste. Veblen, along with Patten and Gunton, reshaped traditional attitudes toward consumption and morality. Although Veblen attacked the conservative moralists he nonetheless agreed with their preference for meaningful work and abhorrence of waste. Finds Veblen to be distinctive in that he appreciated machinery but at the same time emphasized the need for restraint. Veblen's solutions were sometimes vague and contradictory yet Veblen, like Thoreau before him, exposed the false conventions of a consumer society.

11   LOWE, ADOLPH. "What Is Evolutionary Economics?" Journal of
      Economic Issues 14 (June):247-54.
            Agrees with Veblen that neoclassical economics does not
      satisfactorily explain the problems of the real world. Although
      Veblen denounced orthodox economics, he did not himself offer a
      specific alternative. Continues with a set of proposals. See
      also 1980.7.

12   LOWER, MILTON D. "The Evolution of the Institutionalist
      Theory of Consumption." In Institutional Economics: Essays
      in Honor of Allan G. Gruchy. Edited by John Adams. Boston,
      The Hague, and London: Martinus Nijhof Publishing, pp. 82-104.
            States that the earliest coherent treatment of consumer
      behavior from an evolutionary and holistic standpoint was made by
      Veblen. His analysis was and remains an alternative to the
      orthodox theory of consumer behavior.

13   QUALEY, CARLTON C. "Thorstein Bunde Veblen, 1857-1929." In
      Makers of an Immigrant Legacy: Essays in Honor of Kenneth O.
      Bjork. Edited by Odd S. Lovoll. Northfield, Minn.:
      Norwegian-American Historical Association, pp. 50-61.
            Introduces the reader to Veblen's major ideas and provides
      biographical information. Emphasizes Veblen's Norwegian ancestry
      and asserts that Veblen "produced one of the world's great collec-
      tions of social criticism."

14   RUTHERFORD, MALCOLM. "Veblen on Owners, Managers, and the
      Control of Industry." History of Political Economy 12
      (Fall):434-40.
            Argues that several commentators (including Leathers and
      Evans) have not clearly demonstrated the connection between
      Veblen's theory of corporate "owners" versus "managers" and the
      theories of such critics as Berle and Means or Galbraith. While
      admitting that there are similarities between Veblen's "engi-
      neers" and Galbraith's "technostructure," argues that "it must be
      emphasized that in Veblen's scheme of things, as long as business
      institutions remain, profit maximisation will be the primary goal
      of firms and full discretionary power will not pass to the ex-
      perts." Not until he wrote Absentee Ownership and Business
      Enterprise in Recent Times did Veblen fully develop a system in
      which ownership was clearly removed from management. The simi-
      larities between Veblen on the one hand and Berle and Means or
      Galbraith on the other can easily be overstated. Galbraith's
      "new industrial state" is not a mature version of Veblen's "new
      order." Argument addressed to 1973.15. For a reply, see 1980.6;
      for the rejoinder, 1981.9.

15   SIMICH, J[ERRY] L., and RICK TILMAN. "Critical Theory and
      Institutional Economics: Frankfurt's Encounter with Veblen."
      Journal of Economic Issues 14 (September):631-47.
            Delineates lines of convergence and divergence in the
      approaches of the respective schools of thought. Argues that

several of Adorno's criticisms of Veblen's The Theory of the
Leisure Class are either mistaken or overdrawn. Maintains that
Veblen was neither a technocratic elitist nor "anti-intellectual,"
that he was not a "primitivist," and that he was as equally
concerned with exploitation under capitalism as he was with
waste. The diverse intellectual backgrounds of Veblen and the
Frankfurt school are described and an attempt is made to demonstrate how the approaches of the two might be synthesized with an
eye to understanding contemporary social problems. See 1941.1.

16   TOOL, LAURENCE A. "A War for Reform: Dewey, Veblen, Croly,
      and the Crisis of American Emergence." Ph.D. dissertation,
      Rutgers University at New Brunswick.
         Examines the response to World War I of three leading
      spokesmen of modern American liberalism--Dewey, Croly, and
      Veblen. Argues that all three abandoned science for journalism
      and hailed World War I as a great opportunity for reform.

1981

1   BRINKMAN, RICHARD L. "Culture in Neoinstitutional Economics:
     An Integration of Myrdal and Galbraith into the Veblen-Ayres
     Matrix." American Journal of Economics and Sociology 40
     (October):401-13.
        Explicates Veblen's theory of economic development and its
     relationship to technology and culture.

2   BROOKS, JOHN. "The New Snobbery: How to Show Off in
     America." Atlantic Monthly 247 (January):37-44, 48.
        Veblen's conspicuous consumption ideas as set forth in The
     Theory of the Leisure Class are updated and applied to the con-
     temporary American scene. Topics covered include modesty, decor,
     art, nutrition, physical fitness, drugs, graffiti, real estate,
     bereavement, success, telephoning, and a way of life; the last
     category focuses on the exploits of George Plimpton. Writes that
     there are probably millions of Americans familiar with the ex-
     pression "conspicuous consumption" who never heard of Veblen.
     "The Theory of the Leisure Class for the first time gave
     Americans general license to laugh at their economic superiors."
     Excerpted from 1981.3. See also 1979.2.

3   _____. Showing Off in America: From Conspicuous Consumption
     to Parody Display. New York: Little, Brown, & Co., 296 pp.
     passim.
        Updates, elaborates, and extends Veblenian concepts such as
     conspicuous consumption, emulation, industrial exemption, pecu-
     niary decency, and vicarious consumption. Provides extensive
     interpretations of Veblen's ideas put forth in The Theory of the
     Leisure Class. Finds that his anthropological base is outdated
     but his sociological edifice--the dynamic of modern American
     social behavior--has stood the test of time and appears to be

stronger than ever. Topics covered include behavior related to
drinking, eating, working, dressing, giving, praying, talking,
and telephoning, to name just some. Emphasizes the fact that
while many of the overt behaviors Veblen described have disap-
peared or changed, his fundamental analysis and principle are
sound. Notes that current behavior stresses "parody dispay" as
the thing to do. Argues that The Theory of the Leisure Class can
be organized into a logical and consistent whole; it contains
vivid passages and Veblen's writing, at first reading vague and
obfuscating, actually provides precise description in a rolling
style. "Veblen Lives." Incorporates material from 1979.2 and
1981.2.

4   DIAZ, CARLOS OBREGON. "El pensamiento de Veblen" [Veblen's
    thought]. Trimestre economico [Economic trimestral] 48,
    no. 19:411-42.
        Summarizes Veblen's major ideas for a Spanish-reading
audience, to whom Veblen is not a familiar figure. Covers
Veblen's critique of the Austrian, classical, and Marxist schools
of economics and his respective theories of social change and
history.

5   GALBRAITH, JOHN KENNETH. A Life in Our Times: Memoirs.
    Boston: Houghton Mifflin Co., pp. 24-25, 27, 29-31, 69, 267,
    530-31, 533.
        Cites Veblen, after Alfred Marshall, as having the most
significant influence on his economic thinking. Considers Veblen
to be America's greatest social scientist and one of a tiny few
whose roots go back to the nineteenth century but whose works are
still read today. The book also contains scattered references to
Veblen.

6   HUNT, E.K. "The Consolidation of Monopoly Power and the
    Writings of Veblen." In Property and Prophets: The Evolution
    of Economic Institutions and Ideologies. New York: Harper
    and Row, pp. 115-31.
        Describes Veblen's views on property, class, and capi-
talism. Argues that Veblen is America's most "significant,"
"original," and "profound" social thinker.

7   KENDALL, ELAINE. Review of Showing Off in America: From
    Conspicuous Consumption to Parody Display, by John Brooks.
    Los Angeles Times Book Review, 5 July, pp. 6, 9.
        Writes that Veblen was "virtually alone in his contempt for
robber barons and their pretensions." Argues that H.L. Mencken
was wrong in his estimate of Veblen. "Veblen was the True
Prophet; John Brooks is his vicar. Three cheers for the
Founding Father of Conspicuous Consumption—and for his worthy
successor who is carrying on the great American tradition of
valid generalization." See 1981.3.

8   MASON, ROGER S. Conspicuous Consumption: A Study of Excep-
     tional Consumer Behavior. New York: St. Martin's Press,
     pp. viii-x, 1, 5-13, 15, 17, 19-20, 23, 26, 52, 71, 103, 131,
     137.
          Argues that Veblen's work on conspicuous behavior was not
     exclusively an attempt to bring light to that subject; rather,
     Veblen saw it as only one factor in the larger economic scheme of
     things. Feels that Veblen made valuable contributions to the
     study of conspicuous behavior in spite of the fact that his work
     was largely unempirical. Veblen advanced a general theory of
     conspicuous behavior and thus failed to explain the differences
     between the behavior of individuals. Cites the "Veblen effect"
     and notices that not a great deal of work has been done on the
     subject of conspicuous consumption.

9   RUTHERFORD, MALCOLM. "Veblen on Owners, Managers, and the
     Control of Industry: A Rejoinder." History of Political
     Economy 13 (Spring):156-58.
          Responds to the response of Leathers and Evans to an
     earlier article by the author (1980.6). Raises new points of
     clarification and disagreement and reiterates that Veblen's
     Theory of Business Enterprise should not be understood as a
     forerunner to Galbraith's New Industrial State. See also
     1973.15; 1980.14.

10   TILMAN, RICK. "John Dewey and Thorstein Veblen: An Intellec-
     tual Relationship." Review of Institutional Thought 1
     (December):61-62.
          Argues against the idea of a unity of progressive thought
     and points to the differences between Dewey and Veblen. Empha-
     sizes Veblen's radicalism.

11   WEED, FRANK J. "Interpreting 'Institutions' in Veblen's
     Evolutionary Theory." American Journal of Economics and
     Sociology 40 (January):67-78.
          Analyzes Veblen's evolutionary theory, emphasizing his
     theory of social action, instincts, "habits of mind," and "insti-
     tutions." Argues that Veblen utilizes a literary device—a
     hypothetical historical reconstruction of major societal
     institutions—and then goes on to analyze their transformation.
     In spite of his critical style Veblen's works allow for in-depth
     analysis and predictive validity.

                              1982

1   HAYDEN, GREGORY F. "Social Fabric Matrix: From Perspective
     to Analytical Tool." Journal of Economic Issues 16
     (September):637-62.
          Points out that the "evolution of the institutionalist
     evaluation paradigm begins explicitly with Veblen." Provides a

detailed graph depicting Veblen's technological-ceremonial dichotomy and argues that Veblen did not develop the criteria needed to determine whether a process was ceremonial or technological.

2   SIMICH, J[ERRY] L., and RICK TILMAN. "Thorstein Veblen and His Marxist Critics: An Interpretive Review." History of Political Economy 14 (Fall):323-41.
        Finds Marxist reaction to Veblen's work to be mixed. Many Marxists hold positive views regarding Veblen and see important parallels between him and Marx. Others are of the opinion that Veblen should be understood as a bourgeois reformer. Hence, he is variously charged with being a technocratic elitist, a pessimist, and lacking knowledge of class, history, and dialectics. Careful analysis of Marxist writings shows, however, that a significant number of Marxists credit Veblen with having made important contributions to such topics as class structure, imperialism, militarism, consumption, and the business cycle.

3   STABILE, DONALD R. "Thorstein Veblen and His Socialist Contemporaries." Journal of Economic Issues 16 (March):1-28.
        Argues that not only were Veblen and his Socialist contemporaries unable to cooperate among themselves, but they also failed to provide an effective blueprint for labor's role in the achievement of socialism. Suggests that Veblen erred in placing his hopes of the liberating effect of the machine process on the working class.

4   WALLER, WILLIAM T. "The Evolution of the Veblenian Dichotomy: Veblen, Hamilton, Ayres, and Foster." Journal of Economic Issues 16 (September):757-71.
        Analyzes Veblen's concept of "institutions" and his use of the technological-ceremonial dichotomy. Compares his work to subsequent thinkers.

Index

Aaron, Daniel, 1947.1; 1951.1
Abbott, Leonard Dalton, 1946.1
Absentee Ownership and Business
   Enterprise in Recent Times
   (T. Veblen), reviews of,
   1924.1-2, 4-6, 8-10; 1925.5;
   1926.3; 1968.1
"Absentee Ownership Reread"
   (R. Schulman), 1962.8
"Adam Smith: What Kind of
   Institutionalist Was He?"
   (I. Sobel), 1979.19
Adams, Brooks, as subject,
   1979.21
Adams, Henry, as subject,
   1978.14; 1979.21
Adler, Solomon, 1957.1
Adorno, Theodor W.
-as author, 1941.1; 1955.1;
   1962.1; 1967.1
-as subject, 1978.6; 1980.15
Aesthetics, 1941.1; 1962.9;
   1972.2; 1978.17; 1981.1, 3
Affluent Society, The
   (J.K. Galbraith), 1958.4
Afxentiou, Panayiotis C.,
   1978.1
Age of Excess: The United
   States from 1877-1914
   (R. Ginger), 1965.6
Age of the Economist, The
   (D.R. Fusfeld), 1966.5
Age of Uncertainty, The
   (J.K. Galbraith),
   1977.10
Akin, William E., 1977.1

"Algie Martin Simons and Marxism
   in America" (W. A. Glaser),
   1954.9
Alienation, 1942.2-3; 1953.3;
   1954.12; 1955.7; 1956.10;
   1957.3; 1959.9; 1964.5;
   1974.13; 1977.7-8; 1978.7;
   1979.5, 21
"Alleged Revolution in Economic
   Theory, The," (J.S. Gambs),
   1947.3
Allen, Francis R., 1971.1
Allen, James S., 1978.2
Alle origini del qualunquismo"
   [On the origins of indif-
   ference] (R. Banfi), 1949.4
American Democracy, The: A
   Commentary and Interpretation,
   (H.J. Laski), 1948.10
"American Engineering Profession
   and the Idea of Social
   Responsibility, The"
   (E.T. Layton), 1956.6
American Impact on Russia,
   The, 1784-1917
   (M.M. Laserson), 1950.9
American Mind, The: An Inter-
   pretation of American Thought
   and Character Since the
   1880's (H.S. Commanger),
   1950.4
"Americano non edonista, Un"
   [An American nonhedonist]
   (A. Masero), 1931.3
"American Socialism, An"
   (W.E. Walling), 1905.7

1951.3; 1956.1; 1967.6;
1974.6-7
-as subject, 1949.9; 1973.11
Fetter, Frank A., 1927.3
Feuer, Lewis, 1953.3
Fiction. See Novel, The
American
Fields, W.C., as subject,
1973.5
Firm, theory of, 1957.15;
1958.7, 18; 1967.10;
1975.1; 1977.6; 1980.14
Fisher, Irving, 1909.1
Fishman, Leslie, 1958.13
Fitzgerald, F. Scott,
as subject, 1973.10
Flugge, Eva, 1927.4
Flynn, John T., 1948.7
Food Administration,
1934.9; 1968.13
Ford, Henry, as subject,
1934.6; 1948.9; 1953.17;
1969.9
Foreword to Functionalismus und
Irrationalität: Studien über
Thorstein Veblen's "Theory of
the Leisure Class" [Function-
alism and irrationality:
studies of Thorstein
Veblen's Theory of
the Leisure Class]
(T.W. Adorno), 1962.1
Foreword to The Theory of the
Leisure Class (S. Chase),
1934.5
Foreword to The Values of
Veblen: A Critical
Reappraisal (M. Lerner),
1956.7
Foreword to Thorstein Veblen
and the Institutionalists
(L. Robbins), 1975.13
Formalism, 1947.10
Forman, James D., 1974.8
Fossati, Eraldo, 1937.4
Foster, Fagg, 1982.4
Foucault, Michel, as subject,
1979.21
Fox, R.M., 1926.2; 1930.3
Fraina, Louis C. [Lewis Corey],
1917.6; 1934.7; 1937.3
Frank, Lawrence K., 1924.5
Frederick, William O., 1965.5

Frederickson, George M., 1959.9
Freeman, Maurice, 1930.4
Freeman, R.E., 1915.6
Freud, Sigmund, as subject,
1934.8; 1946.5; 1948.16;
1949.18; 1954.11; 1957.19;
1961.6; 1978.2; 1979.21
Freudian Psychology and Veblen's
Social Theory, The
(L. Schneider), 1948.16
Freudian Psychology and Veblen's
Social Theory, The
(L. Schneider), reviews of
1948.5-6
Friday, Charles B., 1954.8;
1968.7
Friedman, Georges, 1971.9
Friedrich, Carl Joachim, 1948.8
"Friendly Product, A"
(J. Brooks), 1979.2
Fuhrman, E.R., 1979.6
Functionalism, 1949.14; 1950.10;
1962.1, 9; 1963.8; 1967.15;
1971.5; 1976.13, 17; 1978.1
Functionalismus und
Irrationalität: Studien
über Thorstein Veblen's
"Theory of the Leisure Class"
[Functionalism and irration-
ality: studies of Thorstein
Veblen's Theory of the
Leisure Class]
(P. von Haselberg), 1962.9
Functionalismus und
Irrationalität: Studien
über Thorstein Veblen's
"Theory of the Leisure Class"
[Functionalism and irration-
ality: studies of Thorstein
Veblen's Theory of the
Leisure Class]
(P. von Haselberg), review
of, 1963.8
Functions, latent and manifest.
See Functionalism
Furnas, J.D., 1969.4
Fusfeld, Daniel R., 1966.5

G., R.B.P., 1935.8
Gabriel, Ralph Henry, 1940.2
Galbraith, J.K.
-as author, 1958.14; 1973.9-10;
1977.7; 1981.3

Knight, Frank H., 1920.5;
1921.7; 1935.12; 1959.11
Kohler, Gernot, 1977.11
Kohn, Hans, 1939.8
Kolko, Gabriel, 1963.5
Kolodny, Julius, 1947.5
Kraetzer, Mary C., 1975.7
Kretschmann, Jenny
Grizziotti, 1949.10;
1958.22
Kuhn, Thomas, as subject,
1979.21

Labor, 1917.9; 1930.2; 1934.7;
1935.1, 17; 1940.3; 1941.4;
1942.5; 1949.15; 1950.11;
1953.5; 1958.10, 13, 17, 20;
1971.3; 1972.10; 1973.15, 17;
1974.1; 1976.7; 1977.8;
1982.3
LaMont, Robert Rives, 1905.6;
1917.10
Landmarks of Economic Thought
(J. Ferguson), 1938.3
Landsman, Randolph H., 1957.18
Lapham, Lewis, 1977.12
Laserson, Max M., 1950.9
Lasker, Bruno, 1917.11
Laski, Harold J., 1919.12;
1925.5; 1948.10
Laumann, Edward O., 1970.5
Law, 1957.4, 15; 1959.5
Law, natural, 1932.6;
1936.20; 1958.26; 1971.13
Lawson, R. Alan, 1971.10
Laxdaela Saga, The,
translation of (T. Veblen),
review of, 1925.14
Layton, Edwin T., Jr.,
1956.6; 1962.4; 1971.11
Leacock, Stephen, as subject,
1979.3
Leathers, Charles G.
-as author, 1973.15; 1974.11;
1977.5, 13; 1978.18
-as subject, 1981.9
LeClair, Edward E., Jr., 1968.11
Lecture Notes on Types of
Economic Theory vol. 2
(W.C. Mitchell), 1949.16
"Lecture on Veblen, A"
(D. Riesman), 1952.11

"Legacy of Thorstein Veblen,
The" (C.E. Ayres), 1964.1
Leibenstein, Harvey, 1950.10;
1968.12; 1969.7; 1975.8;
1976.13
Leiman, Melvin, 1970.7
"Leisure Class" (Anon.),
1957.2
Lekachman, Robert, 1959.12;
1962.5; 1967.11-12
Lenin, V.I., as subject,
1959.13; 1979.14
Lepawsky, Albert, 1949.12
Lerner, Max
-as author, 1931.1; 1935.13-14;
1936.12-14; 1939.9-12;
1948.11; 1956.7; 1977.14
-as subject, 1935.20
LeRossignol, James Edward,
1920.6
Levi, Albert W., 1959.13
Levy, Marion, 1939.13;
1940.3; 1976.14
Lewis, Sinclair, as subject,
1941.3; 1947.10; 1952.1;
1966.3; 1972.7
Liberalism, 1920.10; 1936.21;
1957.18; 1971.10; 1974.4,
10; 1980.16
Liebel, Helen, 1965.7
Life against Death: The
Psychoanalytic Meaning of
History (N.O. Brown), 1959.4
Life in Our Times, A: Memoirs
(J.K. Galbraith), 1981.5
"Life of Veblen, The"
(H.B. Parkes), 1935.17
Life process, 1940.6; 1949.10;
1958.1; 1974.5
Lindblom, Charles E., 1953.12
Lindeman, Eduard C., 1936.15
Lindsay, Samuel McCune, 1900.2
Linguistics, 1958.10;
1960.1; 1968.6; 1979.22
Lipset, Seymour Martin, 1951.5
"Literary Landscape, The"
(H. Brickell), 1933.6
Literary style, Veblen's,
1899.3-5, 7; 1900.1, 3;
1904.4; 1905.1; 1915.1, 5-6;
1916.4; 1917.4, 7; 1919.13-
16, 18; 1920.1, 10; 1924.4,

Social class, 1899.1-7; 1900.1-
3; 1905.7; 1920.6; 1932.6;
1940.1, 5; 1948.8; 1949.11,
19; 1950.8; 1952.13-14;
1953.13; 1954.7; 1955.5;
1956.8; 1957.3, 9, 14;
1958.20, 33; 1959.13, 19;
1960.9; 1962.9; 1964.9;
1965.6; 1966.8; 1974.1, 9;
1975.12; 1977.3, 18; 1978.6-
7, 18
Social Class in American
Sociology (M.M. Gordon),
1950.8
Social Darwinism in American
Thought, 1869-1915
(R. Hofstadter), 1944.13;
1955.4
"Social Discussion and Reform"
(C. Henderson), 1900.1
"Social Fabric Matrix: From
Perspective to Analytical
Tool" (G.F. Hayden), 1982.1
Socialism, 1891.1; 1917.3, 6, 9-
10; 1918.2; 1919.8, 14;
1920.7, 10; 1929.5; 1933.7;
1950.7, 11; 1952.10, 13;
1956.10; 1957.9, 11, 18, 28;
1958.16, 28; 1960.7; 1971.3,
12; 1982.3
"Socialists and War"
(L.C. Fraina), 1917.6
"Socialists and War",
(R.R. Lamont), 1917.10
"Social Philosophical System of
Thorstein Veblen, The"
(L.E. Dobriansky), 1950.6;
1957.11
Social Roots of the Arts, The
(L. Harap), 1949.11
"Social Sciences, The"
(L. Wirth), 1953.23
"Social Status and Social
Structure, 1" (S.M. Lipset
and R. Bendix), 1951.5
Social Theory and Social
Structure (R.K. Merton),
1949.14
Social Thought in America: The
Revolt against Formalism
(M.G. White), 1949.20;
1957.29

"Social Value Theory, A"
(M.R. Tool), 1977.17
Society and Thought in Modern
America (H. Wish), 1952.14
Society: Its Structure and
Changes (R.M. MacIver),
1931.2
Socio-Cultural Dynamics: An
Introduction to Social Change
(F.R. Allen), 1971.1
"Sociologia di Thorstein Veblen,
La" [The sociology of
Thorstein Veblen]
(F. Ferrarotti), 1950.7
"Sociological Elements in
Economic Thought"
(T. Parsons), 1935.18
"Sociological Elements in
Veblen's Economic Theory"
(A.K. Davis), 1945.1
"Sociological Imagination of
Thorstein Veblen, The"
(J. Walton), 1979.25
"Sociological Mind of Thorstein
Veblen, The"
(T.J. Bergen Jr.), 1973.4
Sociological Theory: Its Nature
and Growth (N.S. Timasheff
and George Theodorson),
1976.17
"Sociologist of Money, The"
(D. MacRae), 1975.9
"Sociologo e gli sport, Un"
[A sociologist and sports],
(F. Ferrarotti), 1956.1
Sociology of knowledge, 1956.3;
1971.5; 1972.12; 1974.9;
1975.7; 1976.17; 1979.21
"Sociology of Knowledge of
Thorstein Veblen and
C. Wright Mills: A Study
of the 'Radical' Tradition
in American Sociology"
(M.C. Kraetzer), 1975.7
Sombart, Werner, as subject,
1925.6; 1934.13; 1951.4;
1961.6; 1978.21
"Some Aspects of the Writings
of Pareto and Veblen"
(I.Z. Bhatty), 1954.3
"Some Fundamentals of Peace"
(M.S. Handman), 1917.8

Index

"What Is Evolutionary
Economics?" (A. Lowe),
1980.11
"What Is Positive in
Veblen?" (D. Hamilton),
1956.2
"What Is Usable in
Veblen?" (M. Lerner),
1935.14; 1936.14; 1939.12
What Veblen Taught
(W.C. Mitchell ed.),
reviews of, 1936.2-4, 18;
1937.6
White, Morton G.
-as author, 1947.10; 1949.20;
1957.29
-as subject, 1979.20
White, Ron D., 1978.22
Whitney, William G., 1976.19
Whittaker, Edmund, 1950.20
"Who Was Thorstein Veblen?"
(J.K. Galbraith), 1979.7
"Why Is Institutional Economics
Not Institutional?"
(D. Hamilton), 1962.2
Wilcox, Clair, 1928.5
Wilcox, Samuel, 1949.21
Wild, Joseph, 1935.21
Wilensky, Nathan W., 1920.10
"William B. Dubois and
Thorstein B. Veblen:
Intellectual Activists of
Progressivism, A Comparative
Study, 1900-1930"
(B.N. Namasaka), 1971.12
"William James, Oliver Wendell
Holmes Jr., Thorstein
Veblen: American

Intellectual Prose, 1870-
1910" (C.B. Silver),
1964.16
Williams, William Appleman,
1957.30
Williams, William D., 1972.13
Wilson, Edmund, 1933.14
Wilson, H.H., 1957.31
Wilson, Woodrow, as subject,
1932.5; 1967.14
Winkelman, Richard, 1979.26
Winner, Langdon, 1977.21
Wirth, Louis, 1953.23
Wish, Harvey, 1952.14
Wolfe, A.B., 1936.20;
1939.19; 1952.15
Wolfe, Don M., 1957.32
Women, 1934.14; 1948.4;
1952.11; 1956.4; 1972.8;
1977.7, 12; 1978.6-7;
1979.8
"Work for Thinkers, A"
(W.J.), 1919.11
"Work of Thorstein Veblen,
The" (H.A. Innis), 1956.5
Worldly Philosophers, The
(R.L. Heilbroner), 1953.8;
1961.6; 1980.8
World War I, 1917.10;
1959.15; 1967.14; 1968.16;
1978.14; 1980.16
Wright, John G., 1936.21

Young, Allyn A., 1925.9

Zingler, Ervin K., 1962.10;
1974.14
Zinke, George W., 1958.34-35